Wc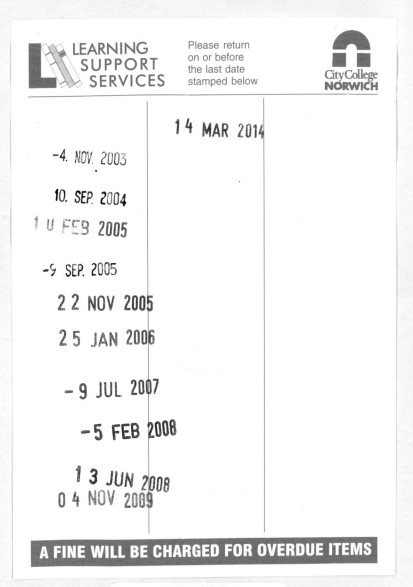

Other books by the author

How to Study Linguistics (1998)
Linguistic Terms and Concepts (2000)

Word of Mouth

A New Introduction to
Language and Communication

GEOFFREY FINCH

palgrave
macmillan

First published 2003 by
PALGRAVE MACMILLAN
Houndmills, Basingstoke, Hampshire RG21 6XS and
175 Fifth Avenue, New York, N.Y. 10010
Companies and representatives throughout the world

PALGRAVE MACMILLAN is the global academic imprint of the Palgrave
Macmillan division of St. Martin's Press, LLC and of Palgrave Macmillan Ltd.
Macmillan® is a registered trademark in the United States, United Kingdom
and other countries. Palgrave is a registered trademark in the European
Union and other countries.

ISBN 0–333–91453–8 ppc
ISBN 0–333–91454–6 paperback

This book is printed on paper suitable for recycling and made from fully
managed and sustained forest sources.

A catalogue record for this book is available from the British Library.

Library of Congress Cataloging-in-Publication Data

Finch, Geoffrey.
   Word of Mouth : a new introduction to language and communication /
Geoffrey Finch.
      p. cm.
   Includes bibliographical references and index.
   ISBN 0–333–91453–8 (cloth) — ISBN 0–333–91454–6 (paper)
      1. Language and languages. 2. Linguistics. I. Title.

P107 .F56 2002
400—dc21   2002026770

Editing and origination by Aardvark Editorial, Mendham, Suffolk

10   9   8   7   6   5   4   3   2   1
12 11 10 09 08 07 06 05 04 03

Printed in China

For Amy, Sally, Liesel and Thomas

ROSENCRANTZ: *What are you playing at?*
GUILDENSTERN: *Words, words. They're all we have to go on.*

(TOM STOPPARD, *Rosencrantz and Guildenstern are Dead*)

Contents

List of Figures   x

Preface   xi

Acknowledgements   xii

1   The Talking Animal: The Origin of Language   **1**
    I talk therefore I am   1
    Our brains and language   3
    In the beginning   5
    An evolutionary detour   8
    The descent of language   10
    The social instinct   14
    Theory of mind   18
    Language and thinking   24
    The power of names   26
    The missing link   29
    Conclusion   32
    Notes   32

**2   Getting the Better of Words: Language and
    Communication**   **34**
    The intolerable wrestle   34
    Words and signs   39
    Ferdinand de Saussure   41
    Sense relations   45
    The power of association   46
    Figurative language   50
    Communicative competence   54
    The cooperative principle   60
    Speech acts   64
    Conclusion   70
    Note   71

3	**Virtual Words: Language and Media**	**72**
	Scripted speech	72
	Electronic language	76
	Talking in cyberspace	80
	Speech and writing	85
	The world of print	91
	The origins of literacy	95
	Alphabetic writing	100
	Conclusion	104
	Notes	105
4	**We Are What We Speak: Language and Society**	**106**
	The problem of silence	106
	Speech communities	112
	Sociolinguistics	119
	Linguistic variables	124
	Dialect mapping	130
	Language and discrimination	132
	Men and women speaking	134
	The gender pattern	139
	Conclusion	141
	Notes	142
5	**The Finite Instrument: The Design and Structure of Language**	**143**
	The structure instinct	143
	Grammatical knowledge	145
	The power of infinity	149
	The modular system	153
	The hierarchic principle	154
	Language universals	159
	Moving things around	166
	Communicative grammar	169
	Conclusion	172
	Notes	174
6	**The Parent of Language: Language and Mind**	**175**
	Mind over matter	175
	Language and the brain	176
	Left-hemisphere dominance	182
	The mind's language processor	186

Garden paths and other distractions   197
Language acquisition   200
Conclusion   208
Notes   209

7   Conclusion: The House of Being   **210**
Language rules, OK?   210
The future of language   215
Accepting change   218
Note   220

Bibliography   221

Index   225

List of Figures

1.1	Chimp vs human vocal tract	6
1.2	The three-tier system of language	14
2.1	Words have signification and reference	42
2.2	Semantic field for *drunk*	49
3.1	A typical web page	79
3.2	The relationship between speech, writing and language	87
3.3	North American Indian pictorial representation of an expedition	96
3.4	Syntactic writing: tablet from Ur, 2960BC, itemising contents of a storehouse	98
3.5	Example of a modern pictogram	99
3.6	Example of a modern pictogram	99
3.7	Phonogram of 'catalogue'	100
3.8	Early history of the alphabet	101
4.1	Children's truce terms	131
5.1	Saussure's model of linguistic structure	150
5.2	A tree diagram of a sentence	155
5.3	A tree diagram of constituent nodes	158
6.1	Broca's and Wernicke's areas	177
6.2	Cookie theft picture	179
6.3	Our phonological processor	188
6.4	Our combined phonological and syntactic processor	190
6.5	The complete language processor	193

Preface

Word of Mouth is a book about the enjoyment and intellectual excitement of exploring language. Over the past twenty years the study of language has changed enormously. The discipline of linguistics has introduced into language study an ever more sophisticated methodology and technical vocabulary. So much so that, for many people, studying language has become an esoteric and specialised activity. This is a pity because language is our common inheritance; arguably, our single most important possession. Many of the ideas about language which have become current in the twenty-first century challenge our ideas about who we are, and to what extent we are special in the scale of evolution. To study language is to study ourselves as well as the world around us.

The chapters in this book all focus on key aspects of language, in its historical, individual, and social dimensions. They demand no special expertise or skill in language study to enjoy and appreciate them, just an interest in the fascinating power of words and the way they shape and influence our lives. Chapter 1 discusses the evolution of language and suggests that the acquisition of language was a cognitive leap forward with enormous repercussions for what we understand by the term 'human nature'. Subsequent chapters each take a major area of language: communication, media, social function, structure, and psychology. In each case the approach begins by considering our everyday encounter with language and then develops a view of the subject which fits with our experience as inhabitants of a new century and a new millenium. All the chapters of the book can be read separately or dipped into for interest or information. In the first instance, however, it will repay you to read through the book as a whole to gain a sense both of the variety of ways in which language affects our lives, and of its distinctiveness as our principal means of communication.

Whether you are a student at school, or college, pursuing a course in communication, or language studies, or just someone eager to catch up with current ideas about these subjects, you will find *Word of Mouth* a valuable and thought-provoking introduction.

Acknowledgements

Some parts of Chapters 2 and 5 previously appeared in *How to Study Linguistics* (Finch, 1998).

For the quotations on language I am indebted to David and Hilary Crystal, *Words on Words: Quotations about Language and Languages*. Penguin, 2000.

Special thanks are due to my daughter Amy for her help in formatting the typescript.

Figures 3.5 and 3.6 are from *The Highway Code*.

The author and publishers would like to thank the following for permission to reproduce copyright material:

Allsorts Licensing for a cartoon by Sally Forth.

Blackwell Publishers for map from P. Trudgill, *The Dialects of England*, Blackwell (1990) Map 30, p. 119.

The British Museum for plate, 'Syntactic writing: tablet from Ur, 2960BC. Copyright The British Museum.

Cambridge University Press for figures from Jean Aichison, *The Seeds of Speech, Language Origin and Evolution* (2000) Fig 7.2; and Andrew Radford, Martin Atkinson, David Britain, Harald Clahsen and Andrew Spencer, *Linguistics: An Introduction* (1999) Fig 2.

The Cartoon Bank for a cartoon by Dana Fradon, 'I can't put it into Layman's language'. © The New Yorker Collection 1975 Dana Fradon from cartoonbank.com. All Rights Reserved.

Creators Syndicate International for the Far Side® cartoons by Gary Larson, "So! ... you *still* won't talk, eh?" (Release date 08/31/81). © 1981 FarWorks, Inc. All Rights Reserved. Used with permission; "So then Sheila says to Betty that ..." (Release date 11/05/83. © 1983 FarWorks, Inc. All Rights Reserved. Used with permission; "Hang him, you idiots! Hang him! ..." (Release date 06/22/83). © 1983 FarWorks, Inc. All Rights Reserved. Used with permission.

Jerry King for his cartoon, 'You should check your e-mails more often. I fired you over three weeks ago.'

Pearson Education for figure from Ray Jackendoff, *Patterns in the Mind: Language and Human Nature*, Harvester (1993) Fig 5.3.

Every effort has been made to trace all the copyright holders but if any have been inadvertently overlooked the publishers will be pleased to make the necessary arrangements at the first opportunity.

1 The Talking Animal
The Origin of Language

Man appears a mere talking animal
JOSEPH CONRAD (Prologue to *Under Western Eyes*, 1911)

I talk therefore I am

Most people, if asked to name the greatest invention of humankind, would probably opt for some kind of technological breakthrough on which hinged the material progress of the species: the creation of modern vaccines, jet propulsion, the microprocessor, perhaps the wheel. Whatever the list, language would probably not feature prominently, if at all. And yet, when you think about it, none of these, or any other invention for that matter, would have been possible without language. We take our ability to speak entirely for granted, which is as it should be of course. Like walking, or breathing, it seems an entirely natural function. But all languages are inventions. The words we speak or write, and the system which underlies their use, have all been made up. More importantly, it is this act of making up which separates us from other animals. For, while all animals communicate, sometimes quite subtly, they do not talk. Animal exchanges in the wild are mostly formulaic, and even when trained beyond this, in captivity, they are incapable of learning language to become independent users. When humans crossed the threshold of language, several millennia ago, they created for themselves the most powerful and delicate tool the world has witnessed, and, in so doing, distanced themselves from the rest of creation.

So powerful is the medium of language that its origin has often been considered magical. To us the idea that language is a tool seems thoroughly normal. After all, we see words on the page; we know that they are assembled from units of type. They are things to work with, visible, tangible entities. But this is a comparatively recent idea. For most of human history, up until the arrival of print, language was not thought of as something we made, but something we were given. It already existed before us, although known only to the Gods. In many non-literate societies language is still viewed in this way. Words are mysterious, semi-

1

THE FAR SIDE® By GARY LARSON

© 1981 FarWorks, Inc. All Rights Reserved/Dist. by Creators Syndicate

The Far Side® by Gary Larson © 1981 FarWorks, Inc. All Rights Reserved. Used with permission.

"So! ... You *still* won't talk, eh?"

magical, things, with the power to create and destroy life. In the mouth of a skilled 'shaman', or witch doctor, they can heal the sick, make the crops grow, or bring down an enemy. And even in western culture, until comparatively recent times, the Bible was regarded as the 'word of God', or God's language, and, as such, not to be tampered with.

The concept of language as divine in origin may not be something which most people believe any longer. Nevertheless, we still intuitively think of language as a 'gift', even if not from God. Like other exceptional talents, the ability to play a musical instrument, or paint, supremely well, it has that sense of unearned, almost miraculous endowment. But with this difference: it belongs, not just to the select few, but to everyone. Under normal circumstances, all children will acquire it. Language is the inheritance, the birthright, of all of us and yet the property of none. No one *owns* it, although some have tried to do so. In this way it is like that other supreme gift: life. Indeed, it is part of the theme of this book that language is, to use the philosopher Ludwig Wittgenstein's phrase, 'a form of life'. Interestingly, language has many of the features we attribute to human life. Not only, as I have said, is it a universal endowment, but it has a similar capacity for creativity and almost endless diversity. Estimates of the number of languages around the world hover at about 5–6000, all of them different, with separate vocabularies and grammars, yet all sharing certain basic design elements. In a similar fashion the human species is spread over the globe in a seemingly infinite variety of physical, cultural and ethnic diversity, but with a common genetic and biological foundation. More importantly, perhaps, language reinforces the instinctive sense we have of our own uniqueness and personal identity. No two people are biologically, or linguistically, identical. We all have our own voice print, which makes us recognisable to others: our own pattern of pronunciation, intonation, use of vocabulary and grammar. Linguists refer to this bundle of features as our **idiolect**. Language is the projection we make of

---

The Dogon view of language

The Dogon people of Mali, in West Africa, traditionally believe that language is a sort of spirit inhabiting everything. Any object, however humble, such as a hoe, or a piece of woven cloth, is thought to consist of words. So powerful are words that they can also impregnate women:

> words spoken by day enter the bodies of women. Any man speaking to any women is assisting procreation. By speaking to a woman one fertilizes her, or at least by introducing into her a celestial germ, one makes it possible for her to be impregnated in the normal way.

M. GRIAULE (1998)

---

ourselves. Hidden within it are our sex, age, ethnic background, nationality, social class, occupation, education, and personality. And also our lifetime experiences, because language does not exist in a vacuum. Every utterance or, in linguistic terms, **speech act**, takes place in a thoroughly unique set of circumstances: different people, setting, place, time, and so on. As observers of language we have to take into account what the Russian critic, Mikhail Bakhtin, has called 'the concrete living totality' of language. Language is inextricably part of a social, as well as a personal, reality, a fact which is intriguingly signalled for us in the term 'world', which in its very form seems to suggest precisely that:

$$W O R \{L\} D$$

Our brains and language

In order to be able to speak a language we need two basic kinds of knowledge. On the one hand, we need a knowledge of the particular language itself: what its vocabulary is, how the items are pronounced, and the method of combining them in meaningful and well-formed strings. This is language information, what linguists call the **grammar** of a language. Most of the language lessons we receive at school are to do with developing this. To enable us to perform this feat, however, we need another kind of knowledge. To put it simply: we need to know how to acquire the grammar. This is a more subtle form of knowledge. After all, parrots can be taught to make the right sounds and put them in meaningful patterns without having a clue what they are doing. The reason we can manage to learn a language and parrots can't is because our brains are equipped with a device which is able to interpret and sort the incoming data in a way which theirs is not. Our brains know what to look for. Think for a moment of how a computer works. At the moment, I'm typing this on a word processor, using a software package called, appropriately, 'Word', which contains masses of information in code about page layout, fonts, editing, and so on. At the same time, my computer has a processor, referred to as its 'hardware', which scans the program, decoding the electrical impulses, and effectively 'reading' the information they contain. Similarly with the human brain. If language programs are the software with which we work, then they require the corresponding hardware to enable them to run. Humans have this hardware, animals don't.

The natural question to ask is 'why?' How is it that one particular species developed this mental capacity and the rest didn't? To begin with, it's clear that our brains have developed differently from that of other animals. They are significantly bigger relative to our body size. In general we have a brain about nine times bigger for body size than is usual in mammals. What this means is that, after we have accounted for everything that is necessary to keep the body functioning, our brains have more spare capacity than those of other species for things like problem-solving, game-playing, and language too. More significantly, one particular part of our brain has grown quite dramatically. This is the area known as the neocortex, a thin coating of nerve cells wrapped around the rest of the brain. The psychologist Robin Dunbar refers to it as the 'thinking' part of the brain, the place where the activities associated with reasoning and thought occur. In most mammals it accounts for 30–40 per cent of brain volume whereas in humans the proportion is 80 per cent.

Bigger brains are not necessarily in themselves a good thing, however. Although our brains account for only two per cent of our body weight they consume about 20 per cent of the energy absorbed through food. This makes them very expensive to maintain. No animal could afford to develop such a drain on energy resources unless there was a distinct evolutionary advantage in doing so. For humans, the development probably meant a dramatic change in diet. The primates from whom we are descended were fruit-eating animals, feeding on a diet of seeds, tubers and tree fruits. This is fairly nutrient-rich and more able to sustain the demands of a growing brain than the leaf-eating habits of other mammals. Indeed, there is some evidence to suggest that the initial impetus towards larger brains may have come from the natural advantage to fruit- and seed-eating primates of developing colour vision. Fruit is rather patchy in its distribution and difficult to detect in dense undergrowth without an ability to distinguish colours. But while such a diet is richer than that of leaf eaters it probably could not sustain the growth needed to produce the super-brain necessary for language. Only one source was available for that: meat. As Robin Dunbar comments, 'The initial increase in brain size about two million years ago seems to correlate with a shift from a predominantly vegetation-based diet in the australopithecines (the early members of our lineage) to a diet with a significantly larger meat component in *Homo*' (1996: 127). From the need for meat eventually came hunting, and hunting in turn places new demands on communication and social habits. Hunters live in large groups and are nomadic. Without the natural speed, teeth and claws of other mammals, early humans would have needed good communication skills to co-ordinate a successful hunt. It's a tantalising thought that the development of brains capable of language in our primate ancestors may have coincided with our development into carnivores. That, at least is the suggestion of William Golding in his novel *The Inheritors* (1955), in which he imagines a group of Neanderthals who have a very limited form of language. Their thought processes are made up of images of the outside world by means of which they communicate telepathically to the rest of the group. They are a gentle people, vegetarian in lifestyle, who are eventually destroyed by a 'superior' race of hunters with far more developed language skills able to reason about the outside world in a more sophisticated way.

In the beginning

No one knows for sure exactly when language began, nor how. There are, of course, no records of language use prior to the invention of writing. All we can go on are the findings from archaeology which indicate changes in the human anatomy essential for the evolution of language. Over the past twenty-five years, the fossil record has been extraordinarily rich, and has enabled archaeologists to piece together the story of our descent. In 1976 the partial skeleton of a small female, named 'Lucy' by her discoverers, was excavated out of the Ethiopian desert. Lucy, one of our earliest ancestors, lived around 3.3 million years ago. In many respects, if Lucy were alive today, she would seem to us more ape-like than human. She was probably very hairy, with strong chest and arms suitable for climbing trees. But with one significant difference: she could walk upright. Bipedalism, as it is called, is

one of those major developments in the evolution of our modern phys-
iology. Among other things, it has left us as a species prone to back
trouble, something apes and chimpanzees don't normally suffer from.
But, more importantly, by standing up, our front legs became our
hands, enabling us to carry things and make tools, in a way that other
animals can't. Additionally, a number of researchers consider it likely
that bipedalism contributed to changes in the lungs and vocal cavity
which enabled us to talk. Lucy clearly couldn't talk.

For one thing she didn't have the vocal apparatus. Her larynx would
have been in the position in which it is located in apes and chimpanzees, too high in the throat to enable recognisable speech sounds to
be made (see Figure 1.1). The larynx is an ancient part of our anatomy,
an echo of a time when we lived in water. Its original function was
probably to prevent water entering the lungs during swimming. In primates this feature has evolved a different function, serving to seal off
the lungs and make the rib cage rigid when extra effort is needed. You
can feel this effect if you lift anything really heavy. Only in humans,
however, has it evolved into a speech organ. The outer case of the
larynx is the lump in your throat, popularly called the 'Adam's apple'.
Inside it are two membranes, or vocal folds/cords, which vibrate
against each other as air rushes between them. In so doing they
produce a phenomenon known as 'voicing', which is crucial to the production of speech sounds. All speech sounds are either 'voiced' – produced when the vocal cords are together – or 'voiceless', produced
when the cords are apart. To get the effect try putting your fingers in
your ears and saying the voiceless consonant s followed by its voiced
counterpart z. The buzzing you should hear when saying z is caused by

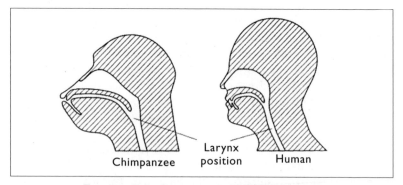

FIGURE 1.1   CHIMP VS HUMAN VOCAL TRACT
Source: Aitchison, The Seeds of Speech (CUP, 1996)

the vibration of the vocal cords. The lowering of the larynx in humans was part of the reconfiguration of the vocal tract which enabled us to expel sounds more easily through the mouth and with a greater degree of resonance. In so doing it also made us more prone to choking, as you will know if you have tried to eat and talk at the same time.

The other way in which Lucy was different from us was in her brain size. It was probably not much different in its dimensions from that of a chimpanzee's. The development of the super-brain able to process language was yet to come. Since Lucy's discovery in 1976, researchers have been looking for evidence to determine whether there were other two-legged ape species which evolved at the same time, and if so, whether they shared the same characteristics. They were rewarded in 2000 when the palaeontologist Maeve Leakey found the remains of a fossilised skull dating from the same period as Lucy in Northern Kenya. 'Flat-faced man' as he is commonly called was much the same as Lucy with the exception of his flat face, a characteristic which makes him more like us, whose facial features are all on the same level, as opposed to apes, where this is not the case. But crucially, he had the same relatively small-sized brain. This discovery has led researchers to suggest that about 3.5 million years ago a number of different varieties of two-legged apes evolved. One of these, perhaps we shall never know precisely which, was our direct ancestor. All we can say for certain, is that between Lucy and her fellow bipeds, and us, lie several stages in development which indicate the evolution of humankind to have been an extremely slow and laborious process:

- *homo habilis*, or 'handy man', able to make and use tools, around 2 million years BP (before the present)
- *homo erectus*, 'upright man', who could use fire, around 1.5 million years BP
- *archaic homo sapiens*, 'archaic wise man', around 300,000 years BP
- *homo sapiens*, or 'modern man', 175,000 years BP.

Comparing the brains from fossilised skull remains during these periods it has become clear to archaeologists that from Lucy to *Homo Sapiens* our brain size has approximately doubled every 1.5 million years. At some point on this vast evolutionary journey language began. But where? And did it happen merely as a consequence of having a bigger brain and a lower larynx or were these changes driven by the evolutionary need for language?

Most researchers put the date for the evolution of language between 250,000 BP and 50,000 BP, in other words, in the final stages of human development. The date for the descent of the larynx to its present position is as yet uncertain, although Jean Aitchison in *The Seeds of Speech* (1996: 81) mentions the finding some years ago of what looks like a modern shaped hyoid bone – which fits at the top of the windpipe – in a skull dated 100,000 BP, conveniently right in the middle of this period. To us this still suggests an enormous time span. But it has become clear since Darwin that evolution occurs very slowly, by what he called 'very short and slow steps'. The theory of evolution has been called humanity's single most important discovery. In contrast with those other significant theories of the nineteenth century – Marxism, and Freudianism – which have faded with time, it has succeeded in becoming the leading explanatory theory in a whole range of physical and human sciences. Despite this, most people still have only a vague notion of it and its key ideas of natural selection and adaptation to environment. If we are to understand the mystery of how we have developed our language ability, however, it's important to have some understanding of Darwinian principles.

An evolutionary detour

Central to changes which occur within species is genetic variation. Although genes copy themselves in passing from parents to children they don't always do so exactly. We are not exact copies of our parents. Most changes, or mutations are trivial: darker hair, smaller noses. But occasionally a mutation is more significant. Let's imagine a group of birds which feed on a particular species of insect by virtue of long beaks able to reach into the recesses of plants. One day the supply of insects begins to diminish, forcing the birds to search harder for their food and facing them with the possibility of extinction. From time to time in the bird population a bird has been born with a longer beak but because the supply of insects has been plentiful this mutation has been insignificant. Now, however, the bigger beaks are a distinct advantage and enable these birds to reach further and get the scarce food. Over time, if these conditions continue, the bigger beaked variety will be more successful and will pass on their genes to more and more offspring.[1] Nature will have selected them because they have adapted to the changing circumstances. In the process many other mutations will not have succeeded, precisely because they provide no advantage in the struggle for life. Survival of the fittest, that much misunderstood principle of evolution, does not mean survival of the strongest, but of the species most successfully adapted to its environment.

If the environment never changed there would never be any need for species to change. They would continue virtually the same for ever. Deep-sea creatures such as sharks, for example, have remained pretty much the same for many hundreds of millions of years, whereas we, on the other hand, have changed considerably from our primate ancestors of four million years ago. The message is clear: evolutionary change is driven by environmental change. And in our case, one particular change may well have triggered the development of the human species. Genetic evidence, particularly from analysis of what is termed 'mitochondrial DNA', now suggests that we all came originally from Africa, from a small group of ancestors. Early religious writers who placed the Garden of Eden in East Africa were, ironically, not far wrong. Around eight million years ago the earth's climate began to change dramatically. In simple terms, the planet started to dry out. Evidence for this comes from the disappearance of the great rain forests which covered much of the earth's surface. By six million years BP they had shrunk considerably, giving place to grass lands and open plains. The immediate consequence of this change was to increase competition among the forest-dwelling primates for food. Less trees meant less fruit. In this battle for survival the advantage lay with the monkeys, who had developed the ability to eat the fruit before it was ripe, something both we and the apes are unable to do. In these circumstances the apes were driven to the forest floor and the forest edge, places more open to attack, to search for food. So began the long decline of the apes, the descendants of which still cling on in isolated areas of Africa and Asia. Before the climate change fifty different species of apes roamed the forests. Afterwards only a handful remained, like the orang-utan, the gorilla, and the chimpanzee. But some groups managed to free themselves from the forest and came down from the trees for good. Evolution as we have noted tells us that this was a gradual process of small adaptations. One of these was the bipedalism of Lucy and flat-faced man.

Climate change was probably the major environmental factor in human evolution, but it coincided with another change, equally catastrophic, which occurred along the African continent around six to seven million years ago. It was a catastrophe probably caused by movement of the earth's plates, resulting in massive earthquakes, which separated East Africa from the rest of the continent, creating what is now called the 'Great Rift Valley'. This major environmental change, occurring over several million years, effectively separated two very different environments. To the west was a land dominated by rain forest, while to the east beyond the new mountain range which had formed lay the open dry grasslands of what is now Uganda, Ethiopia, and Kenya. The catastrophe separated not only land masses but populations of animals too. Our ape cousins were left in the fertile forests of the west whereas our ancestors were stranded in the dry, treeless savannah of the east. This coincides with the fossil record. Today hominid, or early human, fossils are found only in the east of the Rift Valley, while chimpanzees occur only in the west. Forced to adapt to our new environment we learnt to walk upright, change our diet, lose much of our hair, and eventually develop language. Lucy and her fellow hominids, were the first step for humankind on the long path 'out of Africa'.

The descent of language

Most theories about the development of language take as their starting point the advantage for early humans of living in groups. Many animals live in groups. For one thing, it's a useful protection against enemies. The more pairs of eyes there are to see possible predators, the better. It sometimes seems strange to us to see a herd of wildebeest grazing in full view of a pride of lions. Our natural instinct would be to beat a hasty retreat. But while the group makes the wildebeest collectively more vulnerable, individually they are safer. Since the lions can take only one animal, the risk for any single beast is significantly reduced. More importantly, although a single animal can't see the lions when it is bending down and eating, the other animals can. When the alarm signal comes it will follow the rest of the herd blindly, but safely. Unlike primate groups, wildebeest have never been known to 'cry wolf'.

The formation of groups for mutual protection, or in the case of predators, for mutual assistance, is fundamental to the mechanics of survival. The 'herd instinct', so called, is part of our natural inheritance. But the groups formed by primates are significantly different from those of other animals. Defence and attack still play a principal part in their formation, but so does one other ingredient: sociality. Monkeys and apes live in tightly bonded groups with complex kinship relationships. They use these relationships to form alliances, designed to preserve the integrity of the group and promote the interests of individual members within it. As Robin Dunbar (1996) comments, anyone who has lived in a close-knit community where everybody knows everybody else's business and where life is dominated by intense physical relationships, whether of affection, sex, or rivalry, would recognise the coalitions formed in the harems of a troupe of vervet monkeys, or gelada baboons.

There is a growing consensus among anthropologists and linguists alike that the emergence of language was a result of the group dynamics which developed within a particular species of our ape ancestors. Nineteenth-century explanations of the origin of language usually interpreted these dynamics in a rather literal and utilitarian fashion. It was argued that the great advantage of language to early human groups lay in its usefulness in co-ordinating activities more successfully. So, for example, a troupe out hunting or felling a tree or trying to assist injured members could signal to each other and convey more sophisticated meanings via language than through animal cries or gestures. Indeed, it was thought most likely that early words could be traced back to these cries, the names of which formed the titles of the following most popular theories:

- 'bow-wow' theory: the view that language originated in the noises of animals, imitated by hunters in the course of tracking

- 'yo-he-ho' theory: the view that language originated in the grunts which occur in heaving and hauling

- 'pooh-pooh' theory: the view that language originated in instinctive cries of pain and joy.

There are difficulties with all of these theories, however, at least in their simplistic form. To begin with, the first two assume that language was male in origin, since in most primitive groups it is the men who do the hunting and the hauling. This seems odd because among modern humans women are generally acknowledged to have more verbal skills than men. Second, and more importantly, it is not immediately apparent how language offers advantages in the pursuit of any of these activities significant enough to have triggered the biological developments necessary for speech. As we have seen, language demands a huge amount of energy to sustain its operations, energy which could more usefully be spent elsewhere, in mating, for example. It is true, as I said earlier, that an activity such as hunting requires good communication skills, but these need not necessarily be linguistic. If a group of hunters manages to hunt well enough with gestures and cries, why invest in something more sophisticated? As Dunbar argues, imagine a firm which requires someone with good word-processing skills having to choose between two candidates, both of whom have the relevant experience to do the job adequately, but only one of whom has any qualifications. Given an open choice we would expect the qualified candidate to be selected. But let us suppose employing him/her involves doubling the salary. The decision is no longer so obvious. Darwin has shown us that this is how evolution works. Nothing comes free. For natural selection to work there must be an obvious advantage in survival value.

This is not to say that noises connected with activities such as hunting or felling trees or pain did not provide the starting point for language. Language has to start somewhere, and where else we might ask but in animal cries? As we now know, these are capable of extraordinary complexity. Vervet monkeys, for instance, use different calls to identify various types of predators. The anthropologists Cheney and Seyfarth (1990) report that there are at least three separate calls indicating whether the source of the threat is from the ground, the air, or the long grass. So a leopard call will send them climbing into the trees, while an eagle call will cause them to jump out of them. And if they hear a snake alarm they stand on their hind legs and peer into the long grass.[2] Indeed, a visit to any zoo will usually show that, apart from birds, monkeys and baboons are the noisiest animals. They are constantly chattering to each other in what seems at times to resemble speech. Robin Dunbar says of these exchanges, heard in the wild, that they 'involve complexly structured whines, moans, and whinnies expressed with all the intonations of speech. Listening to them with eyes closed is like sitting at the far end of a restaurant or a bar where you can hear the rise and fall of speech, the alternation of voices as speakers take it in turns, but you cannot make out the word themselves' (1996: 49). Perhaps the closest we can come to this is in the cries and calls that infants make in the cooing and babbling stage, before the onset of language proper. The limitation of these as acts of communication, however, is that they are individual to each child and can only be interpreted by the parent. The linguist Michael Halliday (1985) distinguished at least sixteen different sound sequences that his young son Nigel made before he was able to utter his first word.

But, despite the sophistication of animal noises, there is an important difference between them and words. An animal cry may express the meaning 'There's a leopard coming', but it is unable to express the meaning 'There was a leopard here yesterday' or 'My friend thinks there's a leopard coming'. Language possesses a feature, unknown to animal systems of communication, called **displacement**. Displacement allows us to talk about things removed in time and place from the immediate context. Possibly the closest the animal

Nigel's speech	
na	'I want that thing'
yi	'Yes, I want that thing there
a	'Yes, I want what you just said'
an:na	'Hallo Anna'
ɛdɛdɛde	'Nice to see you; let's look at this'
ɛ	'Yes it's me; I'm here'
a::da	'Look, a picture; you say what it is'
æyi	'That's nice'
bwgabwga	'A lot of talk'

HALLIDAY (1985)

kingdom comes to realising this feature is in the ability of bees to convey information to their fellow bees, through dancing, about how to reach flowers which are often at a considerable distance from the hive. But this is a poor second to the complex acts of displacement available through language. No bee could speculate, hypothesise, or express its feelings in the way that we can. The signalling systems of animals, like the early noises of children, can best be understood as a form of **proto-language**, rather than language itself. Proto-languages are invariably two-tier systems in which a sound, or series of sounds is directly related to a meaning. Because of this we can't detach the sounds or recombine them to form alternative meanings. They are fixed in place. Language, however, is a three-tier system. In between the other two tiers lies a middle one, a system of words, or **grammar** (see Figure 1.2). At some stage in his/her development a child leaves the two-tier system and adopts the three-tier one. It is this leap which is unique to humans. Some chimpanzees in captivity have been taught the rudiments of a three-tier system, but the limited repertoire they have acquired suggests they haven't understood the principles on which it is based. As we know, being able to imitate a system is crucially different from understanding how it works. Earlier on we distinguished between knowing the ingredients of a language and understanding the principles on which it is based. This latter knowledge we can now call **linguistic competence**. Its possession is one of the hallmarks of our humanity.

```
Proto-language:        MEANING
                          ↓
                        SOUND


Language:              MEANING
                          ↓
                   SYSTEM OF WORDS
                          ↓
                        SOUND
```

FIGURE 1.2 THE THREE-TIER SYSTEM OF LANGUAGE
Source: Halliday, *Spoken and Written Language* (Deakin University Press, 1985)

The social instinct

But if language did not develop, primarily, as an aid to more effective hunting, or tree felling, how and why did it begin? To answer this we need to return to the distinctive primate feature of sociality and consider the part this plays in language interactions. Living in groups poses particular problems for animals and humans alike. Groups offer protection and security to their individual members but they also can be stressful. Competition for food, accommodation, and sexual partners, increases with group size, particularly in periods of scarcity. Most animal groups are relatively small. Disputes, where they occur, are sorted out quickly, and each animal knows its place in the hierarchy. But imagine a large group of 50 to 55 baboons or chimpanzees with their extended families of aunts, uncles, half-sisters, cousins and so on. How would such a large group manage to survive without either self-combusting in relentless warfare, or splintering into smaller groups, thus making themselves more vulnerable to predators? The reason for the success of such large groupings has emerged over the past decade from research which has been carried out into the social behaviour of primates.

Monkeys and apes spend a great deal of time in establishing and servicing their relationships. One of the principal mechanisms for this is grooming. Grooming occupies anything from 10 to 20 per cent of a monkey's day. By any reckoning this is a significant investment in time which must have some evolutionary pay-off. The most important function of grooming, as we would expect, is to aid hygiene. Monkeys tend to groom those bits of each other which are difficult to reach. But animals will spend far more time grooming than is necessary for hygiene. This is because it is a source of mutual pleasure. The animal being groomed gets a great deal of sensory pleasure, in the way a cat does from being stroked, while the groomer gets tasty titbits to eat. In other words, grooming performs a highly significant social function. Animals which groom each other tend to develop a stronger bond than those which don't. They are more likely to come to the assistance of one another and share food. Large groups work because individual members form coalitions, or self-help groups, which enable them to withstand the bullies who might otherwise get the best food or places to sleep. Grooming is a kind of social lubricant; it eases the otherwise nakedly competitive elements of an animal's life by establishing the importance of interdependency and mutual interest. We might also add trust, too, since animals being groomed are vulnerable and open to attack from their groomers in a way that they wouldn't normally be.

Among humans the activity which approximates most closely to grooming is talking. We use language in a broadly similar way, to form alliances and differentiate between allies and non-allies, the great aim of talking being to increase the former and decrease the latter. Could it possibly be, then, that language has evolved from grooming, that its principal value to early humans was to provide a more effective form of bonding? A number of linguists and anthropologists have been attracted to this idea, principally, the writer Robin Dunbar who popularised it in his *Grooming, Gossip and the Evolution of Language* (1996). As he points out, 'If the main function of grooming for monkeys and apes is to build up trust and personal knowledge of allies, then language has an added advantage. It allows you to say a great deal about yourself, your likes and dislikes, the kind of person you are; it also allows you to convey in numerous subtle ways something about your reliability as an ally or friend' (p. 78). Once language had evolved we could form even larger groups because

THE FAR SIDE®   BY GARY LARSON

"So then Sheila says to Betty that Arnold told her what Harry was up to, but Betty told me she already heard it from Blanche, don't you know ..."

language enables people to exchange information about others without them being present. And larger groups are essential to the dominance of our species. If all the ants of the world could form a large enough group we should disappear overnight. Basic to all linguistic acts of communication, whether of speech or writing, are two dimensions: power and solidarity. Power is the dimension we characteristically associate with language because we use words to get the goods and services we want. We need language to order the latest sales catalogue, or get our bank account changed. Making people do things for us by manipulating them linguistically is part of everyday life. All societies, whether animal or human, depend on distributions of power. In some the power is naked and direct, and accompanied by the possibility of actual violence if a service is not performed. But, as we have seen, a distinctive feature of successful large groups is sociality. Any threat must not be so great as to destroy the group's cohesion. This is where the second dimension of language is so significant. Equally important as the desire to manipulate people is the need we have to signal that we are friendly human beings who are well disposed towards others. A great deal of language activity is taken up with what the anthropologist Bronislaw Malinowski termed **phatic communion**, which roughly means language for its own sake (see Chapter 4). Just think for a moment of what happens when you go into a shop to buy a newspaper. Nothing in the transaction which takes place requires anybody to say anything. The price of the paper is printed on it and all we have to do is hand over the money and receive the change. Yet the transaction is punctuated throughout by superfluous information – 'That'll be fifty pence' – and pointless courtesies, 'please' and 'thank you', as if the actions of giving and receiving money were somehow favours rather than requirements of the sale. What are we doing here but creating allies, ritually grooming each other, if only temporarily? We choose to pretend that the person serving us is doing it out of choice rather than because they are employed to do so. After all, we wouldn't thank a machine. This minor deception is an indication that our primitive linguistic instincts, the ones which lie behind our development as 'talking animals', are not simply concerned with extending the power and control we have over people and things, but with promoting human solidarity. Alongside the competitiveness and blind self-interest which popular accounts of Darwinism often suggest are our heritage, the evolution of language exists to remind us of alternative, subtler instincts which have developed in us through the need to survive. It is, arguably, these that are the source of what the linguist Michael Toolan (1996) calls the 'other-orientedness' of human nature on which language crucially depends.

If anthropologists are right in linking grooming with the evolution of language this may also explain why lying is such a critical feature of language development. Children, of course, are taught never to lie. But, as we know, they do, and manage the operation very successfully, more so than many adults. Being able to lie convincingly involves considerable linguistic skills. We have to convince someone else of the reality of something we know not to be the case: the ultimate in displacement, a key feature, as we have already identified, of language systems. As such, it is the most telling evidence we have of the power of words. Indeed, the linguist Jean Aitchison (1996: 21) suggests that 'the ultimate goal of language learning may be the skill of lying' since it is 'the deliberate use of language as a tool ... with the content of the message unsupported by context to mislead the listener'. On the other hand, however, lying is the only real crime we can commit linguistically. In a court of law it is called 'perjury' and can result in us being sent to prison. People will admit to misleading, being 'economical with the truth', even deceiving, but rarely lying. Lying seems to violate some basic moral principle on which language is based.

There is a paradox here which can tell us something more about the nature of this extraordinary medium. The point is, that while lying seems a denial of what language exists to promote, it is only the existence of language which makes lying possible at all. Words are amazingly effective at deceiving others, but they can only do so because our fundamental expectation when we are conversing with anyone is that we are being told the truth. If we automatically thought we were being lied to the whole basis of meaningful communication would be destroyed. At some deep, instinctive level, lying seems a hostile act. 'I hate a lie' says the narrator in Joseph Conrad's *Heart of Darkness* 'it has the taste of mortality.' Nevertheless, the possibility that we are being deceived in some way is never wholly absent from our minds. No one speaks the absolute truth all the time. Life would probably be intolerable if we did. We all indulge in mild deceptions and exaggerations in everyday conversation. And, as poets and novelists bear witness, many of the imaginative capacities of language rely on powers of inventiveness which bear a close kinship to those of deception.

In other words, it's the very ambivalence of language which makes it so potent. Whenever we listen to someone speaking to us we are automatically evaluating the truth value of what is being communicated. If our neighbour tells us it is going to rain when the forecast has said the opposite we have to work out whether s/he is telling us the truth as s/he believes it to be or playing a joke. And if it is a joke, whether it is malicious or simply playful, in which case we would expect this to be signalled in some way, probably by tone of voice. The very fact that we can be ironical and tell jokes at all is evidence of the duality which is at the heart of language, and which may explain just why it has been so important in our evolution. For, while language may facilitate the 'trust and personal knowledge' important in building up alliances, it also facilitates the reverse. As the anthropologists Dick Byrne and Andrew Whiten (1988) have noted, it is part of our 'machiavellian intelligence'. Something we share with apes and monkeys.

It's an intriguing thought, then, that the principal evolutionary value of language for humans lay in its **interpersonal** function. Only through this development could they negotiate the increasingly complex arrangements entailed by large groups and thus withstand the danger of predators from without and rivals from within. This is what we understand by a society. Our deepest instincts are social because our evolution has rested on the formation of mutually sustaining coalitions as a guarantee of individual security. And with security comes enhanced productivity. If we had to worry all the time about our safety and well being we should not be able to make the implements, and build the constructions, which our larger brains have made possible. Language, thinking, and doing, are inseparably linked in our evolution. This can be seen most significantly in the development of what psychologists refer to as 'Theory of Mind' (ToM).

Paul and the tuber

An interesting example of an animal cry being used to deceive comes from a story told by Byrne and Whiten about a female baboon (Mel) digging out a difficult tuber from the ground whilst being watched by a juvenile (Paul). According to the observers, as Mel managed to pull the tuber free Paul screamed loudly in the manner of an animal being threatened. At which point, Paul's mother rushed out and thinking her son was being attacked chased Mel off, leaving Paul to pick up the tuber and munch it peacefully.

Theory of mind

This is something which all normal human beings possess. Very simply, it means being able to understand that other people have thoughts, beliefs and feelings separate and different from ours. This, seemingly, obvious ability is worth pondering on because it is crucial both to our humanity and our possession of language. Theory of mind is not something we automatically have. Very young children, up until the age of about four, do not have it. They assume that other people see and interpret the world as they do. This is part of the natural egocentricity which surrounds us from birth. Understanding that the world is not necessarily as we experience it, and that other people may have different experiences from us, is a leap forward which our brains are programmed to make. This is significant in our emotional development too, because ToM is necessary in the production of feelings such as sympathy, and empathy, which, in turn, enable us to appreciate that other people have, what the novelist George Eliot called, 'an equivalent centre of self'.

Just how important this cognitive, or mental, ability is to our use of language becomes clear if we think about what goes on in any act of communication. Most of the time we spend talking is taken up with the problem of meaning. What did Susan mean by describing James as a *poor musician*? Did she mean he hadn't much money or that he couldn't play very well? In other words, what was in Susan's mind, what did she intend? Linguistically, the ambiguity of this utterance lies in the word *poor*. Like many words it is **polysemic** (see Chapter 2), that is, capable of many meanings. Language systems have to be polysemic in order to capture the variety of meanings which speakers may wish to express within the finite resources of any vocabulary. If we had to have a different word for every possible use of *poor* we should end up with a vocabulary of unimaginable proportions. Words have to be able to do more than one job. This is why many of them have a figurative as well as a literal meaning. If I want to refer to the piece of wood which goes at the top of my bed I call it the *head*, the same word I use to refer to the person in charge of my local school, and the object on top of my shoulders. Without a theory of mind such uses would be impossible because they depend on my knowing that the world is capable of being described in a variety of ways. I know that *head* can be used differently according to the context. In other words, that the world consists of a plurality of possible descriptions.

There are some people who never develop ToM. The medical term which is now applied to the condition from which they suffer is **autism**. Autistic individuals do not realise that other people may see the world differently from them or that things could be any other than how they seem to be. As a consequence, autistic children are unable to play games which involve pretence, so called 'fictive play', such as pretending that dolls are real, or that a cupboard is a ship. Similarly, they find jokes very difficult to understand and won't usually lie because lying involves the assumption that you know something another person doesn't. Autistic people are locked within a **monosemic** world in which words yield a single meaning. If you ask an autistic child to *push the pram*, s/he may simply give it a shove. Sufferers are unable to read people's minds in the way that most people can, and, as a consequence, their development of linguistic understanding is severely impeded. This inability has significant social repercussions, too, because autistic individuals find it difficult to sympathise with people in pain and may well appear unfeeling and unsocial. At the same time, however, other areas of their general intelligence are usually thoroughly normal and can be above average. Autistic sufferers are frequently good at subjects, such as mathematics, which enable them to think abstractly without the distractions caused by other people's interventions. In some cases, so-called 'autistic savants', these abilities may be exceptional. The existence of such individuals was popularised in the film *Rainman* in which Dustin Hoffman played a man whose linguistic and social skills were so severely handicapped that he had been institutionalised and considered insane. The film centred around the discovery by his brother that he could perform amazing counting feats, in one scene correctly counting the number of matches that spilled out of a box onto the floor.

Observations of autistic sufferers are part of the accumulating evidence that language ability may be specialised within the brain. It is quite clear that language impairment does not necessarily mean that people are unintelligent or unable to reason about things. This is important because a great deal of prejudice still attaches to people who have language deficits. Nevertheless, impairment can have important consequences for the way in which sufferers conceptualise themselves and the world around them. Most significantly, language development does seem to be part of social development. Whatever part of the brain triggers theory of mind also facilitates our full emergence as linguistic beings. All of which raises the interesting question as to whether we are alone as a species in possessing ToM; or, to put the matter more directly, are animals also self-conscious beings?

I have deliberately expressed the question in its most provocative form because to many people this is probably the nub of the issue about our distinctiveness within the animal kingdom. We have consciousness and other animals don't. But it is becomingly increasingly clear that this is a vast over-simplification. The subject of consciousness, or self-awareness, is one of the hottest topics in contemporary psychology. The jury is still out on many of the questions which surround it, but some things are already apparent. First, it is not an all or nothing faculty. There are degrees of consciousness. Second, thinking and consciousness are not necessarily synonymous. A great deal of thought is unconscious. Moving our arms and legs about requires a mental decision on our part to perform the actions, but in most normal circumstances we are thoroughly unaware of making such a decision. We don't think to ourselves 'I will put my left leg in front of my right leg, then repeat the action with my right, and so on, until I reach the door'. If we did so it would take an eternity to accomplish anything. The thoughts which drive these actions are hidden from us; they have become automatic, or instinctive. They clearly do involve a level of thinking, as we see in the attempts of infants learning to walk, and in the deliberate efforts made by brain-damaged people recovering the use of their legs. These people literally have to make the necessary thoughts conscious again, in the manner I have described, in order to reprogramme their brains.

This is a level of thought which we obviously share with other animals, although in the case of animals we tend to label it 'instinct'. The conventional distinction between instinct and thought is that instincts control us while we control thought, but this is an artificial distinction which tends to evaporate on investigation. My cat can't help but feel hungry: it's a consequence of biological changes in the body chemistry over which it has no control. But what about its cry, signalling to me that it wants food? Is this an involuntary action, something it can't help, an instinctive response, like a cry of pain, or a voluntary one, a thought of some kind, involving an act of will? The answer is probably neither. Voluntarism, whether something is willed or not, is a very slippery concept even in human situations and to try and apply it to animals is probably mistaken. It leads us into asking whether, if animals can perform free acts, they have a moral sense and should be held accountable for their actions. We are on safer ground if we stick to labelling my cat's cry as an unconscious mental act, something which at some level of brain activity it must have decided to do, although that decision is not one of which it is consciously aware. The French thinker Condillac labelled such physiological cries 'natural' signs. Much of animal behaviour falls into this category, from the leaving of spoors, to the territorial songs of birds. Young infants indulge in natural signs when, in the early months of life, they cry to be fed or to relieve wind. Very soon, however, the infant discovers that crying is a way of gaining attention, and it then begins to manage its crying in order to manipulate its parents. At this stage the signal develops from being a natural to an artificial one.

Artificial signs are the beginning of what we earlier termed 'proto-language'. They involve a degree of conscious awareness, even though of a limited kind. The vocalisations of monkeys and apes fall into this cat-egory. The story of Paul and the tuber recounted earlier demonstrates a baboon using a natural cry of fear to manipulate his mother into thinking he was being attacked. Artificial signs, however, don't neces-sarily require the possession of ToM. The child who learns that crying brings attention will probably not know how or why the trick works. Nevertheless, the development of ToM allows for greater sophistication in the use of signs and the communicative power attached to them. This is why apes, and in particular, chimpanzees, are the most skilled communicators in the animal world next to us, because there is com-pelling evidence that they possess at least the rudiments of ToM.

The evidence comes from observations of ape behaviour over many years in which researchers have looked for indications of 'tactical deception', similar to the kind illustrated by the story of Paul and the tuber. Tactical deception is linked to the idea we have already discussed that language began primarily as a way of 'gaining friends and influ-encing people'. In order for tactical deception to work an animal must consciously consider what is going on in another animal's mind and deliberately try and influence it. A classic case concerns Jane Goodall's chimpanzees in Tanzania. In order to study the chimps at close quar-ters researchers allowed them to feed from bananas stored in a concrete box sunk in the ground. So that low-ranking animals would get an equal chance of getting the food they rigged up a line which could open and close the lid. On one occasion the researchers opened the lid to enable a low-ranking male to reach inside for some bananas. At this point, however, the chimp noticed a high-ranking male observing him and immediately pretended not to be interested in the box. The other male, fooled into thinking the box was locked, walked away. When he reached the edge of the clearing, however, he hid behind a tree and looked back to observe the chimp at the box, presumably to make sure he wasn't being fooled.

As Dunbar (1996) observes, this behaviour suggests a degree of bluff and counter bluff of quite a high order. Not only is chimp 1 deceiving chimp 2, but chimp 2 is trying to deceive chimp 1 into thinking he's been deceived. The difficulty with all research of this kind, however, is that without being able to communicate with chimpanzees and interro-gate their thought processes we can only assume the presence of ToM. Actions which look calculated to us may simply be the product of learned behaviour, something animals do without knowing why it works. On the other hand, the sheer number of similar accounts which have been given by scientists of chimpanzees would suggest that we are dealing here with something more complex than learned behaviour. It is not unknown, for example, for female chimps to put their hands over the mouths of low-ranking males who are copulating with them to prevent them making the noises which would alert higher-ranking males, a degree of calculation which seems almost human in its duplicity. But while chimps may possess some elements of ToM they don't possess it to the degree that we do. Humans are able to imagine how someone who does not exist might feel or think. We do this all the time when we think about the experience of people in past periods of history and exercise our 'historical' imaginations. But we do it, pre-eminently, when we create literature. The dynamics of writing and reading have complex acts of tactical deception embedded within them. As readers we have to discover what the narrator of a novel wants us to think while taking on board the fact that the narrator is a deliberate construction of an absent author. Not only that, but characters within the narrative have views about each other which we have to evaluate both for their truthfulness and their relationship to what the narrator is telling us. 'Point of view' is a critical issue in the discussion of most texts which writers exploit to their own advantage. It is also a critical issue in life, since much of the time we spend communicating is taken up with evaluating the accuracy, or otherwise, of narratives, whether these are tales of individual happenings, or news accounts of some commercial or political event. The fact that we are able to perform the complex feats of thought demanded by such 'texts' whereas other animals can't is because we have a fully developed ToM. More particularly, we are able to investigate the contents of our own minds in a way barred to them. If the evidence is right about chimps and ToM, they must have sufficient self-awareness to know that they feel hunger, pain, or the desire to mate and that other chimps feel similarly. But the ability to go that step further and ask 'Why do I feel pain?' or 'Why do I want that female?' is uniquely human. We are self-aware, or self-conscious, to an extent that separates us across an unbridgeable divide from even the most intelligent chimp. Because of it we are able to conceive of ourselves in time with a history and personal destiny. In other words, we have an identity: a sense of ourselves as experiential beings with the capacity for controlling and directing our behaviour in a way prohibited to animals. And we know that other humans are like this too. With self-awareness also comes a knowledge of personal mortality. Animals mourn each other and have a sense of danger, but, as far as we can tell, are not able to think the thought 'One day I am going to die'. So, ironically, while they do not have access to the benefits of fully developed ToM in the way that humans do, they are, nevertheless, free from the ultimate burden which it has laid upon us.

Language and thinking

Where in all this does language feature? More precisely, what is the relationship between language and thought, in the sense that I have been describing it? Like the subject of consciousness this is a vexed issue among psychologists and linguists alike. Many people commonly assume that language is just a means by which thoughts are expressed. We think of something and then find the words to communicate it. But this is much too simplistic. To begin with, much of our thinking is done in language anyway. Our heads are full of an internal monologue in which we think out problems and debate issues without uttering a word. A certain kind of mental activity seems to require language. This is not to say that all thinking demands the use of words, however. Day-dreaming is a form of thought which rests not on language but on the power of the mind to create images, something which is utilised by artists. Similarly, composers often hear the music they are composing or visualise it as notes on a score. Many animals, as we have already seen, are capable of quite complex acts of thought without possessing language. And then there are all those thoughts which we have described as unconscious. The ones which make our limbs move, for example. Language is clearly not involved there. Neither is it in those transcendent feelings of beauty or love which we experience at times as being 'beyond words', those occasion where the quality of the thought exceeds language.

Given, then, that the relationship between language and thought is not a simple one of dependency, we need to examine more precisely what function it is that language performs that makes it so indispensable to us as humans. The most important thing that language does is to enable the world of unconscious experience to become present to the mind. In other words, it brings into consciousness all the half-formed ideas floating within us and allows us to manipulate them. In a sense, all systems of representation have this as part of their function, from the images created by artists to the vocalised sign systems of the apes. All thought of any kind creates a pressure to be represented in some concrete way. The unconscious thoughts which govern our limbs find their representation in action: I walk over to the door. And those which indicate the way to the nearest pot of nectar find their expression in a complicated dance by the honey bee. In ape culture the growing complexity of social thoughts created by the demands of living in larger groups is represented both in the physical act of grooming and the great range of noises which they make. But there are certain thoughts which cannot be represented without a system far more sophisticated than anything which exists in the animal kingdom. The pressure of evolution made this level of mental activity a distinct advantage in the struggle for survival. Only language was capable of making us reflective and communicative to a degree previously unknown. Ideas about what occurred yesterday or might happen tomorrow could not be represented in any animal sign system. And without being represented they couldn't be fully conscious to the mind. In other words, they couldn't be fully thought. Enhanced language ability and mental capacity must have gone hand in hand in the emergence of early human society, the one triggering and responding to the other in the demand for ever more sophisticated social arrangements.

Just how this process happened is still a mystery to us and will probably remain so. It is as if a computer with the appropriate hardware and software were to evolve perfectly naturally in the course of nature. Our brains had to expand and develop to cope with language and, at the same time, we had to invent a wholly new program which the hardware could run. Richard Dawkins, in *Unweaving the Rainbow* (1998), suggests that this may have happened by some form of mental explosion, as in an atomic reaction where a critical mass of energy builds up by a series of chain reactions, or, on a more homely level, like the way a book may 'take off' after a series of good reports to become a best seller. This doesn't mean that all of language came into being at one go. Computers, when they first burst onto the scene, were rather primitive. Anyone who can remember trying to use a Sinclair ZX at home will know what I mean. Computer rage is not a phenomenon only of the pentium era. Language, in both vocabulary and syntax, most probably developed over time. Jean Aitchison (1996: 60) uses the image of a bonfire as a way of understanding what might have occurred: 'Probably, some sparks of language had been flickering for a very long time, like a bonfire in which just a few twigs catch alight at first. Suddenly, a flame leaps between the twigs, and ignites the whole mass of heaped-up wood. Then the fire slows down and stabilizes and glows red-hot and powerful'. However it occurred, the intellectual advance from an animal sign system to human language is both dramatic and absolute. As we saw earlier, language is a three-tier system: between the sign and the meaning lies a system of words, or a grammar. The construction of words depends on a principle which is quite special to language known as **double articulation**. Many animals can produce sounds which have definable meanings such as 'there's a leopard coming' or 'feed me', but what they cannot do is detach those sounds from their immediate context and recombine them to make new meanings. We, however, can do this effortlessly. On their own, sounds such as *b* or *t* mean nothing but we can string them together with other similarly meaningless sounds to create an infinitude of words. The only system which compares with this in the animal world is birdsong. As with language, each note in the song of a robin or thrush is meaningless. It is the sequence as a whole which is important. Interestingly, it has been found that these sequences sometimes vary regionally within a single species, rather in the manner of human dialects, so that a sparrow in one part of the country may not sing exactly the same sequence as in another part. But, crucially, the principle of double articulation has very limited application in bird communities. The meanings of songs appear to be restricted to two basic messages, either 'This is my territory', or 'I fancy you'. By contrast, the thirty or so speech sounds which comprise human languages can be recombined almost endlessly to generate new words. Not only that, but we can put the words together to make strings of words which are entirely novel. Most of the sentences in this book have never been written or uttered before in the whole of human history.

What separates our system from that of birdsong is a second principle, which is equally important: **creativity**. Within a finite set of rules for composing new sequences we are able to generate an infinite number of fresh utterances. The nearest equivalent to this is chess, in which a fixed number of pieces are moved in accordance to the rules of the game to create an endless number of actual games. Creativity and double articulation enable a system to take off from contextually-bound fixed meanings to those which are fixed by arbitrary convention. There is nothing to stop me inventing a new word or sequence of words and creating a genuine innovation. This isn't incidentally how most innovations occur, but, nevertheless, the fact that it is conceivable demonstrates that language is an **open** system as opposed to the **closed** ones of animals. There is an important conceptual leap here on which the whole edifice of language is based and which makes possible the other design features which we have been talking about. It has to do with the way words refer to the world about us.

The power of names

Animal sequences are like the **holophrastic** utterances of infants. These are one word utterances such as *shoe* or *daddy* which are meant to signify whole clauses 'I want my shoe' or 'Here comes daddy'. Similarly, the calls of the vervet monkeys indicating the presence of a predator mean something like 'Watch out here comes a leopard' or 'snake' as the case may be. But although the cries vary according to the nature of the predator, the cries aren't pure acts of naming. There isn't an isolable bit of the cry which means 'leopard' or 'snake'. If there were it could be recycled to make other messages. Words in any language refer to the outside world in a totally different way than do the calls of animals. This is because words have a naming function. The word *shoe* doesn't mean 'I want my shoe'; it means the object into which I put my foot. Even verbs name things, although in this case it is activities or events. If I describe someone as *throwing* something I am naming the activity s/he is engaged in. Similarly, adjectives name qualities and attributes, while adverbs name the manner in which activities are performed. It's important to bear in mind that these are not grammatical criteria for describing nouns, verbs, and so on (see Chapter 5). What we are considering here are their semantic functions, that is, their meaning as linguistic items. Even so, of course, it's true that not all words name. Small, grammatical words such as prepositions *of, to, in,* and determiners like *the,* or *a,* can't be said to name anything. These are words which provide the grammatical framework, or scaffolding of sentences. In many cases we could leave them out and still convey enough sense. *Beware dog* would tell us all we need to know without the bits in-between. Most probably the grammatical scaffolding was a late development in the evolution of language, as it is in the speech of children, and consequent on the first initial breakthrough.

The 'naming insight' appears to be definitive in the development of language. What words do is enable us to **nominalise** experience: to objectify things, activities, processes, and events in sequences of sounds. The realisation that things have names comes to children normally at about 18 months, after which a 'naming explosion' often takes place. Occasionally, the onset is delayed because of some impairment, but when it eventually occurs, the insight can be a revelation. Here is Helen Keller's account of her discovery at six years old, after being blind and deaf from the age of two, that things have names:

> As the cold stream gushed over one hand she spelled into the other the word *water*, first slowly, then rapidly ... and somehow the mystery of language was revealed to me. I knew then that 'w-a-t-e-r' meant the wonderful cool something that was flowing over my hand. That living word awakened my soul, gave it light, hope, joy, set it free! ... Everything had a

name, and each name gave birth to a new thought ... every object which I touched seemed to quiver with life. That was because I saw everything with the strange, new sight that had come to me. (Keller, 1923)

Interestingly, Helen Keller says that 'each name gave birth to a new thought'. Nature is rethought in language: re-imagined as sound, and in so doing seems to take on new life. In other words, language endows nature with meaning. No wonder it seemed a God-like activity to her. It's worth recalling that in the Jewish and Christian religions the first privilege God confers on Adam, before even the creation of a helpmate, is that of naming the animals. The crucial breakthrough, then, is the realisation that sound sequences can have symbolic value, that is, they can 'stand for' objects, processes, events, and activities in the world around us. This 'stands for' relationship is important at all stages of language development. When the child begins to read, for example, it has to learn the phonetic principles on which the alphabet is based, that is, that the letter <t> stands for the sound *t*. Once the symbolic system underlying language is grasped the door is open for its manipulation to articulate the whole range of human experience, a process which subtly changes and interiorises it, and is instrumental in forging our individual identity.

Animals never crossed this threshold because they never learned to name things. Over the past thirty years a number of experiments have been carried out to see whether this is inevitably so, that is, whether under certain conditions animals might be able to acquire language. Most experimenters in this field have used animals closest to us, chimpanzees, as subjects. Chimpanzees obviously can't talk as such – their vocal apparatus, as we have seen, won't allow them to make human speech sounds – so they are normally taught to use American Sign Language (ASL), or to use a keyboard with symbols. The results of these experiments indicate that, even when taught in captivity, chimps find it very difficult to use words as naming devices. This is not because the task is beyond them, but rather that their normal instinct is to use them as one would a call, to represent a request or instruction of some kind. With a great deal of effort they can be coaxed into developing the ability of a $2^{1}/_{2}$-year-old child, with a vocabulary of around 150 words and the capacity to form three word utterances. But no chimp has yet progressed beyond this. So although they can name things, the kind of explosion which takes place with children never occurs, nor does the ability to invent sequences effortlessly as children do. Language just doesn't seem important to chimps in the way it is to us. And it may well be this lack of importance which resulted in the chimpanzee brain staying the way it did. In the wild their vocalisations

Chimp language

There have been two major projects involving 'educated' chimpanzees. The first, and most famous involved a chimp named Washoe reared by Beatrix and Alan Gardner from the age of 10 months. 'Project Washoe', begun in 1966, eventually included a number of chimpanzees, all of whom were taught to use American Sign Language. Their progress was followed until they reached the age of five. When the project finished the chimps had a vocabulary of 140 signs acquired at about the rate of three a month. More recently, Duane Rumbaugh and Sue Savage-Rumbaugh have duplicated the Gardners' results with a pygmy chimpanzee called Kanzi. Evidence published in 1993 shows that Kanzi can follow an instruction such as 'Go to the refridgerator and get the melon'. Critics have pointed out, however, that this does not necessarily indicate any understanding of syntax since it is clearly possible to understand the sequence simply from knowing how the words 'go', 'get', 'refridgerator' and 'melon' are normally used.

are invariably tied to the immediate demands of their emotional life. As Jane Goodall comments, 'the production of a sound in the *absence* of an appropriate emotional state seems to be an almost impossible task for a chimpanzee ...' (Lieberman, 1998: 32). This is something we are familiar with from the sounds of young children. But language allows us to do more than this. Not only can it **express** emotion, it can also **suppress** it. By extending the power of thought language enables us to manage our inner life in a manner unavailable to any other animal. As we have seen, this ability is of crucial importance in the complex social and interpersonal arrangements of human society.

The missing link

There remains, however, one final piece of the jigsaw. If, as seems clear, language represents a significant development from the vocalisations of even the most intelligent animals, how can we visualise the first step on the ladder? How can we imagine language coming into being? We have established that it must have involved an increase in the brain size and a lowering of the larynx to allow the full range of speech sounds to be made. No language could be formed out of the grunts and whoops of ape communication. Clearly words would be impossible, for example, without the ability to form the vowels /i/ ('beat') /a/ ('hat'), and /u/ ('boot') which is dependent on the expanded vocal tract exclusive to humans. But how could a primitive group move from grunting to talking? It's the difficulty of establishing such a link which has led some theorists to suggest a different source entirely for the origin of speech. There has long been a minority view that the inspiration for language came not from animal vocalisations, but from gesture. It's a view given recent currency by Michael Corballis in *From Hand to Mouth* (2002). Corballis points to the fact that the part of the brain responsible for fine motor control is located in the same area responsible for speech. The changes in brain structure which allowed us to develop skills of aimed throwing and the making of tools also facilitated the control over our lips and other vocal organs necessary for speech. So maybe language seized first on our hands, not our mouths, for its evolutionary beginning? Clearly hands are important in communication. Gestures have always accompanied speech. Most of us would find it a severe restriction on communicating if we were not allowed to use our hands. And, as we know, we are not the only animals to use gestures. Chimpanzees and other apes do so constantly. However, Corballis argues that rather than simply accompanying vocalisations, as they do in the case of chimpanzees, early hominids developed gestures into a form of sign language. The move from hand to mouth, that is, to autonomous speech, he argues, happened relatively late, around 50,000 BP, principally because by then early humans needed their hands free for other things.

Intriguing as the theory is it has some major drawbacks. There is a big difference between gesturing and sign language and it is difficult to see how one could have evolved from the other. Although we use gestures to communicate we do so only in a very basic way. Gestures can't express abstract concepts or subtleties of opinion about things distant in place and time. And apart from that, gestures have to be seen in order to communicate. A species relying on hand movements couldn't communicate at night, nor to anyone out of eyesight. The only advantage such a system possesses is that of secrecy, which is one reason why it remains useful today. But for any larger purpose gesturing is severely limited. In addition, as Corballis acknowledges, a language based on gesturing would impose an extra task on the hands, which for a species heavily reliant on hunting, foraging, and fighting for its existence, would be an inconvenience. Why use hands in the first place when the mouth is free to use?

Perhaps we can do little better than return to those nineteenth-century theories of the origin of language. But with this difference. It's unlikely, as I suggested earlier, that language began as a direct means of enabling logs to be felled or animals to be hunted more efficiently. It's more probable, given the argument about the interpersonal significance of language, that it began as some kind of ritual accompaniment. In other words, as a form of **paralanguage** accompanying action. The anthropologist Chris Knight (1990) has shown that ritual is a very ancient element in human culture as a way of emotionally bonding groups. And we should remember that language consists not simply of words in sequence but of rhythm and intonation too. Language and singing are intimately connected. It may well be that the earliest words were syllables strung together musically. These are some of the earliest sounds made by children when they are imitating the noise of human speech. Syllables are in themselves totally meaningless. They are pure units of sound whose purpose is to carry the rhythmic pattern of speech. Derek Attridge (1982) likens them to the step in dancing. We can imagine how a grunt or pant-hoot might develop into a syllable which, in conjunction with others, could form a word. Such noises attached to regular occurrences – the birth of a child, the hunting of an animal – could over time develop the necessary displacement to become the name of the activity rather than simply its ritual accompaniment. This would bear out the argument of the linguist Michael Toolan (1996: 109) that the principal stimulus for language lay in what the anthropologist Malinowski termed its 'magical' function, one of the main purposes of which is to create 'ties of union ... by a mere exchange of words'.

All of this is speculation. It is likely that there were a number of routes by which humans arrived at their first words. Language represents a point of convergence, rather like a motorway, onto which a number of smaller roads feed. Its development co-ordinated several changes occurring over many millennia. Some of these were anatomical, involving changes to our vocal tract and musculature, others were biological, involving the growth of new tissue, principally in the brain, others mental, involving the development of sophisticated programming devices in the brain. And, outside of ourselves, there were changes in the climate and ecology, in that part of the planet where we evolved, forcing us to walk upright, change our diet, and develop more complex social organisations. We shall never know what the first real word was, nor who spoke it, but we do know that, once the genie was out, there could be no putting it back.

Conclusion

This chapter has been concerned to show that language is a distinctively human acquisition. Animal signalling, although capable of complexity, both in structure and function, has nowhere near the sophistication and range of uses that language has. Comparing them is like comparing a bicycle as a mode of transport with a modern car. While some animals in captivity have been taught the rudiments of language they have never advanced beyond a very limited stage. They lack the appetite for learning language which young children possess, and which quickly enables them to work out grammatical principles. This is because chimpanzees, our nearest relatives on the evolutionary scale, have never become genetically programmed for language in the way we have. For captive chimps, trying to learn language is rather like trying to break a code, jolly hard work, whereas, for us, it is more like discovering something we already potentially know, and which only requires the right environment to produce. Just how and why this capacity entered our gene pool we are still finding out. But one thing is clear. Acquiring language was not just a matter of developing a superior signalling system. It also meant acquiring a new and enhanced mental landscape, one which enabled a quality of thought and reflection essential to what we understand as 'human nature'. And it has also allowed a quality and complexity of personal interaction that represents an advance on what is possible elsewhere in the animal kingdom. I say 'advance' conscious of the knowledge that any invention is double-edged in what it allows us to do. There is something of the 'Pandora's box' syndrome about language. But that is a risk which as humans we have had to take on board. In one sense the breakthrough into language was a technological advance. For language is a code or system with design features light years ahead of animal codes. And in another sense it was a breakthrough in evolutionary terms, since we can now say that to be human is to possess the capacity for language.

Notes

1 This imaginary scenario is similar to a classic case observed by researchers studying the beaks of finches on the Galapagos Islands, but in this case it was the advantage for larger beaked varieties of cracking open certain seeds which was significant.

2 Interestingly, Cheney and Seyfarth also discovered that vervets distinguish between alarm calls made by younger, inexperienced, members of the troupe, and adults. In cases of the former, the nature of the threat

will be verified before it is passed on. In this way, infant vervets learn to adjust their calls to the conventions of the troupe and avoid calling out unnecessarily.

Design features of language
Formal features

- **Arbitrariness:** the use of tokens which bear no natural relationship to the world, for example neither the individual sounds in *coin* nor the word itself are motivated by the thing represented, as opposed to animal cries, where the reverse is the case

- **Double articulation:** the ability to combine essentially meaningless sounds into units of meaning at a higher level, for example /h/+/a/+/t/ = *hat*

- **Nominalisation:** the ability to use sound sequences to represent things, events and processes, for example *water, global-warming, driving*

- **Displacement:** the ability to refer to things, events and processes removed in time and place from the present, for example *Caesar, tomorrow, global-warming*

- **Creativity:** the ability, from a finite set of rules, to generate an infinite number of sequences, for example the rules for constructing sentences allow any speaker to utter entirely novel examples.

Functional features

- **Ideational function:** the ability to conceptualise the world as an instrument of thought, that is, to bring the world into being linguistically

- **Interpersonal function:** the ability to service our relationships and express our interests and feelings, that is, to bring ourselves into being linguistically

- **Textual function:** the ability to construct 'texts' from utterances, that is, to string linguistic items together to form connected discourse as in narratives, whether oral or written

- **Poetic function:** the ability to manipulate forms for our own pleasure (for example sound symbolism – alliteration, onomatopoeia, puns, eccentric spellings), that is, to express our delight in novelty and play.

2 Getting the Better of Words

Language and Communication

The limits of my language mean
the limits of my world

LUDWIG WITTGENSTEIN (*Tractatus Logico-Philosophicus*, 1921)

Words strain
Crack and sometimes break, under the burden,
Under the tension, slip, slide, perish,
Decay with imprecision, will not stay in place,
Will not stay still.

T.S. ELIOT, *Four Quartets*

The intolerable wrestle

T.S. Eliot's lament in his poem *Four Quartets* about the frailty of language is one with which most writers, certainly creative ones, would empathise. If you have ever tried to write a poem you will know just how difficult it is to find the right word to match your feelings. You struggle to create the exact formulation to express what you mean, rather in the way people try on clothes, discarding various possibilities either because they are too ordinary or too ill-fitting, eventually settling on something which approximates to what you have in mind. By which time it may well be too late because the idea which began the search may well have altered. As with language, our mental and emotional life is in a constant state of flux. Here is Eliot again some lines later:

One has only learnt to get the better of words
For the thing one no longer has to say, or the way in which
One is no longer disposed to say it

Not surprisingly, writing poetry tends to be a rather specialised activity. If we were to spend as much time writing a note to the milkman, or asking for a bank loan, human life would probably cease to exist. None the less, what Eliot calls 'the intolerable wrestle with words' is experienced by us all at times, and it highlights a problem which is basic to language as a communicative medium. The problem has two inter-related parts which we can put as questions: first, 'How can we control language so that it expresses exactly what we want it to?'; and second, 'How can we control the minds of others so that they understand us as we wish to be understood?'

> *Fumbling for a word is everybody's birthright*
> ANTHONY BURGESS

Conservative models of communication used to show an idea leaving the head of a speaker and going via a language tube to the head of a listener. It's known colloquially as the 'conduit' view of language because it visualises language as a container of meaning. The speaker encodes the meaning and the listener decodes it. But this is an unreal view of communication. It's very rarely that we understand an idea in exactly the same way the speaker intends us to. Language is not suffi-cient to achieve that.

Language hoodwinks us into thinking that problems of communi-cation are our fault. We haven't expressed ourselves clearly, or our lan-guage skills aren't good enough. We never blame language. Yet it's not such an innocent medium, for while it solves problems of communi-cation, it also creates them. To begin with, the meanings of many words are not stable. If you are a student you will probably have been told the importance in developing any argument of defining your terms, that is, saying exactly what you mean. But how can we define words like *civilisation, democracy, culture,* or *liberty*? They seem to be subject to what has been called the 'law of accelerating fuzziness' by which words expand in meaning and decline in precision. As we saw in the previous chapter, the naming capacity of language enabled a signif-icant advance in our ability to represent the world, both to ourselves and to others, but at the same time it also imposed a limit. Any circle which we draw, however big, will leave out space as well as enclose it. So it is with language. As the nineteenth-century philosopher Jeremy Bentham pointed out, there is a tendency, because many nouns like *table* and *chair* refer to real substantial things, to think that other nouns like *democracy* and *crime* are also real in the same way. We call them **abstract** nouns but often treat them as **concrete** ones. This is really a trick of the mind. The truth, as we soon discover when we

Newspeak

Newspeak is the official language of Orwell's imaginary, totalitarian society of the future, in *Nineteen Eighty Four*. Its aim is to make revolt impossible by making it unthinkable. As one of the principal characters puts it, 'In the end we shall make thoughtcrime impossible because there will be no words in which to express it. Every concept that can ever be needed will be expressed by exactly one word, with its meaning rigidly defined and all its subsidiary meanings rubbed out and forgotten.'

explore further, is that we are surrounded by mysteries, kept conveniently at bay for us by the conventional categories of language.

Attempts to make language logical and precise, like George Orwell's Newspeak in his novel *Nineteen Eighty Four*, usually entail trying to get rid of ambiguity and nuance in language. The slipperiness of language is something that has been bewailed by philosophers for centuries. In his *An Essay Concerning Human Understanding* (1690) the seventeenth-century philosopher John Locke moans that: 'every man has so inviolable a liberty to make words stand for what ideas he pleases, that no one hath the power to make others have the same ideas in their minds as he has, when they use the same words as he does' (Locke, [1690] in Woozley (ed.) 1964: 262). Words mean different things to different people; they are laden with connotations and subject to the influence of fashion. We have only to think of the debate about colour prejudice to see how difficult it is to find a vocabulary which is truly neutral and non-discriminatory. A few years ago the term *black* was considered racist because in European culture it is associated with evil and death, and *white* with purity and goodness. As a consequence, the term *coloured* became fairly common, but that, of course, entailed regarding *white* as not a colour and therefore more statusful.

> *As a matter of racial pride we want to be called* blacks. *Which has replaced the term* Afro-American. *Which replaced* Negroes. *Which replaced* colored people. *Which replaced* darkies. *Which replaced* blacks.
>
> JULES FEIFFER quoted in *Language Maven Strikes Again*

At the same time, however, in many non-European cultures, and to a certain extent in European, the term *black* was associated with vitality and power, while *white* suggested frigidity, coldness, and death. This reversal of values allowed the term *black* to be rehabilitated as a positive, instead of a negative, term. People of an older generation in Britain, who are not aware of this movement in language, will still use the term *coloured*. To them *black* remains an offensive term.

What I have referred to as the 'slipperiness' of language is one of its glories and also one its chief irritations. For people producing advertising copy it is a godsend. Exploiting the associations which words have is a vital means of planting suggestions in the mind of the consumer. The name *fairy liquid* – used in Britain for a popular brand of washing-up liquid – counts on us responding to the connotations of *fairy*. The advertisers clearly hope that it will suggest something soft, gentle and effortless, thus kind to the hands as well as the clothes. And, perhaps, there is also the possibility that the solution might remove the dirt by magic. On the other hand, *fairy* is not a completely innocuous word. In some contexts it is used as a prejudicial term for someone effeminate or homosexual. All advertising takes a risk that we might not access the 'right' associations. In this particular case, as most washing-up liquid adverts are targeted at women, the risk is factored out. For politicians, too, slipperiness can be an invaluable ally. A few years ago, former President Clinton was able to deny that he had 'slept' with a particular woman since neither of them had done any sleeping, ignoring the fact that for most people the term is a euphemism for sex. He also denied that he had ever 'smoked' marijuana because he didn't inhale. But for scientists, philosophers and lawyers, the looseness which is built into language can be a major hurdle. If you've ever wondered why legal treaties are written in such fiendishly ponderous prose it's precisely to prevent the merest possibility of misunderstanding.

But probably the biggest difficulty most of us have in determining meaning has to do with the influence of context on utterances. In working out the meaning of what is said to us we have to take into account not only the words themselves as individual items, but also the circumstances in which they are uttered, the medium used, and the person who is addressing us. All these factors have a bearing on how we understand the words. The same message delivered verbally can have a different meaning for us when written down. Many years ago a North American academic, Marshall Mcluhan, popularised the idea that the medium, or channel of communication used, is itself a message, irrespective of the words contained in it ('the medium is the message'). In its extreme form the idea has gone out of fashion, but nevertheless, Mcluhan performed a valuable service in drawing attention to the channel of communication in the determination of meaning. But perhaps more important for us in determining meaning are the circumstances of the utterance and the relationship of the **addresser** to us. Let's take a brief example: a declaration of love – *I love you*. Clearly, the meaning we assign to this is different if the speaker is our lover as opposed to our parent or child. In other words, the person who is addressing us influences the meaning we give to what s/he says. Similarly with the situation in which the declaration is made. If it is prompted, or said to get out of the washing up, it will have a different meaning from an unprompted, non-manipulative declaration.

What we are faced with here is not simply the difficulty of meaning but the larger problem of interpretation. It's not enough to know what words mean in isolation. We have to be able to interpret them in concrete situations. This entails more than linguistic knowledge. It involves a knowledge of the world, and of practical realities. If we came across the sign *Dogs must be carried* at a railway station our knowledge of dogs and trains would prevent us from rushing out to beg, borrow, or steal a dog, not our knowledge of English grammar. Just think how differently we would interpret a corresponding sign *Passports must be carried* at an airport.

But the situation is even more complicated than this because meaning is not the sole prerogative of language. We also convey meaning through our bodies, by gesture, posture, and looks, that is, by **non-verbal communication**, and through our voices, by intonation and rhythm. All of these can have a **paralinguistic** function, in other words, they can run alongside the words contributing to the total meaning of the communication, either by reinforcing the word meaning, or, sometimes, contradicting it. The daughter who asked her father, 'When they teach us French at school, why don't they teach us to wave our hands?' (Bateson, 1972: 13) was not asking a frivolous

---

Children and comprehension

Young children make numerous mistakes in comprehension because of their relative lack of contextual knowledge, as in the case of the Sunday School child who, when asked to illustrate the story of the Fall in the book of Genesis 'drew a picture of a car and three persons in it, with the explanation that this was "God driving Adam and Eve out of the Garden of Eden."'

CITED IN BARON (1981:10)

question. Being able to speak another language fluently means taking on some of the physical mannerisms and characteristics of native speakers. To learn French we have, in some measure, to become French. Not surprisingly, interpretation is a difficult skill, and one which involves more than simply decoding the language. We have only to think of the way two people can have a conversation and come away with entirely separate interpretations of what has been said, to realise this. Commentators on discourse point out that in any speech context there exists the possibility of at least four interpretations: a **surface**, or 'open' meaning – one of which all parties are aware; a **speaker's**, or 'concealed' meaning – one intended by the speaker but not consciously known to the listener; a **hearer's**, or 'blind' meaning – one perceived by the hearer but not consciously known to the speaker; and a **listener's**, or 'hidden' meaning – one apparent to someone overhearing the exchange but not to the participants themselves.

These are just a few of the principal reasons for what we can term the **indeterminacy** of linguistic meaning: the impossibility of determining, absolutely, what a given string of words actually means. Other reasons would include the way in which words change their meaning over time, so that we cannot always be sure, for example, when reading a text from the past, what the words meant in their original context, and the influence of fashion, which is continually bringing words into prominence and giving them extra semantic 'spin'. Given all this, it might seem surprising that communication takes place at all. But, obviously, it does, and for the most part very successfully. This is principally because of two things: first, while we may not be able to establish the total meaning of any given string, we can usually establish enough for an exchange of meaning to occur. And second, irrespective of the slipperiness of words and the unfixed nature of 'context', we know, as speakers of the language, and members of particular language communities, the chief processes by which words signal meaning. This is part of what we referred to in Chapter 1 as our **linguistic competence**, and it is aspects of this competence which we need to consider more closely.

Words and signs

In the previous chapter we saw that the breakthrough into language involved the development of a three-tier system in which sounds are related to meaning via a level of words, as distinct from the two-tier system that we find in animal communication, in which sounds are directly related to meaning. So, for example, an animal cry of warning is interpreted by other animals in the way we might interpret the presence of a rain cloud. Both are natural 'signs', that is, signs that are motivated by, or arise directly from, the context of their occurrence. As a consequence, cries cannot be detached from their context and used as parts of other utterances. This is not the case with language, however. The word 'beware' also operates as a warning. But in-between the meaning and its expression lies a series of individual sounds which have been assembled specifically to make the word and which bear no relation to its meaning whatsoever. In other words, language is a digital system. Each of the individual sounds can be reassembled to make other words. Not only that, but 'beware' can be used in any number of utterances, not all of which are warnings. As distinct from most animal communication, language is an artificial sign system. It consists of a carefully constructed code in which individual items are sequentially related to each other to form, first, words, and second, sentences.

Words, then, are artificial signs. This is not to say they didn't arise from a natural origin, at some point in the past. In all likelihood they did. But this plays no part in the way we use them today. Except in the case of a few **onomatopoeic** words, such as *splash* or *cuckoo*, where the sounds are said to echo the sense, the relationship between sound and

---

Children and signs

The difficulties which young children often experience in understanding the conventional nature of signs is well illustrated by the experience of Stephen Daedalus in Joyce's *A Portrait of the Artist as a Young Man*:

It was very big to think about everything and everywhere. Only God could do that. He tried hard to think what a big thought that must be; but he could only think of God. God was God's real name just as his name was Stephen. Dieu was the French for God and that was God's name too; and when anyone prayed to God and said Dieu then God knew at once that it was a French person praying. But, although there were different names for God in all the different languages in the world and God understood what all the people prayed said in their different languages, still God remained always the same God and God's real name was God. (1966: 16)

the meaning is completely conventional. Words are not facts of nature like rocks and trees, but cultural objects, products of the human brain. The fact that they are able, despite an in-built slipperiness, to allow successful communication to take place is because of two systematic relationships which they enter into. The first is an internal one, something called their **signification**. This has to do with the way words are related in meaning to each other. The second is an external one, their **reference**. This is concerned with the way they refer to events, processes and objects in the world around us, whether real or imaginary. Consider again the declaration, *I love you*. We said that the meaning of this depended on the context in which it was uttered. But this is not entirely true. Even out of context the sentence has a meaning of sorts. We may not know who *I* and *you* refer to, whether lovers, family, or friends, but we know *I* refers to the speaker, and *you*, to the person being addressed. Similarly, while we can't be sure what the nature of the love is that is being declared, we do know, as users of the language, what range of feelings the word is capable of expressing. And this is true even if we have different views about what love is. We know, for example, that it means more than *like* and less than *adore*. Our sense of what the word means comes from our knowledge of where it fits in the vocabulary of words which relate to the declaration of feelings. In other words, we know what the word signifies. Each of us carries the vocabulary of our native language in our heads. It's called by linguists, a **lexicon**. This is a mental inventory of words, their meanings, and the relationships they have with other words. No one's inventory is precisely the same as another's. That's why we have so many arguments about what words mean. At the same time, however, there is sufficient shared understanding of the system and how it operates to enable communication to take place. I may not agree with you about what it means to love someone but we would both agree that it is somewhat different from merely liking them, significantly different from adoring them, and completely different from hating them.

Ferdinand de Saussure

The linguist principally responsible for developing the concept of words as signs is Ferdinand de Saussure, sometimes referred to as the 'father of modern linguistics'. Saussure was a Swiss linguist who lived around the turn of the last century. After his death some of his students put together a book from their lecture notes and published it with the title *Cours de linguistique générale*. Despite its slimness it had, and continues to have, a seminal influence on linguistics. According to Saussure a word combines two elements, a sound image, which is its physical form, and a sense, or meaning. The first, he refers to as the **signifier**, and the second he terms the **signified**. The signifier and signified together constitute the total sign. In the case of *tree*, which is the example Saussure himself gives, what this means is that the word acts as a sign comprising a sound image, or signifier, /tri/, and a sense, or signified, indicating 'treeness'. In other words, the signifier acts as a label, not for an object, but a concept. Real trees, or **referents**, are referred to by the sign as a whole. This is logical if you think about it because before you can identify something called /tri/ you must already possess the concept 'tree'. To recap, words have two kinds of semantic meaning: first, they signify one or more senses, or signifieds, that is, they have **signification**; and second, they refer to things or activities in the outside world, so they have **reference**. If this isn't sufficiently clear have a look at Figure 2.1.

Reference and signification are semantic relationships which apply generally to items in our mental lexicon, but, at the same time, not all the words we use are equally rich in these two linguistic dimensions.

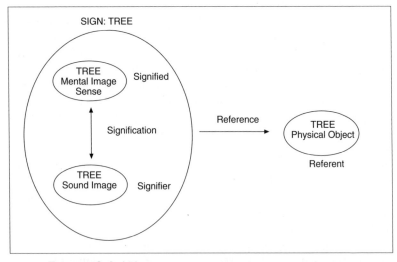

FIGURE 2.1 WORDS HAVE SIGNIFICATION AND REFERENCE

Words like *truth, sincerity, virtue* – or **abstract nouns** – have a complex signification. Their sense is very full, but we would be hard pressed to say what they referred to in the outside world: thus the title 'abstract noun'. On the other hand, words such as *Gloria* and *London* – or **proper nouns** – which refer to unique entities, have very little signification, at least in conventional terms. A fact which makes them, as W.H. Auden observed, 'Like a line of poetry … untranslatable'. If someone were to ask 'What's the meaning of Gloria?' it would be very difficult to make a meaningful reply. And finally, 'function' words – *of, and, if,* for example – seem to be weak in both reference and signification when compared with either abstract or proper nouns. These are words which provide the scaffolding for sentences and often play a crucial part in establishing logical relationships. Their signification is grammatical in nature, rather than lexical. We can say they have **grammatical sense** as opposed to the **lexical sense** of nouns and verbs.

An important corollary of Saussure's approach is that the meaning of words, or, more particularly, their 'sense', is a product of the linguistic system as a whole. Each sign, by virtue of its relationship with other signs, occupies a certain amount of territory, or semantic space, in the system. The total extent of this territory is the sign's 'value'. In order to know this we have to know where the sign fits in the language to which it belongs. Saussure illustrates this by comparing the English word 'sheep' with the French word 'mouton'. A simple definition of the words would suggest they meant the same thing but there is a crucial difference in semantic space. In English, 'sheep' only applies to the living animal. We use separate terms 'mutton' or 'lamb' to refer to the flesh. We wouldn't go into a butcher's and ask for a leg of sheep, for example. In French, however, the term 'mouton' can signify both the living animal and its meat. In other words, it occupies more semantic space. The value of a sign is continually expanding and contracting in relation to the other signs around it. We can see this most clearly if we take a brief look at the history of certain words. Old English, for example, used to have a word *mete* which meant food; at some point in our history it came into competition with a rival, possibly from Old Norse, *foda*, also meaning food. Since words rarely, if ever, occupy exactly the same space, one of

> 'Must *a name mean something?'Alice asked doubtfully. 'Of course it must,'* Humpty said with a short laugh: *'my name means the shape I am – and a good handsome shape it is too. With a name like yours, you might be my shape, almost.'*
>
> LEWIS CARROLL, *Through the Looking Glass* (1872)

these had to alter its signification. In this case *mete* shrank in meaning to signify the 'flesh of animals', that is, a particular kind of food (our *meat*), leaving *foda* to have the larger meaning. We can still get a glimpse of the older meaning of *meat* in the proverb 'One man's meat is another man's poison'. In the nineteenth century both words came into competition with a word of French origin, *victuals*, from *vitaille*, but it didn't survive the contest and is now obsolete. Similarly, Old English *steorfan*, meaning 'to die', lost ground to another Old Norse word *deyja*, and came to have the more limited meaning of 'die through lack of food' (our *starve*).

We could say, then, that while words are not creatures of nature, they are still subject to the survival of the fittest. Fortunately, English is such a large and generous host that words which are forced to contract in one sense are often able to expand by generating another, related, one. As well as its specific sense, for example, *starve* can also have the looser meaning of 'be hungry', as in *I'm starving*. Many words which would otherwise have a very limited use have acquired a more general sense in this way, for example, *horrible, frightful, ghastly*. Some people hold up their hands in dismay at the increasingly loose usage of such terms. The eighteenth-century writer Samuel Johnson referred to them as 'women's words', regarding them as a female affectation, while, in the nineteenth century, Oliver Wendell Holmes called the phenomenon 'verbicide'. Others have called it 'weakening', or 'distortion'. But before seeing it as an instance of language decay, it's as well to bear in mind the point made by the linguist Nelson Francis (1967: 119): 'Words do not have meanings; people have meanings for words'. If we no longer use the word *horrible* with the meaning 'full of horror', it may be that we no longer need it to carry that precise sense. In Saussure's system words are a form of currency. Just like coins of the realm their value is not derived from the substance of which they are made. There was a time when coins were made of gold, silver and bronze, but not any more. Their value derives from what they signify, that is, represent, in the system as a whole. When the dollar or the euro go up or down in value so do all the other denominations to which they are tied. Similarly, when the sense of a word alters it affects the sense of related items in the language. This means that when speakers of different languages, or even dialects, communicate, it isn't enough simply to translate terms. They have to know the semantic space individual terms occupy in the language or dialect of which they are a constituent. American and British English, for example, divide up the area of sweet and savoury biscuits differently:

USA	BRITAIN
cookie	biscuit (sweet)
biscuit	scone
cracker	biscuit (savoury)

Even here the translations are not exact; there is no real equivalent to the British 'scone' in American English.

Sense relations

What I have been describing is a form of linguistics sometimes referred to as **structuralism**. According to this approach, meaning, and thus communication, depend on a structured set of relationships. The philosopher Ludwig Wittgenstein put it most succinctly when he said 'the meaning of a word is its use in the language'. We may well

Synonymy: a relation which exists between words which have a similar sense, for example *drunk/intoxicated, mad/insane*

Antonymy: a relation which exists between words which are opposite in sense. There are three main types of opposition:

- Gradable antonyms: *wide/narrow, old/young*
- Complementary antonyms: *alive/dead, married/single*
- Relational antonyms: *husband/wife, above/below*

Polysemy: a relation in which a word has acquired more than one sense, for example *Flight*, which can mean i. An air journey, ii. The power of flying, iii. a series of steps, iv. A digression, v. a unit of the air force

Hyponymy: a relation in which the sense of one word is included in another, for example the sense of 'flower' is included in that of *daisy, daffodil,* and *rose*. These items are referred to as hyponyms of *flower*

Meronymy: a part–whole relation between the sense of words, for example *cover* and *page* are meronyms of *book*

Incompatibility: a relation between words in which the senses are mutually exclusive, for example *banana/apple.* *This fruit is an apple and a banana.*[1]

feel, in view of the difficulties in communication, which we touched on earlier, that there is more to it than this. And indeed there is. None the less, Wittgenstein's dictum does alert us to an important base line in our linguistic competence. Whenever we speak or write to one another we assume the existence of a stable set of relationships within the language even when they are departed from. These relationships exist at all levels of analysis, whether of sound structure (phonology), syntax (grammar), or meaning (semantics), and much of linguistics is concerned with describing them. And so it is with words. Their signifying power derives, in part, from their place within a large, and continually changing, family. Just like the members of any real family they preserve their individuality through a shared, corporate, identity: that is, they define themselves in relation to each other. These relationships are known as **sense relations**, the most important of which are set out above.

The power of association

If words only had the kinds of stable meanings we have been describing then linguistic communication would not be so fraught with ambiguity and uncertainty as it is. But knowing what words **denote** only gets us so far, because the sense of a word does not exhaust its meaning or its possible use. We all know people who think it does and who insist on pinning words down to a so-called 'literal' meaning. They will tell us that it's wrong to say we're going *up the park* since *up* means 'to ascend'; one goes *up* a mountain but *to* the park. But a moment's reflection will show us what an unreal view of language this is. *Is the kettle boiling?* we say, and yet, thankfully, kettles never do boil, merely the water inside. The problem with trying to 'fix' words in this way is that we have many more meanings to communicate than language can easily accommodate. Just imagine buying a machine to do a job, say wash our clothes, and then discovering that we need it to do the dishes, vacuum the floor, and a hundred other things as well. Language has to represent all of our humanity, not just part of it. As we shall see in a moment, this is why **metaphor** is such an integral part of language use.

Perhaps a better analogy is an archaeological, rather than a mechanical, one. If you chip away a piece of rock from an outcrop and examine it in detail you will find within it the record of its existence on the planet. There will be a substratum, or sedimental core out of which it was formed, but there will also be traces and deposits of other minerals acquired over time which give it its particular character. So with words. If you look up the word *man* in the dictionary you will find its denotative meaning: what we can call its **conceptual sense.** This will be made up of the **semantic features** 'human', 'adult', 'male'. But knowing this will not give you the full meaning of it were someone to say to you *He's a real man.* The conceptual sense is only partially helpful here. We need to know what extra qualities the speaker judges a man to have; and we might hazard a guess at 'bravery', 'resilience', 'strength', 'lack of sentiment', and so on. There is no absolute limit to what we might infer here because we are dealing with what the word connotes, or **connotative** meaning, which is more open-ended than conceptual. Similarly with *She's a real woman.* Again, we might surmise 'attractive', 'shapely', 'sexually mature'. In Anglophone cultures the term *man* typically connotes positive, character-forming qualities, while woman has acquired more sexual connotations. The terms are only equal in their conceptual sense, whereas their associative senses differentiate between them on the basis of mental, or moral, versus physical attributes. What a word connotes often gives a clearer insight into social and cultural attitudes than what it conceptually means. In this particular instance, the connotative differences between *man* and *woman* are a reflection of current assumptions about what constitutes maleness and femaleness. This has a direct bearing on language use since we cannot always use the term *woman* as the female counterpart of *man.* In some contexts it is still considered rude to refer to someone as a *woman.* Compare, for example, *Give it to the woman, Give it to the lady,* and *Give it to the man,* as instructions to a child to return a dropped coin. And occasionally, the connotations of a term are so strong that they are more dominant than their conceptual sense. This is why, despite the contradiction in conceptual sense, it is possible to refer to a man as *an old woman.* Here, the denotative meaning has been totally submerged by the connotations surrounding the phrase *old woman.*

What we are dealing with here is a much less stable kind of meaning than the conceptual kind, and one which will differ according to the social and cultural context. Given the changing sensibilities towards issues of gender, for example, we might well access a less favourable set of connotations from the term *man* than those listed above. This is all because we have more meanings in our heads than the word itself can convey. Yet another source of instability is the way in which words that apparently have the same conceptual sense acquire extra layers from the linguistic contexts in which they are used. *Strong* and *powerful,* for example, are clearly synonyms, but *strong language* means something entirely different from *powerful language*. And in a café we ask for our tea to be strong but never powerful. One of the ways in which we know the meaning of a word is, as the linguist John Firth says, by knowing 'the company it keeps' (Crystal, 1987: 105). This is referred to as a word's **collocation** (from the verb 'collocate' meaning 'to go with'). A word takes part of its meaning from the other words it is used with. If you look up the adjective *clear* in the dictionary you will find at least ten different meanings, from *clear conscience* and *clear sky* to *clear case* – as in *a clear case of theft*. In each instance the meaning of clear is slightly different; *clear conscience* means 'without guilt', whereas *clear* in *clear case* means 'unmistakable'. At the same time, however, we should not want to say there was a separate conceptual sense in each instance. We can see enough commonality of meaning to assume an underlying sense. All the examples I have given have the meaning 'free from', whether free from complications – *clear case* – free from guilt – *clear conscience* – or free from clouds – *clear sky*. The differences between them come from the words *clear* is put with. We could say, then, that in order to know the meaning of a word in the language we need to know its **collocational range**, that is, all the linguistic contexts in which it can occur. We need to know, for example, that while both humans and cows *wander*, only humans *stroll*. Part of the natural evolution of language is in the development of new contexts and the demise of old ones. And one of the ways in which creative writers experiment with language is by generating odd collocations. In 'Fern Hill', for example, a poem by the Welsh poet Dylan Thomas about the world of childhood innocence, Thomas alters the phrase *once upon a time* to *once below a time*. The novel collocation now suggests, strikingly, the timelessness of being young.

Words also acquire associations from the different styles, or **registers** to which they belong. One of the consequences of the way in which English has developed over the past 1500 years has been the emergence of different registers of English. This has been partly due to the influx of new words from other languages, such as Latin and French, and partly to the variety of social needs which English has had to fulfil. If we are in a court of law, for instance, we might need to use the term *larceny*, which is of French origin, whereas talking with our friends we would probably use the term *theft*, which is from Anglo-Saxon, or Old English. Doctors talk of *haemorrhaging* (Greek), and *lacerations* (Latin), rather than *bleeding* and *wounds* (Anglo-Saxon). In all these cases there is no real difference in conceptual sense between the terms used. The difference has to do with levels of formality. Part of being able to use language effectively is the ability to switch between these levels when it is socially appropriate to do so. Consider the following terms, for example, all of which are conceptually the same: *steed, horse, nag, gee-gee*. We can see that they belong to different contexts. *Steed* is poetic in style and would be appropriate in a literary work about the knights of the round table; *nag* is slang and is normally used only in colloquial English; while *gee-gee* belongs to the nursery and is used with children. Another way of putting it is to say these terms are stylistically marked. The least marked is *horse* because it can be used in any context and, as a consequence, we can refer to it as the **normative** term.

As a further example, think about the following terms, all of which are used to describe living quarters: *domicile, residence, abode, home, pad*. As in the case of words for horse there is one normative term, in this case *home*, and several marked terms, all of which can be slotted into various linguistic contexts. It's possible to take many linguistic categories and sort the individual items into groups of this kind. These are sometimes referred to as **semantic fields**. Figure 2.2 shows a possible semantic field for *drunk*.

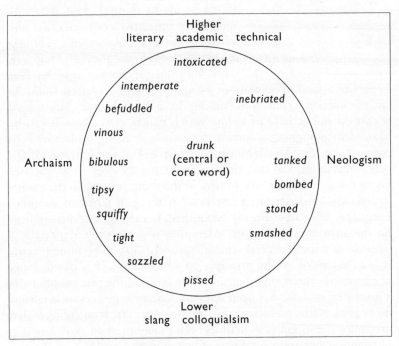

FIGURE 2.2 SEMANTIC FIELD FOR *DRUNK*

Figurative language

In the previous chapter we saw that language arose as a representational system. That is, we use it to represent the world to ourselves and to represent ourselves to other people. Language is not unique in this. Other forms of communication, painting and music, for example, also represent experience, and in some ways more successfully than language. Much of our experiential life is inward and intangible, whether it be of love, joy, suffering, or the passing of time. All of these are complex dimensions involving elusive states of being, or modes of awareness. How often have we felt unable to put into words exactly what we feel, whereas a piece of music, or a painting, can capture it exactly, with the added advantage that it can be transmitted to, and shared by, people who do not have a common language?

As we have amply seen already, language struggles to do justice to the inarticulate and formless world of experience which exists within us. That it manages as well as it does is because of systematic relationships between words and meaning of sufficient stability to ensure mutual comprehension. But language has another trick up its sleeve. It allows words to transfer their senses to apparently unrelated contexts. Take the following unremarkable sentence *The ship ploughed through the water.* Obviously, ships don't plough; they sail or steam. Nor is the sea a field. The sense of *plough* is being transferred from the entirely unrelated context of farming. In so doing a small shaft of light is cast on the activity of sailing which makes us see how it can be likened to ploughing a furrow. One thing is being understood 'in terms of another'. This is how the linguists Lakoff and Johnson (1980) define metaphor. But isn't this what all language does we might ask? Using the sound string /tri/ to refer to the thing growing in the garden is precisely 'understanding one kind of thing in terms of another'. Language, as we have already established, is a representational system. So the answer must be 'yes'. Metaphor is really only a specialised instance of a more general semantic property. Or, to be more precise, it is an extension of the principle on which language is based. Linguistic systems internalise their own processes. In the past twenty years a great deal of work has been done on figurative devices in language, more particularly, on metaphor. The consensus that is emerging is that metaphor is not, as has sometimes been thought just an extra function of language, but an integral part of how it works. And this, as the pio-

> *Experience is always larger than language*
>
> ADRIENNE RICH

THE FAR SIDE® By GARY LARSON

© 1983 FarWorks, Inc. All Rights Reserved/Dist. by Creators Syndicate

The Far Side® by Gary Larson © 1983 FarWorks, Inc. All Rights Reserved. Used with permission.

"Hang him, you idiots! Hang him! ... 'String him up' is a figure of speech!"

neers in the field, George Lakoff and Mark Johnson, suggest, is because our mental processes, that is, the way in which we reason and think, are metaphorical in character. Human beings are symbolising creatures.

To see how language utilises this capacity of the human mind, let's consider a few examples:

(a) *The bus is coming to take me to town*
(b) *The time is coming for me to leave*

In both of these sentences the verb *come* signifies the arrival of something. It's a verb of action. However, in (b) it has a different sense from (a) – although we recognise a relationship between them. Time is visualised in (b) as an approaching object, not necessarily a bus, of course, but an object none the less, moving through space. The underlying metaphor here could be expressed as 'time is a moving object'. We know that it isn't, but that is how we often experience it to be. We feel ourselves to be stationary, unchanging, while time moves inexorably past us. This is the source of expressions such as *time flies* and *time passes*. There is nothing inevitable about this way of perceiving time. Another culture might well perceive time to be stationary while people do the moving. In this respect a culture's metaphors are an invaluable guide to its values and outlook. In the case of time, because of the complexity of the concept, we use a variety of metaphors to express its significance for us. In the following example the process of transference centres on the verb *spend*, to give us the underlying metaphor *time is money*:

(c) *How do you spend your money?*
(d) *How do you spend your time?* (cf. *Don't waste my time; this will save you time*)

A majority of these metaphors are an indelible and integral part of language which we take on board quite unconsciously. And perhaps we can now see why. Metaphors provide an essential means of articulating what would otherwise remain inarticulate. They allow us, by a process of transference, to make the intangible, tangible. Characteristically, metaphors take material verbs such as *come* and *spend* and transfer their senses to non-material situations. In so doing they exploit the associative meanings of words and create fresh collocations. Something is always lost in the process of transference since no single metaphor can express the whole of an experience, but language gets round this by providing a variety of metaphors for any one concept. Here is a selection from Lakoff and Johnson (1980) of metaphors for love:

(e) *His whole life revolves around her* (love is a physical force)
(f) *She drives me out of my mind* (love is madness)
(g) *He's bewitched by her* (love is magic)
(h) *She fought for him* (love is war)

These metaphors are what Lakoff and Johnson call 'structural metaphors', that is, they structure our experience in some way. In addition to these, however, there are two other types of metaphor: orientational metaphors and ontological metaphors. The first sort – orientational ones – are concerned with the way in which we give a transferred sense to physical space and movement. Consider the way in which the prepositions *up, down, in, out* take on metaphorical meanings in the following examples:

(i) *Things are looking up*
(j) *I'm feeling down*
(k) *Count me in/out*

With these transferences we are using our bodies and our spatial awareness to construct metaphors. They reflect the biological importance we attach to standing up as opposed to lying down, and the priority we give to the inside of our bodies as against our exteriors. As a consequence, *up* becomes associated with conditions which are positive, *down* with those which are negative, and *in* with those which are seen as privileged in some way. In other words, there is a physiological basis to these metaphors. And finally, ontological metaphors. These are the least visible to language users of all the three groups distinguished by Lakoff and Johnson. Language works by translating experiences into concrete entities so that they can be talked about. For example, a judge at the end of a court case sums up the evidence. This is an activity, an event in time, not an object. Language allows us, however, to turn it into one, and talk about *the summing up* as in *The summing up was severe*. Ontological metaphors are typically used to 'comprehend events, actions, activities and states' (1980: 30). They enable us to extend entity status to a wide range of experiences based on processes of referring, quantifying and identifying. We might say of someone *She's got a lot of life left yet*, and create a metaphor in which life is quantified in object terms as if it were a substance. So deep rooted are such processes, however, that most of us wouldn't register them as metaphorical unless alerted to their presence by a poet or novelist. In his poem 'The love song of J. Alfred Prufrock', for example, T.S. Eliot takes the 'life as substance' metaphor a stage further when Prufrock says of himself 'I have measured out my life with coffee spoons'.

The power and centrality of metaphors to our conception of the world have been extensively explored by **cognitive linguists**. These are people who are interested in the way in which we organise and imaginatively construct the world through language. One such way is by developing **image schemas**. These are conceptual structures, or ways of thinking about experience which are metaphorical in character. A good example of an image schema is the 'containment' schema (Mark Johnson, 1987), based on an orientational metaphor deriving from the experience we have of inhabiting our own body. This instinctive sense of containment links with other, similar experiences – being in rooms, buildings and beds, and putting things in bottles and jars – to establish a schema, or framework, which extends over other areas of experience. So, for example, the visual field is often conceived of as a container, *He's coming into view now, The car's out of sight*, as are states *She's in love, He's in a temper*. Other schema examples are 'path' schemas, which derive from our experience of moving around the world, and 'force' schemas which reflect the sense we have of interacting with animate and inanimate entities. On the basis of the former we conceptualise our lives as journeys and talk of *rushing* to do something, and not getting *sidetracked*, while the latter give rise to expressions like being *held up* or feeling *bogged down*.

Communicative competence

So far we have been considering communication from the standpoint of the linguistic system on which language relies. All languages utilise processes of reference and signification and draw on the resources of metaphor to expand their expressive capabilities. But equally important are the communicators, the people doing the talking or writing. Us. What competencies do we require, as users of the linguistic system, for successful communication to take place?

The principal thing we need sounds simple enough: the ability to understand the logical basis of linguistic communication. Straightaway I can imagine a few eyebrows raised. Is language really logical you ask, after all that has been said about the indeterminacy of its use? The answer is 'yes', but in a way peculiar to itself. Logic, or more precisely, **formal logic**, is concerned with the rules which govern valid argument. We draw on these all the time when we communicate. So, for example, we know that the statements *I have lived in Manchester* and *I have never been to Manchester* are contradictions. They can't both be true. Similarly, we know that *My sister is a spinster* and *My sister has never married* are synonymous. At one level all linguistic communication consists in the utterance of propositions. These are more abstract than sentences. If we take the sentence *Washington is the capital of America* it's easy to see that we can produce several different sentences and yet preserve the underlying proposition: *The capital of America is Washington, It is Washington which is the capital of America, The teacher said that Washington is the capital of America,* and so on. Some linguists, notably logical semanticists, see all language as predicated on formal logical relationships which can be represented and analysed using symbolic formulae. They concentrate their attention on the **logical connectives** of language, that is, with words such as *not, and, if, then, or, so,* and *either.* These are the logical hinges of language which link propositions together. They enable us to understand the subtle difference in the use of the *either … or* construction in the following sentences:

(a) *Either John will go to the meeting or I shall*
(b) *Either John will go to the meeting or he won't*

In the first of these it is logically possible for both propositions to be true. John going to the meeting does not exclude the possibility that I might go as well. In the second, however, the propositions are mutually exclusive: there is no way in which John could both go and not go to the meeting.

But formal logic only gets us so far in understanding the basis of communication. In most conversational exchanges, excluding those between logicians, the normal assumption would be that the propositions in a) above were mutually exclusive. In other words, that there was an unspoken *but not both* tagged on the end. To be communicatively competent we need a knowledge of **natural logic**. This is significantly different from the formal type used by mathematicians and philosophers. All of us implicitly understand and consent to natural logic as an agreed element in communication. For example, if I ask you whether anyone passed the language exam and you reply *Some did* I am entitled to draw the conclusion that some people failed. If I subsequently find out that in fact everybody passed I should consider myself misinformed. *Some did*, in other words, means 'not everybody did'. But, as I'm sure you've spotted, this isn't a strictly logical deduction since *Some did* does not conflict with *Everybody did*. Clearly if all passed then some must have. Or, again, consider asking a stranger *Can you tell me the way to the station?* and receiving the answer *Yes* and no more. Logically, we might say the utterance had been answered impeccably. None the less, most people would conclude either that the stranger was being difficult or that s/he didn't understand what was said. This utterance is in reality a request, not a question. Natural logic, in other words means understanding the **speech acts** which form the basis of linguistic communication. Or, to put it another way, speaking is a form of doing, and being communicatively competent involves knowing what people are trying to do through language. This is not always straightforward. But more of that in due course.

In order to comprehend what is said to us, then, we need to understand more than the literal sense of an utterance. We need to understand its **force**. Force is an interesting concept in language study and a vital part of natural logic. The force of an utterance is the meaning it has in a particular situational setting or social context. If someone says *I like your hat*, we need to know more than the sense and reference value of the words in order to interpret them correctly. We have to be alert to the possibility of irony in the speaker's tone, particularly if there is anything odd about the hat, in which case the speaker might be implying the reverse. Indeed, ironical statements characteristically oppose force and sense, as in *nice one* said sarcastically. One of the ways in which we interpret the force of utterances is by paying attention to

---

'Short people got no reason to live'

The title of a popular song, recorded in the 1980's in America by the singer Randy Newman, which caused a great deal of offence because it appeared to cast a slur on short people. The song was banned in Boston, and attempts to ban it were also made in Maryland. Newman's defence was that he was being ironical because his intention was to expose the absurdity of prejudice. At issue is the question of what speech act is being performed here: viz. is the statement a judgement meaning 'short people do not deserve to live,' or a complaint meaning 'short people have nothing to live for'. We can only decide this by providing a context in which the words might be uttered.

Cited in STANLEY FISH, 1989

---

the intonation pattern of speakers. It's often the case that we object to the *manner* in which something is said rather than just *what* is said. We know instinctively, as users of a language, that the meaning of an utterance is a product of the total speech event of which words are just a part. Intonation is a **paralinguistic** feature of communication which enables us to indicate subtleties of attitude and personal response not present in the words themselves. Conveying the same nuances through written language, where the resources of intonation are not available, is, by comparison, much more difficult. If we want to recapture the force we have to mentally turn the script back into speech and imagine it being said. The act of reading is, in part, an attempt to recreate a lost voice. Intonation is not the only non-verbal means of communication, of course. It often acts in conjunction with gesture, facial expression and posture to convey meaning. Sometimes these devices may reinforce the sense of an utterance, or, as in the case of irony, contradict it. The study of intonation falls within what is termed **prosody**. It's sufficient enough for us to note here that language is part of a much broader system of communication in which verbal constructions are a vital, but not stand-alone, component.

Another way of indicating the force of an utterance is by making the key part of it more prominent. In spoken language we can do this most easily by stressing the particular word(s) we want to emphasise.

Consider the following statement, for example, and think about how stressing a different word might alter its force: *I can't drive there.*

(i)   *I can't drive there* (but s/he can)
(ii) *I can't drive there* (it's out of the question)
(iii) *I can't **drive** there* (but I can go some other way)
(iv) *I can't drive **there*** (but I can drive somewhere else)

We can also make parts of utterances more prominent by thematic arrangement. This is a process which involves changing the sequence of information in an utterance for greater communicative impact. A common way of doing this is by putting important items first, or **thematising** them. Newspapers frequently draw attention to the most dramatic bits of the news by putting them first. We are far more likely to read *The President lied on oath according to his mistress, Monica Lewinsky,* than *According to his mistress, Monica Lewinsky, the President lied on oath.* The force of the first arrangement is to highlight, or **foreground**, the accusation, whereas that of the second is to highlight its source. Subtleties of emphasis such as these are significant in the persuasive effect they have on readers. Creative writers also rearrange sentences to convey the force of items more powerfully. Changing *The rain came down* to *Down came the rain* doesn't affect the sense of the line but it does alter its impact because the emphasis now is on the physical descent of the rain rather than its simple existence. And how much more arresting is Shakespeare's *To be or not to be, that is the question,* in comparison with its pallid alternative, *The question is, to be or not to be.*

But important as intonational and thematic clues are in the process of communication they would be of little value if we were not able to relate utterances to an appropriate context. To a considerable extent interpreting the utterance meaning of sentences depends upon the degree of assumed knowledge which exists between speaker and listeners. This assumed, or shared knowledge, is called by philosophers, **presupposition**. On a formal level presupposition deals with the necessary preconditions for statements to be true *My cat was run over yesterday* assumes as a necessity the truth of *I have a cat.* But on the level of natural logic it has a much broader function than that, because presupposition allows us the freedom not to make everything explicit in our communications. If we had to

> *The whole force of conversation depends on how much you can take for granted.*
> OLIVER WENDELL HOLMES

spell out all the details every time we spoke, then communicating would be an extremely lengthy and tedious business. Being able to assume a certain amount of knowledge on the part of listeners makes it possible to take shortcuts. If someone said to you *Your room is a pigsty*, they would be presupposing that you knew what a pigsty was, and more importantly, what was characteristic of them in Anglophone cultures. If you belonged to a culture where such places were revered, you couldn't understand the speaker's meaning. Based on the right presupposition, that is *pigsties are disgusting places*, we can draw the correct **inference** – *your room is disgusting*. Presupposition and inference are part of the logical machinery we use to interpret utterances. But they don't work in a vacuum. They need the raw material of shared knowledge and cultural understanding on which to operate. As a consequence, a good deal of our meaning is implied: we assume the listener can draw the correct inference. Just consider how much is implied in the following utterance: *The picnic was ruined. Someone forgot the corkscrew.* On the face of it there is no necessary connection between these two statements, but the speaker is implying a link and assuming we have enough prior knowledge to make the right inference. To do so we have to know what picnics are, that wine is often taken on them, and what function corkscrews perform. This would allow us to arrive at the inference, 'The picnic was ruined because we couldn't have any wine.'

The majority of inferences which we draw are, fortunately, automatic. They allow us to link consecutive sentences together in a coherent manner. In the examples below, the words in bold are inferred by the listener to refer back to an antecedent noun phrase (*the vase* and *the boss* respectively):

(i) *I dropped the vase yesterday.* ***It*** *broke*
(ii) *I saw the boss yesterday.* ***The old fool*** *still doesn't recognise me*

Similarly, general, or background knowledge often allows us to fill in the gaps between consecutive sentences, as in:

(i) *I entered the room.* ***The ceiling*** *was beautiful*
(ii) *I walked on the beach.* ***The tide*** *was out*

In these cases, because it is a matter of general knowledge that rooms have ceilings and that tides occur on beaches, the listener is able to draw the appropriate inferences linking the two statements. This is

More about presupposition

Stylistically, presupposition is exploited in a range of discourse types, including advertisements, newspapers, and fiction. The injunction *Don't put up with back pain*, for example, carries the implicit presupposition *You have back pain*. Similarly, the headline *President cracks down on political corruption* presupposes *There is political corruption*. Presupposition is sometimes triggered by certain words. Verbs such as *realise* and *regret* – factive verbs – for example, presuppose the truth of their complement clauses. In the sentences below only 1(a) and 1(b) presuppose 1(d). The non-factive verb *think* in 1(c) has no such presupposition:

1(a) *Sarah realised it was raining*

1(b) *Sarah regretted it was raining*

1(c) *Sarah thought it was raining*

1(d) *It was raining*

Other presuppositions depend on our knowledge of the world rather than anything present in the language. In the following sentences 3(c) is presupposed by 3(a) but not by 3(b). The reason for this is that we know that someone who has died cannot get into a car:

3(a) *She tripped before getting into the car*

3(b) *She died before getting into the car*

3(c) *She got into the car*

not so with all inferences, however. In many communications there are, in addition to these automatic or conventional inferences, a widening penumbra of possible inferences, which are, so to speak, up for grabs. To return to our picnic example for a moment – *The picnic was ruined. Someone forgot the corkscrew* – we might think, from the way the speaker is emphasising *someone* and looking in our direction that s/he is accusing us of being the culprit. In which case we would draw an extra inference –

> *Nothing can be so clearly and carefully expressed that it cannot be utterly misinterpreted*
>
> FRED HOUSEHOLDER,
> *Linguistic Speculations*
> (1971: Preface)

You have ruined the picnic. In other words, because a certain amount of utterance meaning, or force, depends on implication, or **implicature**, as linguists term it, we can never be entirely sure of the full extent of the meaning. Most of us know people who read all sorts of meanings into what seem apparently innocent statements. In a sense there is no way, linguistically, of proving whether they are right or wrong, because it is we who are the arbiters – it is we who decide on the contextual meaning. Others might feel we are over-reacting in thinking ourselves accused of forgetting the corkscrew. But, equally, they could be missing something. We are back again to a point made earlier about the essential indeterminacy of linguistic meaning.

The cooperative principle

It is because of the sheer volume of possible meanings which could be inferred from utterances that we depend most crucially on a process of cooperation in our everyday exchanges. There is an unspoken pact that we will cooperate in communicating so as to understand and be understood. This pact may be broken, but it exists as a norm against which deviations, such as lying, or exaggerations can be measured. All communication assumes an intention to communicate. We go a long way before we abandon the attempt to make sense of what someone says to us, simply because the idea that they may be speaking without wishing to communicate seems nonsense. This is reinforced by the phenomenon known as **accommodation**, or **convergence**. When two friends are speaking together they will tend to copy each other's speech patterns. Features such as accent and dialect will normally converge. This is often an unconscious process and one which allows us to switch from speaking to our friends, to our boss quite easily. On the other hand, one way of stressing our difference from someone we do not like is by diverging. In this case, we deliberately adopt a different speech pattern in order to stress the mental, or emotional, distance between ourselves and the person(s) with whom we are communicating.

The writer who is most closely associated with the concept of cooperation is the American philosopher Paul Grice. He elaborated what he termed 'the cooperative principle' together with its constituent maxims of quantity, relation, manner, and quality. Basic to the principle is the belief that communication involves an ethical imperative to cooperate. Grice defines it in the following way, 'Make your contribution such as is required, at the stage at which it occurs, by the accepted purpose or direction of the talk exchange in which you are engaged' (1991: 26). This sounds too legalistic and bureaucratic to be of much use. Indeed, it is arguable that all attempts to give the principle the force of commandment in this way are bound to be unsatisfactory. It is after all a principle, not a rule. But, if we bear this in mind, it can provide a useful starting point for considering the unconscious assumptions which are implicit in our expectations of linguistic usage.

Grice's first maxim, that of **quantity**, is concerned with the amount of information which we expect from any conversational exchange. When we speak to someone we feel obliged to give them enough detail to enable them to understand us. If we don't, we are not really being cooperative. At the same time, however, we have to avoid providing too much information and obscuring the point we are making. Being able to judge the boundary between too little and too much is part of our communicative competence. If you ask someone whether they have any pets and receive the reply *I've got a budgerigar* you would naturally assume that is the limit. But if you then discovered they had several other pets you would feel the reply inadequate. It is simply not detailed enough. Learning to provide sufficient information is a skill which has to be acquired; as is learning not to provide too much. Most of us know people who are over-circumstantial in their conversation and weary the listener with excessive detail. Knowing what counts as an answer is not something we are born with. Young children, in particular, find it difficult to be sufficiently informative. At the same time, however, once we know the convention about quantity, it is possible to use it to our advantage. Being 'economical with the truth' is a frequent phenomenon in everyday life. Politicians, for example, frequently under-report issues in order to avoid embarrassment. As do all of us on occasions.

The maxim of **relation** directs us to organise our utterances in such a way as to ensure their relevance to the conversational exchange. People who change the subject abruptly, or who go off at a tangent, are usually considered rude or inconsiderate. We normally feel under an obligation to link any new contribution to the existing topic to preserve some sense of continuity. At the same time, however, utterances can be relevant in a variety of ways. So strong is our assumption of cooperativeness that we will try our utmost to wring some meaning out of a reply before deciding that it is irrelevant. In so doing we draw heavily on presupposition, inference and implicature, as in the following exchange:

Angela: *Where's my chocolates?*

Brian: *The children were in your room this morning.*

OR

Brian: *I've got a train to catch.*

In neither case are Brian's replies explicitly relevant. But they can easily be made so by relating them inferentially to the context. Indeed, so powerful is the maxim of relation that the linguists Dan Sperber and Deirdre Wilson (1986) have seen it as subsuming the others. They argue that all of them can be seen in terms of the requirement to relate our utterances to the situational context, whether by direct, or indirect, means. One form of humour, for example, lies in deliberately mistaking the relevance of a remark, as in the following:

Lecturer: *You should have been here this morning.*

Student: *Why, what happened?*

The lecturer's statement is capable of being interpreted in two different ways, either as an exclamation, or a reproof. It is only the situational context which enables us to decide which is correct. The humour here lies in the student choosing not to interpret it as a reproof while knowing that it is.

The maxim of **manner** obliges us to organise our utterances in an orderly fashion, that is, to provide information in a way which can be assimilated by the listener. We have only to imagine what recipes, car manuals, and other sources of information would be like if instructions and details were not provided in a sequential order. But even in less functional contexts there is an assumption of orderliness. This is even the case where the natural sequence is disrupted in some way. Many novels, for instance, change the normal order of events by flashing back, or anticipating the future, but underlying these disruptions there is usually, except in the most experimental works of fiction, a chronological framework which is being departed from and returned to. Orderliness is, or course, one of the first things to go out of the window when people are upset or angry. But again, we could say that the violation of the maxim is precisely one of the ways in which strength of feeling is communicated. In other words, the departure from the convention serves, among other things, to confirm its existence.

The maxim of **quality** in a sense underlies all the other maxims in that it assumes we are speaking what we believe to be true. Lying is an obvious violation of the cooperative principle. If you know someone is lying there are a number of options open to you. You can either confront them with the fact and force them to cooperate, or withdraw your own cooperation and go through the motions of communicating. Difficulties arise, however, when it seems necessary to lie in order to preserve cooperativeness – so-called 'white lies'. We may feel obliged to say nice things about a neighbour's art work, for example, even if we really think it's terrible. Because of this, the linguist Geoffrey Leech (1983) has proposed a politeness principle, in addition to Grice's. The effect of this is to moderate the force of the quality maxim and allow for cooperative departures from it. The politeness principle enjoins people to be tactful and polite unless there is a specific reason not to be.

At first sight one limitation of Grice's maxims appears to be their assumption that communication is simply a process of exchanging information. Clearly there are many other reasons for engaging in conversation, including the need to express, and sometimes to hide, our feelings. The Danish philosopher Soren Kierkegaard, in a rather sombre moment, even suggested that people use language not merely to conceal their thoughts but to conceal the fact that they have no thoughts. Be that as it may, the cooperative principle does not account for all that goes on in communicative situations, nor did Grice intend that it should. The most useful way of viewing the maxims is to see them as representing a kind of core requirement for communicating, a baseline of expectations against which we can measure individual departures. Unless there is evidence to the contrary, we assume, as listeners, that speakers will tell us what they believe to be true, estimate what we need to know, package the material accordingly, keep to the topic, and give some thought to us being able to understand them. The maxims are *public* expectations. The fact that they are frequently departed from merely serves to alert us to the *personal* agendas of those with whom we are communicating.

But we need to distinguish more exactly what we mean by departures. Some are plainly so only in name. A novelist disrupting a story with a flashback, or a digression is clearly not attempting to violate the maxim of manner, and many exaggerations, such as *I've told you a million times* are not intended to violate the maxim of quality. These are creative and expressive departures designed to enhance our understanding or appreciation of something. Linguists call them **floutings**.

Floutings are apparent rather than real violations. They allow for a certain measure of creativity in communication because participants are aware of an underlying tension between the simple maxim and its flouted form. A good deal of irony and figurative language employ floutings and give us the added pleasure of seeing the variety of ways speakers and writers find of obeying the maxims even while seemingly breaking them. Unlike floutings, violations are uncooperative departures from the maxims. They arise from situations in which the normal conventions of communication are set aside, neglected, or ignored. Such departures may indicate the presence of an emotion too strong to be articulated coherently; in which case the end result could well be a resort to tears or shouting. As we have seen already, language can't cope with everything. Or, more usually, they may indicate that we are too bored, inattentive, or inconsiderate to respond appropriately. Violations will always communicate something even if it is only the state of mind of the person who is talking, or failing to talk, as the case may be. But the important distinction from floutings is that either the intention, or the ability, to cooperate is lacking. Classic literature is dotted with characters who are individualised for us by the extent to which they violate the principle of cooperative speech. Benjy's violations of the maxim of manner in Faulkner's *The Sound and The Fury* are symptomatic of his mental disturbance, while Miss Bates's violations of the quantity maxim in Jane Austen's *Emma* are indications of the way prolonged spinsterhood has marginalised her in genteel society.

Speech acts

Earlier on I suggested that being able to communicate successfully involved understanding what language is being used for, that is, what act is being performed through its medium. We can now develop this further. Traditionally philosophers have distinguished between actions and speaking on the basis that speaking about something is quite different from doing it (although as we saw in the previous chapter this division doesn't exist in some preliterate cultures). And to a large extent this is true. Fixing a plug is fundamentally different from talking about fixing it. At the same time, however, they also have something in common. *Actions speak louder than words* we say, and in so doing ironically suggest that actions are also a form of communication. If your partner slaps your face s/he is quite clearly telling you something. The fact that we use the metaphor of speaking to capture this is an indication of how strong is the connection between communication and language. In reality, we employ all sorts of non-verbal gestures to signal meanings, not just words. Language is simply a highly specialised code which we have developed to convey meanings of greater subtlety, and with greater efficiency, than is possible via other means. But practically everything we do is a communication of some sort. Even mending the plug.

Instead of seeing actions and speaking as totally dissimilar it's more useful to see them as twin aspects of the process of communicating. If actions can speak, words can also 'do'. Indeed we could change the metaphor round and say *Words perform better than deeds*, or, as the proverb has it, *The pen is mightier than the sword*. The concept of words as deeds of some sort owes its origin to the work of two Oxford philosophers, J.L. Austin and, latterly, J.R. Searle. They distinguished three types of acts which utterances can be said to perform: a **locutionary act**, an **illocutionary act**, and a **perlocutionary act**. A locutionary act, or locution, refers simply to the act of saying something that makes sense in the language: in other words, that follows the grammatical rules of the language. An illocutionary act is one which is performed through the medium of language: stating, warning, wishing, promising, and so on. And finally, a perlocutionary act is the effect of the illocution on the listener: such as being persuaded, convinced, deterred, surprised, and so forth. A good example of these three acts in operation would be requesting a favour, where the locution consists of the words being uttered in a grammatical sequence, the illocution, the act of requesting, and the perlocution, the granting of the favour. Speech act theory tends to concentrate on illocutions. Locutions and perlocutions, coming before and after the illocutionary act, although important, are of less central interest. When Austin first began his study of speech acts, published in 1962 as *How to do Things with Words*, he attempted to distinguish between a class of utterances which he called **performatives** and those which he termed **constatives**. Performatives are a special group of utterances, the saying of which actually performs the action named by the verb. For example:

Act of marriage: *I pronounce you man and wife*

Act of naming a ship: *I name this ship* The Saucy Sue

Act of closing a meeting: *I declare this meeting closed*

| Act of a wager: | *I bet you a fiver* |
| Act of apology: | *I apologise* |

In order for these utterances to count as performatives various conditions have to be met. Only certain people can pronounce you man and wife, for example, while if you apologise and clearly don't mean it you have not really apologised. The right context has to be matched with the right form of words. Austin termed these conditions **felicity conditions**.

Constatives consist of all those other utterances, such as statements and questions, where actions are being described or asked about rather than explicitly performed, as in *I cooked the cake* and *Can you cook the cake?* The test of whether an utterance can be classed as a perfomative or not is whether the word *hereby* can be inserted before the verb. In this respect *I hereby declare this meeting closed* is unproblematic, whereas, *I hereby cooked the cake*, or *Can you hereby cook the cake?* are not. But Austin quickly realised that the distinction between performatives and constatives was artificial since even constatives are performing some kind of act, although of a more purely linguistic kind than performatives. *I cooked the cake* is performing the act of stating. We have only to recast it as *I hereby state that I cooked the cake* to see this. And similarly, *Can you cook the cake?* is performing the act of enquiring. We can recast this as *I hereby enquire whether you can cook the cake?* As a consequence Austin abandoned the distinction between performatives and constatives and distinguished instead between **explicit** and **implicit** performatives. Explicit performatives are those which have a perfomative verb, that is, a verb which names the act being performed, for example, *affirm, allege, assert, forecast, predict, announce, insist, order, state.* These are sometimes referred to as speech act verbs since they are all acts of 'saying'. Implicit performatives lack a saying verb, but none the less assume the presence of one. So, for example, *Beware of the bull* can be expanded to *I warn you to beware of the bull*, and *Come and see me sometime* is expandable to *I invite you to come and see me sometime.*

So we arrive at the view that all utterances are speech acts of one kind or another. In some cases the type of act is explicitly marked by a speech act verb, whereas, in others, it is more implicitly signalled. But two questions arise here: first, 'How can we categorise these acts?', and second 'What are the rules which govern their formation?' To some extent the first issue has been traditionally handled in grammar under the domain of **mood**. Conventional grammars tell us that there

---

Taxonomy of speech acts

1 **Representatives:** these commit the speaker to the truth of the expressed proposition (paradigm cases: asserting, concluding, telling, claiming)

2 **Directives:** these are attempts by the speaker to get the addressee to do something (paradigm cases: requesting, ordering, pleading, inviting)

3 **Commissives:** these commit the speaker to some future course of action (paradigm cases: promising, threatening, offering, vowing)

4 **Expressives:** these express a psychological state (paradigm cases: thanking, apologising, welcoming, congratulating)

5 **Declarations** (previously 'performatives'): these effect immediate changes in the institutional state of affairs, and tend to rely on extra-linguistic situations (paradigm cases: excommunicating, declaring war, christening, marrying, firing from employment)

---

are three principal linguistic moods: indicative (consisting of interrogative, and declarative), imperative, and subjunctive. All of these have distinctive grammatical forms. We use indicatives for asking questions (interrogatives) and making statements (declaratives), imperatives for giving commands, and subjunctives for expressing wishes or hypothetical possibilities (*God save the Queen*; *If I were you*). But this is a very simplistic taxonomy of acts. For one thing, grammatical form isn't always a sure guide to the act being performed. A statement such as *You're doing the cooking* can easily become a question or even a command by altering the intonation or stress pattern. But apart from that, we clearly perform many more acts than these. Since the early days of Austin much effort has been directed towards categorising the types which are recognised linguistically. Classificatory systems vary in detail but one of the most widely used is that proposed by J.R. Searle (1976: 10–12).

As we can see, the paradigm cases for all these acts involve the use of speech act verbs. As with the cooperative maxims, which they work in conjunction with, they serve as norms for communicative behaviour against which we can measure actual linguistic usage. In order to do this we have to know the felicity conditions which constitute each act.

This is where speech act theory is particularly interesting because it recognises that the meaning and value of any utterance arise in part from the situation in which it is uttered. Felicity conditions, or appropriateness conditions, are the social prerequisites on which communication is founded. Here are the conditions for asking a question:

1. speaker does not know the answer

2. speaker believes it possible hearer knows the answer

3. it is not obvious that hearer will provide the answer at the time without being asked

4. speaker wants to know the answer

These conditions are all fulfilled in the typical question, for example *Is it still raining? What won the two-thirty?* and so on. Against this norm we're aware of questions which deviate in terms of their felicity conditions. So called rhetorical questions, for example, *What's the point in going out?* in which there is no genuine request for information since the speaker does not believe 2 above, or teacher–pupil questions *What's the capital of Peru?* where the speaker already knows the answer. The deviations from the prototypical case alert us to the fact that there are other speech acts being performed here. The rhetorical question is really a complaint while the teacher's question is an act of testing, and as such a demand rather than a request for information

What speech act theory sets out to do is to differentiate all the possible acts we might perform in terms of their felicity conditions. These effectively match utterances against the situational context and the relationship of the people communicating. Thus, pleading, commanding, and requesting are all directives but they differ according to the relationship between the speaker and hearer. The act of commanding, for example, requires the speaker be in a position of authority, while that of pleading requires the reverse, and that of requesting requires either that they must be peers or else the hearer should be in authority. Similarly, suggesting, insisting and hypothesising all belong to the class of representatives but they differ in the degree of commitment towards the truth of what is being represented. All of these can be expressed as differences in felicity conditions similar to those for questions. Part of the complexity of communication, however, lies in the fact that very frequently more than one act is being performed at the same time. There are many occasions in which the performance of one act is really the vehicle for the performance of another. This is the case with the example of the test question above, where what looks like a request for information is something else. We characteristically employ a degree of indirectness in communicating. In many cases this is due to Leech's politeness principle. Very few people when directing someone to do something, for example, employ a command, for example *Open the window.* The usual form is to frame a question about the ability of the person to perform the act, for example *Could you open the window?* We know this doesn't fit the paradigm case for asking a question and consequently interpret it as an **indirect**, as opposed to a **direct**, speech act. The point about indirectness is that it seems to respect the freedom of the hearer and thus preserves a sense of solidarity, which as we saw in Chapter 1 is an important ingredient in the socialising aspect of language. This is particularly marked in situations of obvious inequality such as employer–employee relations. A boss is likely to request an employee to see him – *Can you come and see me?* – although the employee would be unwise to treat it as a request. Again, it's the felicity conditions which enable us to know that the sentence *You must have another piece of cake* uttered by our hostess at a tea party is an invitation, not a command. The situation simply doesn't fit the paradigm for giving a command. By the same token we know that many people feel shy at accepting offers of food in case they appear greedy. In this case, by uttering what looks like an order the hostess takes on herself the responsibility for us consuming her food.

Human beings are subtle, not to say, devious, animals, and language affords us tremendous power to perform all kinds of communicative acts as part of our evolutionary drive to thrive and prosper. But we know instinctively, as social animals that our own interests are best

SALLY FORTH
Source: North American Syndicate

served communally. Because of this we have developed a whole array of linguistic devices for mediating the acts which we perform through language. We hedge our suggestions with *perhaps*, *maybe* and *possibly*, we thank people for things they are required to do, and qualify convictions with *I feel* or *I think*. Indirectness is built into the fabric of our discourse. It's easy to dismiss such devices as so much insincere flannel, and indeed a whole discourse composed of qualifications and hedges would be insufferable. But they send out an important message. They indicate an awareness of our audience. And this is ultimately the case with indirect speech acts. Why bother to trouble ourselves with framing them except that they help us accomplish our needs and at the same time avoid unhelpful confrontations? As with floutings they enable us to conform to the basic conventions of communication with a degree of freedom and imagination. Both as speakers and hearers we interpret them with the aid of the cooperative and politeness principles, because we assume that speakers, unless they have sufficient reason for behaving otherwise, are attempting to be relevant, coherent, truthful and considerate.

Conclusion

We have been pursuing a number of themes in our account of linguistic communication. We began first by considering how language underspecifies meaning because we have many more meanings to communicate than language can easily handle. As a consequence, we rely on all sorts of paralinguistic and non-verbal devices to assist us. We then considered some of the resources of sense and reference which language has at its disposal and which enable stable communication to occur. But even these are not of sufficient determinacy to eliminate obscurity and ambiguity. To cope with these we rely on interpretative strategies which are fundamentally communal and conventional in their basis, taking as their *raison d'être* the mutual responsibility of communicators to cooperate. Cooperation is built on an understanding of what speakers are trying to do through words, knowing their force, not just their sense. This means being a party to the natural assumptions and implications which underlie language use. These are as much institutional as linguistic, because in the final analysis all utterances have their life and being in social situations. We understand them, and the nature of the acts they are performing, because we belong within social groups which operate tacit agreements about interpreting utterances. In other words, we exist within what linguists call 'speech communities' (see Chapter 4), local, educational, political, domestic, occupational, national, which have common forms of expression and common procedures for mediating meaning. Which is another way of saying that a communication means what we can agree with others that it means, or, alternatively, what we can convince them it means.

Note

1   The symbol * is used to indicate an unacceptable sequence.

3 Virtual Words
Language and Media

A word is dead
When it is said
Some say.

I say it just
Begins to live
That day

EMILY DICKINSON (c. 1862–6, *Complete Poems*, no. 1212)

Scripted speech

Imagine this. You are watching a man talking to you. He is sitting down in what looks like a cross between a boardroom and someone's lounge, while you are standing in the kitchen clutching a mug of coffee. Miraculously the man speaks without any hesitation, repetition, or deviation. His voice flows at an even, well-regulated pace, with a varied pattern of intonation and stress. His manner is relaxed and conversational yet this is unlike any normal conversation. Occasionally, you murmur something in response, but he shows no sign of hearing. Your role is passive in an event which appears to be controlled by the man on the screen. Until, that is, you change channels.

This is an experience which, for most of us, occurs everyday, and such is its routineness that the dynamics pass unnoticed. But it is anything but ordinary. As a linguistic event it rests on a complex net of social and cultural assumptions, so accepted as to be almost transparent. But the largely unexamined, and powerful, illusions on which these assumptions are based, shape our sense of reality, and of ourselves in relation to it. To begin with, the speaker is present in our kitchen only as an image and a voice. How else could a complete stranger have such free access to our home? His physical being is elsewhere. But where? The desk behind which he is sitting is most probably computer generated. We locate it, notionally, in something called a 'studio', but the term is practically meaningless. We couldn't find it, and even if we could, he most probably wouldn't be there, especially if the event was recorded. The time and space in which the speaker exists are unreal, and yet they seem as real as the mug we are holding. A word has entered our vocabulary to describe such an experience: it is 'virtual'.

The primary illusion which a virtual experience creates is that of 'presence'. People, things, and events are present in our homes. Not literally, otherwise we should feel unhappy undressing, or doing anything else personal, in front of the screen. But they are there in essence: we can examine their appearance, their mannerisms, their ideas, their speech without the inconvenience of having to entertain them. They are there as personalities to whom we have privileged access. Or apparently so. Because it is all carefully edited, scripted, and arranged for our viewing. We know that, and they know it too. It's a fundamental convention on which all forms of representation are based. We allow ourselves to be taken in. But for what reason? What is the gain for us in such an arrangement? The answer to this would take us far into the psychology of representative acts, but one thing is paramount in the medium we are considering, because it provides one of the most powerful illusions of all: the illusion of intimacy.

The man speaking on the screen appears to be addressing himself to us alone. That's why he tries so hard to make his speech sound like spoken English. In fact, we know he's reading it from a teleprompter. What we are hearing is written English meant to sound like spoken English. He's called a 'newsreader', not a 'newspeaker'. His language is more orderly and formal than spoken language, although peppered with the occasional colloquialism and sentence fragment to disguise the fact that it is written. And here comes the best part of all. We don't have to listen if we don't want to. Being addressed by a virtual rather than a real person means we can turn our backs and get on with the washing up, or just mentally switch off and think about his accent or his tie. We are free to indulge in behaviour which would otherwise be considered rude. The television can be left on to provide background noise, ready for us to tune in and out as the fancy takes us. It's an impersonal medium made to appear personal, because our property. The language it uses is an artefact. Even a conversation in a studio is not a natural conversation, because overheard by us, and carefully stage-managed to provide the appropriate interest and entertainment. Television is a deeply oral medium but at its heart lies the concept of the script, even in those programmes which simulate spontaneity. Moreover, it capitalises on the fact that spoken language is contextualised. That is, it arises from a particular person in a particular place.

Unlike radio where we have to imagine the context, television provides it for us. It can direct where we look, and at what. It entertains the eye as well as the ear. If a news item involves the Prime Minister, the news-reader will stand outside No. 10 Downing Street, although the item would be exactly the same delivered from the studio.

The kind of orality we have been considering is described by the writer Walter Ong (1982) as 'secondary orality', as opposed to the 'primary orality' of non-literate cultures. Secondary orality develops in highly literate cultures concerned to recover the values of an oral medium, presence, intimacy, spontaneity, and contextualisation, by using the skills developed from writing, orderliness, control, and clarity. People who study media argue that the development of such complex modes of expression has been enabled by technology. In Chapter 2 I referred to Marshall Mcluhan, whom many regard as the originator of media studies, and his idea that 'the medium is the message'. What Mcluhan meant was that the medium through which language is conveyed, whether radio, telephone, television, or print, is never neutral. The same words printed convey a different message when spoken over the telephone, because of the different possibilities of the respective media. Printed words strike us as less personal because lacking the contextual features of intonation, stress, and voice quality.

What kind of message, then, do electronic media such as television convey to us? What aspect of language is promoted by the newsreader, the chat show host, the interviewer? The fundamental one, attached to our attempt to recover, electronically, an oral society, is the sense of community. Television creates in our own homes a cast of people who enact for us situations in which we are on the receiving end of a wide variety of speech acts (see Chapter 2). We are advised, warned, amused, and informed, and at the same time left free to join and unjoin without obligation. The ideal community has become the virtual com-munity, what Mcluhan termed the 'global village'. It's another illusion, of course. But then we know that too. And to support it a special kind of language style has evolved. Geoffrey Leech (1966) calls it 'public colloquial'. Very simply, this entails the breaking down of the divide between public and private English in an attempt to make all language look and sound conversational. It's a consequence of large-scale changes in society, in particular increased social mobility and the decline of deference in public life. If we compare the language of news-readers of twenty years ago with those of today there has been a marked increase in informality. We know their first names now, and from the teasing and banter which regularly goes on between them, a lot about their opinions and habits too. The language of 'journalese', with its political 'rows', police 'dashes', and domestic 'tragedies' is now commonplace in news reports.

The linguist Norman Fairclough (1996), in common with a number of other discourse analysts, refers to this merging of styles in public discourse as 'border crossing'. He sees it as a phenomenon of post-industrialised societies in which traditional boundaries have shifted radically. There are many professional situations now in which people are quite happy to use a style of language previously thought sloppy. Fairclough argues that one of the main agents of change has been the advertising industry and its need to create new markets. Advertising style is predominantly oral in character, even when written. Negatives and auxiliary verbs are always contracted (*isn't*, *we'll*), interactive interrogative forms addressing the reader directly are common (*Have you had ... ?*), there's a good deal of colloquial vocabulary (*kids*, rather than *children*, *guy* rather than *man*), and much use of sentence fragments. Characteristics such as these now regularly crop up in books, journals, and government information leaflets. The following is from a government-inspired publicity campaign to encourage small businesses:

> **Take advantage of us while you can.**
> **Don't worry. We hope to get a bit back later.**
>
> It's a kind of 'you scratch my back'... arrangement. The Government is helping smaller businesses grow more prosperous. Because prosperous businesses help the country grow more wealthy. So, if you run your own business, or are tempted to start one, take all the incentives you can get. And there are plenty. Many more than most people realise. You may well get special tax reliefs, for example. And did you know that you could get a loan up to £75,000 guaranteed by the Government? Or that you can get the services of a technical or production advisor, free, for five days? You can get introductions to new export markets. Or help in finding new premises. Or you might get a grant to develop new products. In the last few years 86 special schemes have been introduced to help growing business grow bigger. Some of them might make all the difference to you. To find out which send the coupon and get our new comprehensive guide 'How to make your business grow'. Or dial 100 and ask for Freefone Enterprise. The sooner the better – for all of us. (cited in Freeborn, 1987: 232–3)

The chummy, ingratiating style of this is a good example of the conversationalising of language which Fairclough argues has happened at all levels of public discourse. Sentences are no longer units of grammar, but of style. The model for written English has become spoken English. Ironically, we have emerged from a long period in which the reverse was the case, and it has forced on us a revision of some of the staple injunctions of traditional grammar: 'Never start a sentence with a conjunction, never end it with a preposition', and so on. Language is at the forefront of social change and nowhere more so than in the secondary orality of electronic media. But despite the innovative 'scripts' of television and radio, the virtual communities they construct are essentially one dimensional. Apart from the highly controlled format of 'phone-in' programmes, we cannot talk back. For a more interactive and more dynamic linguistic form we need the technology of the computer.

Electronic language

For most of us, writing used to seem a relatively uncomplicated process. A matter of pen and paper. And although we knew the tools were products of an advanced process of manufacture, it was hidden from us at the point of use. Matters are very different with electronic language, however. The computer makes it abundantly clear to us how far language has become technologised. We have to learn a whole new set of skills before we can begin writing on it, or reading its products. Some of these, like moving and positioning the mouse, are reminiscent of the motor skills we acquired when learning to hold the pen correctly, others require learning to 'read' new symbols, or icons. Powering up the computer, logging on, locating and opening folders and files, are intricate procedures, taking several minutes of actual time during which the mechanical whirring of the machine simulates for us the operation of a brain. To all intents and purposes, the computer appears to be thinking. Indeed, like our brains it can perform several functions at the same time, enabling us to print off a document and compose a new one simultaneously. The ideal computer would simply be an extension of the human mind so that we could 'think' it on and 'wish' it to do something. People who study robotics tell us that such a day will come, at which point the dividing line between human and machine will have shifted quite radically.

It has, of course, already shifted. The language of computing has deeply penetrated all aspects of our consciousness. We routinely hear our brains described as processors, programmed to perform in a certain way. Indeed, I have used the same image on numerous occasions in this book. Our DNA is coded in binary form, and our mental faculties are modularised. Evolution often appears, in scientific terms, to be a vast piece of software of unknown authorship and uncertain destiny. And in turn we often think of the computer as human. It 'reads' new discs which we insert into it. It polices what we do and tells us off if we perform an 'illegal' procedure. It reminds us to 'save' our material and gets sick, occasionally, with a virus. And most humanly of all, it has a linguistic register of its own. To communicate with our computers we have to understand terms such as 'automatic reformatting', 'centering', 'cursor movement', 'file management', 'split screen', 'on-line database searches', 'zip drives', 'menu-driven programs', 'pull-down menus', 'on-screen pagination', and 'windows'. Becoming a competent user of a computer means becoming newly literate, or 'computer literate'.

Once language is seen as mechanically produced, or 'processed', it dynamically alters the relationship between writer, text and reader. In one sense, all of these are liberated from their dependence on each other. This dependence has already been loosened by print. Print serves to hide authorship. A page of a book or newspaper is essentially anonymous. It has no 'signature'. There is no way we could surmise the character of the writer from the shape of the ascenders or the flourish of the descenders. In most cases, even being told the name of the author makes no difference, since the mass circulation which print makes possible means we are unlikely to know him/her. One consequence of this is that, as readers, we are freer to interpret the text. Writers are constantly seeking to control how their texts are read. Much of the history of typography and punctuation has to do with attempts to substitute graphic controls for those exercised by intonation and gesture in oral communication. But once a text is floating in the public domain who is to say, with any certainty, what it means? In Chapter 2 I mentioned a story about the American singer Randy Newman who got into trouble because of a line he wrote, 'Short men got no right to live'. To some it was an attack on those who, in politically correct terms, were 'vertically challenged', while to others it was an ironical statement in support of such people.

Electronic language loosens the moorings of writer, text and reader, even further. As an author I can hide the traces of my authorship, not only from others, but from myself. In producing this typescript I have altered practically every sentence, often more than once. Word processing allows me to move script around, delete, and amend paragraphs, with a minimum of effort. There are no drafts of this book. If anyone should want, inconceivable as it might seem, to reconstruct the process by which the finished version had been produced, they couldn't. But although there are no drafts, there are copies. Word processing allows me to make an endless number of copies, on disc or on other machines. Each one is exactly the same. Usually, that is, On occasions I forget to update the copies and then, by default, I get drafts. And if I forget which is the earlier version, I get into a muddle. But the point I'm making is this: strictly speaking there is no original text. They are all versions, and I can work on any one of them and update the rest. The original text is the one I'm working on now, but tomorrow I may be using another copy on another machine. The text, in other words, has become radically dispersed in time and space. It has become 'virtual'. Once I shut the machine off it disappears, and I live in terror of accidentally deleting it. Hence the numerous versions.

We've grown up with the idea of the text as immutable, fixed, incapable of change. It's a benefit conferred on language by writing and secured by print. 'Fixity' is the ability to ensure that the form and content of a message doesn't change over time and space. In print, words are locked in a certain format, run off in identical copies, and circulated all over the world. But a word-processed text has no such fixity. I can download a page from the internet, change it in any way I want and make it my own. Similarly, I could, conceivably, put parts of this book on the internet and leave them to the mercy of unknown readers to adopt and rear as parts of their own productions. Morally, I might feel the material should be acknowledged, but issues of copyright and intellectual property are notoriously difficult where the web is concerned. In what sense are pages placed freely on the web for anyone to use actually 'published'?

And if the text and the author have parted company, what of the reader? Anyone who has tried to read anything substantial on a computer screen will know how tiring and tedious it is. Conventional line-by-line reading practices do not sit comfortably with the new technology. One can obviously print the material off, but if it's available in book form, it's much more pleasurable to obtain a copy and read it. Novelists do publish novels on the internet, but no one in their right mind would want to run off hundreds of loose pages. The internet has promoted a new non-linear form of reading. A normal web page is quite unlike a conventional page in a book (see Figure 3.1). It consists largely of what the trade calls 'hypertext'. Hypertexts are made up of links to other texts on the web. The reader clicks on highlighted words, or phrases and jumps to these new segments. S/he

FIGURE 3.1 A TYPICAL WEB PAGE

Source: www.nature.com

can then go back again, or move forward on another link to a fresh piece of text. In this way the reader creates his/her own text. S/he follows pathways through related texts which reflect his/her own interests. Using the jargon of the trade, the reader 'surfs' the pages rather than 'reads' them in a conventional linear fashion. Surfing is a little like the channel hopping of television viewers. In both cases the expectations of the audience in terms of immediate gratification are very high. Viewers will decide in a matter of seconds whether a programme is worth sticking with before sampling something else. Similarly, surfers will give up on links which do not connect quickly. Electronic media of all kinds speed up the transmission of material which in turn affects the degree and amount of attention which we are prepared to give. The electronic reader scans the text, rather than peruses it. This is partly because the material which is mostly on the web is information. Hence the term 'information processing'. As a rule, people don't use the web to read poetry or fiction, although they may use it to locate information about them. Electronic readers are information processors. But very skilful ones. It is increasingly easy for readers to collect large amounts of text, and of different kinds. Multi-media texts combine pictures, words, and sound. They allow readers to become authors, and in so doing free themselves from the fixity of conventional texts.

Talking in cyberspace

Multi-media authoring is just one new freedom opened up by the new technology. Many people also use computers to 'talk' to each other. In so doing, they are part of another revolution in language use. Some of the most frequent transmissions on the net are in the form of electronic mail. E-mails are superficially like conventional letters, but increasingly they are becoming a genre all of their own. For one thing, we can, and often do, ignore the traditional courtesies. A short while ago, a study of electronic messaging revealed an increase of rudeness on the net. This is not an uncommon finding. Many people, for instance, abandon conventional methods of address, like 'Dear John/Mabel', and don't bother signing off with 'Yours sincerely', or 'Best Wishes' and so on. All you get is the message, because everything else, including your name and electronic location is done for you. In this sense e-mails resemble memos, rather than letters. But unlike either of these, they have the great advantage of being instantaneous. E-mails can occasionally get held up in cyberspace but for the most part they travel in seconds. Their nearest equivalent are the secret notes children pass around in the classroom. Like them they expect a quick response, and like them no one is bothered very much about spelling and grammar. E-mails are notorious for lapses in both. Exchanges like the following are common: *Thnaks for the bok its great a read.* We excuse the errors because users share the convention that the only thing which matters is speed. E-mails are a bit like telegrams, which in many cases they have replaced. They carry the message of urgency, or haste. The apparent increase in rudeness is often a consequence of this. We can dash off a few lines without reflecting on them as we might in a conventional letter. E-mail allows the almost instantaneous transmission of thought. And also of reply. And there's the rub, because electronic mail is insistent. We might happily leave a letter a week or more before replying, but not so an e-mail. Within organisations e-mails have vastly increased the volume of internal communications and, in so doing, the measure of control. E-mails can be tagged to ensure the sender receives a receipt once they have been read, and if they are ignored they can be flagged up repeatedly until they are answered.

Nevertheless, the experience of most people, outside of big corporations, is that electronic mail is enormously liberating. And it is easy to see why. Some years ago, the actor Stephen Fry left the set of a British play in which he was a central performer, and fled suddenly to the continent. His disappearance caused a major panic about his safety. The newspapers speculated that he'd had a breakdown and might have been

"You should check your e-mails more
often. I fired you over three weeks ago"
Source: www.jerryking.com

driven to harm himself. Writing after the event, Fry said how important to him at the time was e-mail in making him aware, not only of the concerns of his friends and family, but also of his bemused public:

> It may be ... that we shall look back on the last 80 years or so as constituting a blip in human communications, during which mankind lost the art of letter writing and fell in love with the phone. Consider (especially, I would contend, if you are British) how dreadful the telephone is as a means of communication.
>
> It operates in real time ... and carries the human voice. Which is to say all the embarrassments of accent, gender, articulacy, shyness, class and age are brought into play whenever you speak through it. I was not in a state where I could trust my voice to carry my meaning without it cracking or failing or succumbing to pressure. I felt an urgent need to get across a message which revealed neither my whereabouts nor forced me to speak in real time.
>
> Letters take an age to arrive, but e-mail is more or less instantaneous ...
>
> Once armed with the paraphernalia of German telephone socketry, I moved to Hamburg (someone had seen me at the station in Hanover and I wasn't brave enough to risk being found by the press) and went on-line to tell my agent that I was more or less all right and hoped I might be left alone to wrestle with my demons before coming to some conclusion about what I was up to and what I should do. It was then I checked my digital doormat and saw the vast heap of e-mail awaiting me.
>
> There was mail from friends and from family that communicated more than telephone conversation ever could have done. There were letters from complete strangers; letters that joked, coaxed, chivvied, wheedled, hugged, clucked, reproved, wondered, wailed, applauded, doubted, damned, supported and forgave. Alone and fretful in a hotel room overlooking the Alster I could read them slowly, without the need for an instant response. A few hours later I swallowed my pride and a bockwurst, pointed the car towards Holland and drove home to family, friends and help.
>
> If the majority of 'netizens' are really still nerds, geeks, dweebs, anoraks, phreaks and hackers, as we like to think, the 'Net' is living proof of the superiority of the written word. Put the average geek on the telephone and he or she will not be up to much. Put them behind a keyboard, however, and the act of literary composition forces a wit, an integrity, an insight, an emotional and moral honesty that would amaze even an optimist ... .(Fry, 1995, cited in Goodman and Graddol, 1996: 134–5)

Stephen Fry's experience is salutary in two respects. First, it is quite clear that for him, electronic mail performed an important socialising function. This is ironic, given the usual stereotyping of computer users as isolated and socially inadequate. Typical of such views is the newscaster Jon Snow's, who sees the internet as a 'lone male world,' full of people who are 'self-seeking, self-serving, and self-fulfilling' (Goodman and Graddol, 1996: 135). Sitting alone in front of a computer screen takes the user deep inside 'a world of "me", "my choice", and "fuck you"'. And there is an argument to suggest that compulsive computer usage is a form of regressive self-preoccupation. But the second thing to emerge from Fry's account is equally important here. If the internet takes us, as Snow argues, into a deeper 'world of me', it also offers the opportunity to become a different sort of 'me'. Fry was surprised to discover the creativity of the average 'netizen'. People who might be tongue-tied over the phone, and who might be put off by the formal paraphernalia of letter writing, are suddenly able to express a new side of themselves. This is partly because, as we have already said, electronic writing is much more casual than any other genre. People are far more likely to write as they speak. Nowhere is this more so than in the use of chat rooms and bulletin boards. People use computerised bulletin boards to pass messages back and forth about things they wish to buy and sell, or to ask and answer questions about areas of mutual interest. Users don't give their address or telephone numbers unless absolutely necessary, and are identifiable only by a single name, which may be fictional. This enables people to communicate, on a very casual basis, with complete strangers, in a way that would never happen with any other form of communication. This is particularly true of chat rooms. These practically oblige the user to disguise his or her identity. In the process virtually everything which distinguishes us can be hidden: nationality, sex, age, appearance, career, marital status, and so on. One can choose which kind of room to go in: men or women only rooms, mixed sex rooms, public areas for general chats, and so on. The possibilities for constructing completely fictional identities are endless. As Mark Poster comments:

> Conversationalists are in the position of fiction writers who compose themselves as characters in the process of writing, inventing themselves from their feelings, their needs, their ideas, their desires, their social position, their political views, their economic circumstances, their family situation – their entire humanity … .(Goodman and Graddol, 1996: 138)

This is possible because of two crucial factors. First, chat rooms work in real time, so people are conversing spontaneously, and second, users are guaranteed complete anonymity. The nature of the medium means there need be no actual consequences from the interaction. The relationships which are formed are virtual. This is not to say that some genuine friendships are not formed in this way, nor that what takes place is always entirely innocent. We read from time to time of people who have disappeared after arranging to meet someone they have contacted over the internet. But in the main, what goes on is an extension of our natural human instinct for play. The contact is our technological equivalent of the masked ball. We saw earlier that one consequence of electronic writing was the lack of fixity accorded to the text. This is also true of writers and their correspondents. Both are dispersed in time and space over the internet. We cannot say where any of them really are. In such a situation we could say that not only has writing become technologised, but so have its subjects. This is also evident in the recent phenomenon of text messaging, a technique which allows us to use the mobile phone as a form of e-mail. Particularly popular with teenagers, it is one of the fastest growing forms of communication. 'Texting' has already generated its own form of discourse using a mixture of signs and abbreviations (YKWYCD = *You know what you can do*, :-o zz z z ZZ = *I am bored*)

One important consequence of electronic communication has been the increased dominance of English as a global language. Because America has been responsible for much computer and software development, the discourse of computing (its technical terms and programming languages) is inevitably based on American English, as are the operating systems. This doesn't mean that it's impossible to translate the software into local languages, but such translations tend to lag behind US versions. Communication in languages other than English does take place on the internet but, in general, linguistic diversity is considerably reduced. It has been reported that no more than twenty languages are used as the primary medium of message posting internationally, with the overwhelming number of these being in English. Probably the language most threatened by English dominance is French, the most common lingua franca after English. The French government has gone to the lengths of establishing its own World Wide Web site with the aim of promoting the use of French internationally, but it remains to be seen how successful this will be. It may be that, as the technology becomes more available, and more widespread, more, not less linguistic diversity will result. Indeed, there are some indications that this is already occurring. Those who keep a watch on

---

Emoticons

Typographical devices which are used by text messagers to indicate a state of mind:

;-) winking happy face for comments said tongue-in-cheek

:-(sad, disappointed face

:-p face with tongue stuck out

8-) smiling face from someone with glasses

:-] I am very jolly

:-[I am down

:-I I couldn't care less

---

internet use have commented on the growing number of language groups, running into hundreds, which are exploiting the new technology. In the meantime, the English which is used, particularly in countries where it is a second language, exhibits a refreshing capacity for novelty and innovation. Users feel much more comfortable, for example, about slipping into non-standard English than they might with other forms of written communication. The researcher Hock (1995) gives an example from Singaporean English where users resort to non-standard spelling to give their writing a more spoken flavour. In particular, they pepper their exchanges with sentence end particles (in bold), a characteristic of colloquial Singaporean English:

> gimme his act **lorr**
> u dating larry **ah**
> huh din see her **leh**
> work got money **wat** (cited in Goodman and Graddol, 1996: 133)

Speech and writing

The electronic channels we have been talking about all utilise the two principal media through which we encounter language: speech and writing. There are other media, as in semaphore, morse, and sign language. But, with the exception of sign language, where ideas and concepts are translated into movements of the body, they are dependent on some form of writing, or script. It may seem strange to talk of speech as a medium of language. For most people speech and language mean much the same thing. And it's easy to see why. We can't imagine a language unable to be spoken. Even 'dead' languages at one time had their speakers. On the other hand, there are plenty of examples of languages which have no written form. If we look at the history of linguistic representation it is clear that speech predates writing: there is no instance of a society where writing developed before speech.

Not surprisingly, popular understanding tends to regard writing as simply a transcription of speech. But this is not so, and it quickly becomes apparent as soon as we examine the relationship between the two. For one thing, all languages have some written symbols which are unpronounceable. A good example is the number system, *1, 2, 3, 4,* and so on. Numbers like these have no phonetic form and every language which uses the system has its own way of pronouncing them. Linguists call them **logograms** because they represent the conceptual, not the spoken, form of words. Chinese uses logograms extensively. Stylised drawings of objects are used to represent concepts, or ideas. As a consequence people are able to read Chinese without necessarily being able to speak a word of it. In a country where there are scores of mutually incomprehensible dialects this is a great advantage. Everyone can read the same script while speaking a virtually different language. The downside, however, is that an enormous number of symbols, or characters, are needed to represent all the many concepts expressible in language. There are some 50,000 characters in Chinese, although basic literacy requires a knowledge of only 2000. In Chinese a stylised picture of two trees doesn't represent the words 'two trees' but the word 'woods', and similarly, the picture of a woman and child together represents the word 'good' (Ong, 1982: 86). They stand for the words in their conceptual, not spoken form. Apart from logograms, languages have many abbreviations which, strictly speaking, bear little relation to the spoken form. The symbol *cf.* in English is an instruction meaning 'compare', and the initials *BBC* have achieved the status of a word even though that letter formation is not pronounceable as a word.

So although writing emerged, in historical terms, after speech, it doesn't mean it has a secondary, or derivative status. Writing relates to language in a different way from speech, and in so doing, realises a another dimension of language. Rather than seeing the relationship as in 1, we should see it as in 2 (Figure 3.2).

Writing makes us aware of language as a human instrument. It's with the emergence of writing that technology becomes important.

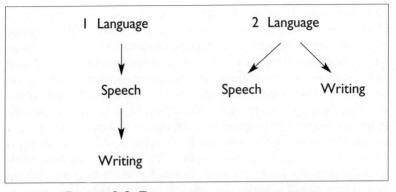

FIGURE 3.2 THE RELATIONSHIP BETWEEN SPEECH, WRITING AND LANGUAGE

Tools are necessary in order to make the symbols, whether chisel and stone, pen and paper, or typeface and printing press. With writing words become objects, detached from us. They can be seen, moved around in space, even touched. Suddenly fixity is conferred on something which before was fluid and impermanent. I suggested in Chapter 1 that one of the achievements of language was to bring thought into consciousness: to make us aware of ourselves thinking. With writing language itself comes into consciousness: we become aware of the underlying code. This represents a considerable cognitive advance and changes our whole mental map. Words now consciously exist for us as signs. The marks on the page are symbols of ideas and meanings in our own minds. And, equally importantly, they can serve as symbols for the same ideas in the minds of others. For the first time we have access to other people through a medium which is essentially impersonal. We don't have to know, or even to have met, people to understand what they think. Ideas and thoughts become detached from thinkers and enter a public domain, which collectively we call literature.

In recent years, a number of linguists have argued that being able to read and write is not just the acquisition of a linguistic skill but an essential element in our development as thinking, self-aware beings. Theorists such as Walter Ong, Jack Goody, and Ian Watt have been concerned with what they call the 'psycho-dynamics' of literacy, that is, with the way writing structures consciousness: with the way we have become interpenetrated by language. Most developed societies took a long time to become fully literate, and even today there is a sizeable residue of the populations of most countries which is illiterate. For the majority, the illiterate past remains something to be excavated by historians, but in so doing we understand a key feature of our modernity. Oral societies are inherently conservative. A good deal of mental energy is concerned with remembering the past and recording it verbally. The tales and poems which survive in oral societies, passed down from father to son, are predominantly backward-looking. They exist as resources for knowing how to carry out sacred rituals and practices and ensuring the society keeps faith with its past. Once it becomes possible to use writing for this purpose, then the mental and emotional energies devoted to recalling the past can be directed towards changing the present. Literacy is inherently dynamic. Part of this may have to do with the different senses involved, although there is no hard evidence here. The poet W.H. Auden, for example, suggested that the ear enjoys repetition while the eye enjoys novelty. He illustrated this by referring to the way in which people tend to listen to their favourite music repeatedly and like to hear the same stories over again, but will rarely read the same novel twice. Whatever the truth of this, when we look back at the development of writing we can see the first steps taken by our ancestors in exchanging a linguistic world dominated by sound, for one predicated on sight.

A key element of that exchange, and of the modernity to which we have become accustomed, is a knowledge of ourselves as subjects over against a world of objects. The rise of modern science with its methods of empirical investigation is dependent on concepts of objective, independently verified, evidence. What the scientist discovers are truths which are meant to hold good for everybody. They are detached from him or her just as written words are detached from their authors. Of something which is definitely true we say it is 'literally' true. There is a persuasive argument to suggest, as does David Olson (1994) among others, that the habits of mind which underlie the rise of science are deeply literate. Studies of the growth of literacy in England during the Middle Ages by Michael Clanchy (1993) have shown just how significant an impact it had on the concept of truth and verifiable evidence in the field of Law. In the early Middle Ages the guilt or innocence of people was established by oral declaration before witnesses. Uttering something under oath was powerful evidence of an accused's 'trothe'. A person's 'trothe' was his or her integrity or dependability. We keep this sense in the idea of someone plighting his or her troth in the marriage service. Gradually, however, written evidence assumed more importance as the use of charters and writs became more widespread. And at the same time courts became more demanding in their requirements of proof. By the time of Chaucer a new sense of the word 'trothe', or 'trouthe', as it was now spelt, had emerged, meaning 'conformity to fact', or 'something independently verifiable'.

What writing does, then, is to focus on language in a new way and in so doing to change the way we experience the world. Writing is solitary whereas talking is communal. More importantly, we have actively to learn to write whereas we acquire speech unconsciously. Putting it another way, speech is the product of nature, writing of culture. For most of us, writing is hard work compared with speaking. We have to think how words are spelt, how punctuation works, and how to express ourselves so we shall be understood by someone we can't hear or see. Writing is a much more severe task master than speech. It won't allow us the repetitions, hesitations, and muddled syntax we are accustomed to in talking. On the other hand, it will allow us to edit and deliberate longer over how to put things. More conscious thought goes into writing than speech. Necessarily so, because we get no direct feedback from our audience and have no second chance to correct ourselves. Compared with speaking, writing is decontextualised language; it doesn't come with a ready made living, breathing human context. Of course, no act of language is entirely context free, but in the case of writing the context is less immediate and more obscure. In writing we have to imagine our audience and fashion our script accordingly. Not only that, but we have to do it without the aid of intonation, or gesture. Much more of the meaning is in the words themselves. Scrupulous attention to wording is a feature of literate habits of thinking. Some psychologists have even suggested that people in traditional oral societies reason differently from those in developed literate societies. A well-known example of this comes from the Russian psychologist Aleksandr Luria, who conducted a series of tests with literate and non-literate people in Central Asia. He found that in response to tests involving classification and reasoning, those who were literate set about solving them in a more abstract and principled way, while those who were non-literate approached them in a concrete and context-bound way. When asked the following, for instance,

> In the far North, where there is snow, all bears are white. Novaya Zemlya is in the far North and there is always snow there. What color are the bears there?

a non-literate would usually answer: 'I don't know. I've never been to Novaya Zemlya. There are different sorts of bears.' (cited in Olson, 1994: 34–5). Luria saw this as a failure to be able to logically infer from the syllogism. But it is so only if we take the question to be a linguistic one rather than one about whether bears in Novaya Zemlya are really white or not. What the example suggests is not that non-literates don't think logically, but that their reasoning is not linguistically based. Logic, as it has been developed in the West, is a form of language game. To play it properly you have to know the rules.

This has important implications for the development of children's linguistic competence. Young children, typically, don't think of questions in terms of the precise wording they take. So, for example, pre-school children, shown a picture of five toy cars, four of which are in garages, and one outside, and asked the question *Do all of the garages have cars in them?* will tend to answer *No* (cited in Olson, 1994: 125). The answer is thoroughly logical if we think of the concrete situation the children are presented with, that is, all of the cars, bar one, are in garages, garages are normally where cars are put, so there must be an empty garage somewhere. Being able to interpret the question properly means knowing that the term 'the garages' refers solely to those shown in the picture. It's the same issue as in the example from Luria. For non-literates, Novya Zemlya is a real place being asked about, whereas for literates it's a linguistic item. Non-literates characteristically use language to refer externally, outside the linguistic context, or *exophorically*, while literates use it *endophorically*, or internally. Even where children are literate, however, they can still retain oral habits of thought. A classic instance of this is an experiment conducted by the education-alist Basil Bernstein. Bernstein showed groups of children a series of pictures which told a story and then asked them to describe in their own words what was going on. The story was a fairly simple one about a football game which results in a broken window and a couple of irate householders. He found that accounts tended to fall into one of two types. The first, in which the objects, participants, and action are made verbally explicit, and the second, in which they are not:

(i) Three boys are playing football and one boy kicks the ball and it goes through the window. The ball breaks the window and the boys are looking at it and a man comes out and shouts at them because they've broken the window so they run away and then that lady looks out of her window and she tells the boys off.

(ii) They're playing football and he kicks it and it goes through there and it breaks the window and they're looking at it and he comes out and shouts at them because they've broken it so they run away and then she looks out and she tells them off. (cited in Gregory and Carroll, 1978: 83)

The difference between these two accounts is solely a matter of reference. The first is independent of its context and can be understood on its own terms, while the second is dependent on access to the pictures. Bernstein used the terms **elaborate** and **restricted code** to refer respectively to the differing kinds of account, and because the first was provided by middle-class children and the second by working class, this had the consequence of suggesting that working-class speech was somehow inferior. This is a pity because it detracts from the real difference here which is between a mode of expression penetrated by literacy and one which retains a greater orality. In the context of providing an adequate description for someone not looking at the pictures, the first account is clearly better, but we should be wary of making evaluative judgements about middle-class as opposed to working-class speech, on the basis of it. 'Restricted' here should not mean 'impoverished' but 'dependent on the immediate context'. In so far as education is based on the acquisition of literate skills it is concerned with the development of context-free modes of expression. Education teaches us to speak in a literate fashion. But, as the upsurge in electronic communication has indicated, we don't always need, or want to speak in such a manner.

The world of print

Literacy has taken two major steps forward in its historical evolution. One was the development of print in the fifteenth century and the other was that of electronic writing in the twentieth. We began by considering the second of these, but it could not have happened without the first. Print is one of the great inventions of humankind on which rests practically the whole of modern culture. In a manuscript culture ideas circulate slowly among a religious or educated elite. Every book has to be copied out painstakingly from its original, or from another copy. All the monasteries of medieval Europe had scriptoria – rooms devoted to copying out ancient texts. The consequence of this was that books were precious objects, individually prized, each copy unique in its own way. Scribes would embellish texts with drawings and other devices, and use different colours to ink in. Such texts, ironically, are closer to the multi-media texts of electronic writing than the more uniform world of print. As with multi-media texts, a manuscript culture is producer oriented. Each copy is different and bears the individual mark, or 'signature' of the copyist. A print culture, on the other hand, is consumer oriented. This is not simply to make the obvious point that books are printed to make money, but that they are produced to make circulation easy. And to do that means making them simple to read and cheap to buy. Both of these objectives have taken time to achieve. The first books were neither of these. But once a print culture began there was an inexorable logic to its development. Looking back from the twenty-first century, in which books are a staple diet of life it is difficult to imagine the consternation caused by the influx of printed matter into early modern Europe. Books which before could only be read in religious houses or libraries, could now be purchased. In so doing language itself became a commodity, with profound effects on social and individual consciousness. The principal linguistic commodity was the Bible. It is difficult to conceive of the Reformation ever being more than a little local trouble in Germany without the invention of print. In Tudor England, Thomas More, the Lord Chancellor, attempted to ban the circulation of William Tyndale's translation of the Bible from Latin into vernacular English. For the first time it was available to be read by people other than the clergy. And if it could be read by them it could also be discussed and disputed by them. Latent within a developing print culture is the notion that ideas do not belong to any one person but potentially to everybody. In that sense they are a universal commodity. Many regimes with totalitarian tendencies have attempted to control their populations by destroying books, but whereas a manuscript, once burnt, is gone for ever, a printed book is practically immortal. As long as there are people who still want to read it, more copies can always be run off.

Printed books are also an individual, as well as a universal, commodity. They are owned and read in a different way from manuscripts. In his great work of autobiography, *The Confessions*, Augustine, a fourth-century professor of Latin and an early Christian saint, mentions seeing a friend, Ambrose, Bishop of Rome, reading. The manner of his reading was remarkable enough for Augustine to describe it for us: 'his eyes scanned the page and his heart sought out the meaning, but his voice was silent and his tongue was still. Anyone could approach him freely and guests were not commonly announced, so that often when we came to visit him, we found him reading like this in silence, for he never read aloud' (cited in Manguel, 1996: 42). This is one of the first recorded instances of something which we take absolutely for granted today: silent reading. The overwhelming evidence is that when reading first began it was anything but silent. The norm for many centuries was reading aloud. Most people today complain of the noise in public libraries, but it would have been nothing to that in the ancient libraries of Alexandria, Carthage and Rome, where scholars consulting scrolls would routinely have mumbled their way through texts. The history of punctuation shows that it developed initially as an aid to the oral delivery of texts, to assist speaking, rather than reading. Once begun, however, punctuation became an invaluable aid to the advancement of silent reading. The earliest of such readers were most probably the scribes working in the scriptoria of the great monasteries. Indeed, it is to ninth-century Irish scribes that we owe many of the punctuation marks in use today. It is from this period that the first regulations instructing scribes to be silent in the scriptoria date. Before then scribes would have copied either by dictation or by reading aloud to themselves. But scribes were among the elite of readers. As far as the general populace was concerned, reading aloud remained a staple of literacy throughout the medieval period. Public readings of documents, such as the *Magna Carta*, were an important method of publishing them, and it is clear from the way in which medieval authors addressed their audience that they expected them to 'hear', or 'listen' to what they had to say.

In a manuscript culture, reading aloud has obvious advantages in allowing non-literates access to the text. This is the case for both authors and readers. We do not distinguish today between the tasks of authoring and writing but it was common to do so in medieval times. Writing in the sense of authoring was covered by the Latin word *dictitare* (literally, 'to dictate'). Literary compositions were frequently dictated. Indeed, the skills of dictation were part of the system of rhetoric taught in schools. As a consequence kings and high officials did not need to be fully literate. The word used for the physical act of writing was *scriptitare* (literally, 'to make a script'). It simply meant making a fair copy of a parchment. At both ends of the process, then, both in composition and in reading, a manuscript culture is much more oral in character than a print culture. As Michael Clanchy remarks (1993: 265) 'Manuscript culture puts the emphasis in any text on its current presentation rather than its archaeological correctness'. Readers and listeners are concerned with making immediate sense of the text rather than with literal accuracy. Copying large texts inevitably means that mistakes will occur requiring correction by readers. Moreover, medieval scribes were quite used to inserting emendations if they considered they made better sense of the text. As Clanchy points out, the copies of the *Magna Carta* which have survived from the twelfth century, all differ in ways which would be unacceptable in a modern printed legal document. Both writers and readers were concerned with the gist of the text rather than the exact words. This was the case for silent as well as vocal readers. Traditional monastic reading was an aid to meditation not an end in itself. 'It was more a process of rumination than reading, directed towards savouring the divine wisdom in a book' (Holdsworth, 1961, cited in Clanchy: 269).

Concern for literal accuracy, as a number of commentators have pointed out, is a consequence of the development of printing. Printing gives writing a greater degree of independence than is possible in a manuscript culture. It becomes possible for workers to reproduce texts mechanically which have not passed through their mouths or their minds. The old oral connections, in other words, become looser. It's with printing that anxieties over plagiarism become significant. A consumer buys a book but does not thereby own the words within it. These remain the private property of the author even though contained in a volume offered for sale. Words, paradoxically, take on a dual identity in a print medium. They exist both as physical entities and as tokens. A printed text has a kind of sacredness conferred on it because, as Walter Ong (1982: 132) comments, it is 'supposed to represent the words of the author in definitive or "final" form'. As such it cannot be tampered with or borrowed from without the author's consent. While we know that texts are invariably composed of other texts and other people's words, nevertheless, originality becomes a prime goal of a print culture, as opposed to a manuscript one, where it is incidental.

With the availability of books in a portable and relatively cheap form the scene was set for the expansion of private, as opposed to communal, reading. A manuscript culture is a more social one both in the way texts are circulated and the way they are performed. By comparison, the printed book is comparatively anonymous. Our model of the reader is one which stresses the privacy and individual nature of the process. We imagine someone undisturbed, in a quiet corner, lost in the book s/he is reading. The development of concepts of privacy, individualism, and the subjectivity which goes along with them, has been the subject of much debate in recent years. Marxists have argued for some time that it is linked to the rise of capitalism. The old feudal world of hierarchy and community gradually gave way in the early modern period to a new commercial reality in which people became private consumers. The relationship between social and economic structures and modes of human consciousness is highly contentious. And to what extent changes in one can cause, or simply trigger, changes in the other is itself debatable. Nevertheless, a number of writers and thinkers have argued that a new sense of the self, in particular, of its interiority, emerges in European culture of the early modern period, that is, the sixteenth and seventeenth centuries. Harold Bloom (1998) in his book on Shakespeare, significantly titled *Shakespeare: The Invention of the Human*, even goes so far as to make Shakespearean drama the focal point of this, arguing that in the character of Hamlet we glimpse the first modern individual, because here we see a human mind debating with itself in a way that is recognisably modern. Since Shakespeare's time, he suggests, it is this internal debate which typifies great literature. Whether or not Bloom's thesis is right, we are only just beginning to appreciate what I referred to earlier as 'the psycho-dynamics' of a print culture. It is not that literacy generates more consciousness, but that, in Ong's more carefully worded formulation, it 'restructures consciousness'. There is no better evidence of that than the way in which the new electronic writing is once again changing our sense of self and community.

The origins of literacy

Just when and how human beings first made the leap into literacy is uncertain. Like most major developments it seems to have consisted of a series of small steps rather than one big one. What also seems to be true is that writing systems developed independently of each other in various parts of the world. Ancient scripts have been found in China, the Americas, Egypt, Mesopotamia, and elsewhere. There is no one writing system from which all others have descended. None the less, despite their variety the great majority of ancient scripts owe their origin, directly or indirectly, to picture writing of some kind.

At around ten thousand years ago humankind embarked on one of the significant changes that have marked its social and cultural evolution. It's referred to, in archaeological terms, as the 'Neolithic revolution'. Our forebears changed from being hunter gatherers into agriculturalists. Instead of moving on from place to place, they settled in fertile areas and began erecting more permanent settlements. This period is marked by the beginnings of pottery making, food preparation, more elaborate rituals for the burial of the dead, and the development of domestic agriculture. It is also marked by the development of picture writing. We are all familiar with the ancient rock drawings and paintings scattered around the world from Europe, to the Far East, the earliest of which date from the Paleolithic period, around 30,000 BP. Many of them are hauntingly beautiful, despite the ravages of time.

An echo of a vanished era. It has been clear to scholars for sometime now that these drawings are not simply art objects in the manner of modern paintings. They have a purpose of some kind, whether religious, magical, or secular. From about 10,000 BP onwards the drawings seem increasingly to have been used in a narrative sense. The writers Brooks and Wakankar (1976), in their extensive analysis of Indian rock art, distinguished 20 separate styles of art, many of which, they suggested, were linked to different representational purposes, including recording events, and providing directional signals, in addition to simple decoration. In another part of the world, the Ojibway, an aboriginal people of North America, inscribed a number of pictures on birch-bark to depict the rituals of their culture, including the creation of the world. Using pictures to tell a story is a common method today of teaching children to read. By associating the words of a story with the pictures, they learn that words symbolically represent things in the outside world (Figure 3.3).

There is no indication, however, that ancient picture writing of this kind was meant to serve as a script in the modern sense. Representations probably served as an aide memoire for a shaman, or holy man, to narrate a story but the pictures would not have represented linguistic units. When a fully literate child comes across the set of symbols 'pig', s/he knows they stand for the word *pig*, not just the animal in the farmyard. There is a significant difference between a graphic system which represents language and one which only represents things or events.

FIGURE 3.3 NORTH AMERICAN INDIAN PICTORIAL
REPRESENTATION OF AN EXPEDITION
Source: D.R. Olson *The World on Paper* (CUP, 1994: 71)

That difference, difficult though it may be to pin down, is what we understand by literacy.[1] Of all the functions which pictures served, however, arguably the recording one was the most significant for the development of literacy. Ancient cultures needed to be able to keep records of various kinds, commercial transactions, debts, details of ownership, and the like. Many instances of recording devices are known to have been in use around the world, from tally-sticks and knotted cords in China to the 'winter-count' calendars of the American Plains Indians, and the 'quipu' of the Incas (a stick with suspended cords onto which other cords were tied). One of the most important graphic forms from which most western writing systems probably developed was the token system developed for accounting purposes in Mesopotamia. Around the beginning of the ninth millennium, the Sumerians, a people living in what is now Southern Iraq, began using clay replicas of sheep, cattle, grain, oil and other goods as a way of recording the day to day buying and selling which accompanied the move from hunting and gathering to farming and trading. By about 4000BC these tokens had increased to such an extent that exchanges were becoming cumbersome. People began keeping them together by piercing them and stringing them. But a better method was to put them in clay envelopes, or 'bullae'. These could then be marked on the outside to indicate the contents. To start with the bullae were marked by impressing the tokens on the wet clay before baking. But once the contents are marked on the surface there is no real need to bother with the tokens themselves. As Olson (1994: 72) remarks 'The envelope has become a writing surface...' In time it becomes possible to economise on space by using one symbol to represent the commodity and another to represent the quantity. So instead of representing *three sheep* by three representations of the animal, all that's needed is one representation plus an indication of quantity. Such a system is, arguably, a script, however primitive, because it has a 'syntax': 'it permits the combination and recombination of symbols to express a broad range of meanings' (Olson: 73). Interestingly, the invention of abstract numbers seems to have coincided with the invention of syntactic writing. Early tallies and counting systems of the kind previously mentioned used a one-to-one method of recording objects, one token for each object. But when the Sumerians began using marks made by tokens to indicate numbers in the abstract an important cognitive and linguistic step forward had been taken. A mark on a clay surface could now, undeniably, represent a word.

Most archaeologists agree that the symbols on the bullae were the basis for the sign system used in the earliest tablet writing of the

FIGURE 3.4 SYNTACTIC WRITING: TABLET FROM UR, 2960BC,
ITEMISING CONTENTS OF A STOREHOUSE
Source: D.R. Olson *The World on Paper* (CUP, 1994)

Sumerians. These tablets were again made of clay but instead of recording simply individual transactions, they served more in the way that they might in modern business, for stock control, tax accounting, and land sales.

Some 1500 symbols have been listed from the ancient city of Uruk, alone, most of them abstract in character. Figure 3.4 is an example of a tablet from around 2960BC itemising the contents of a storehouse. Early writing, then, seems to have been pictographic in character. This is so in whatever part of the world we look. **Pictograms** are, as the word suggests, pictorial representations of the real world used to convey a message. But the problem with pictograms is that the link between what they represent and the message they are meant to convey is not always clear. This is because pictograms are not of themselves linguistic entities, that is, they don't necessarily represent an utterance. Clearly, in the case of the Sumerian bullae, the depiction of a sheep together with the symbol for three can be literally translated as *three sheep*. We are at least moving towards an utterance, if we don't have one already. But many pictograms need to be heavily contextualised to convey a meaning. We only have to consider a couple of modern examples (Figures 3.5 and 3.6) to see this.

FIGURES 3.5 AND 3.6 TWO EXAMPLES OF A MODERN PICTOGRAM
Source: The Highway Code

In Figure 3.5 we have a sign warning travellers of road works and in Figure 3.6, one warning drivers to take care as the road ahead leads to water. But we do not interpret these signs by any system of wording. We have learnt them individually in the same way we have learnt that cowpats in a field mean it is used for cows. Indeed, as David Crystal (1987) points out, the road works sign could be warning us not to put up an umbrella on a windy day. Because they are not linguistically based they can be interpreted by people who speak different languages, which is, of course, their one great advantage.

Historically, pictograms are a form of proto-writing. We know that they have become linguistic signs proper when they are used to bring words into our minds as opposed to just things, or events. One of the earliest indications of this is when pictures are used as **phonograms**. The modern equivalent of these are the rebus, a child's puzzle in which a picture represents the sound of an object rather than the thing itself. A collection of pictures can then be strung together to make a word. So for example, a picture of a mill, a wall and a key can make the word Milwaukee. Or a picture of a bee can be used for the verb 'be'. In some instances, where the pictures won't quite stretch to make the whole word, they may need supplementing with a sign indicating the insertion of a single sound, or syllable, as in Figure 3.7, which makes the word 'catalogue'.

Various kinds of phonograms can be found in Egyptian hieroglyphics, one of the most complex of surviving scripts, dating from around 3000BC. The picture of the sun, for example, could be used for the word *sun*, but it could also represent *son*. The way Egyptian writers distinguished the two was by adding an indicator sign, a picture of a man in the case of *son*. Indicator signs, or determinatives,

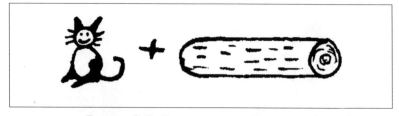

FIGURE 3.7 PHONOGRAM OF 'CATALOGUE'

are not pronounced. They are there as a guide to word identification. In some instances signs clearly represent separate sounds in the manner of letters. So, for example, the first sign in the name Ptolemy, a small square (□) is the same as the fifth sign in the name Cleopatra. Most probably, therefore, it represents a single sound, in a similar way to the letter 'p' in English. Another way in which pictures are used in hieroglyphics is as logograms (see above). Here the link between the sign and the word is with the sense of the word rather than its sound. So the drawing of two legs means 'go'; a large wading bird looking for food, 'find'; and a person with their hand to their mouth, 'eat'. Egyptian hieroglyphs provide a fascinating insight into the way early writing systems combined different methods of word representation in order to link pictures more securely to meaning. The deciphering of the Rosetta Stone in the early nineteenth century, from which comes our understanding of Egyptian writing, shows that here at last we have a fully worked out graphic code capable of representing a wide variety of utterances. Similar scripts have been found to exist in other cultures, Hittite, Mayan, and along the Indus valley, but the Egyptian code is the most sophisticated in the ancient world. It continued to be used for three thousand years until it was eventually replaced by what is, arguably, the most dynamic and innovative system of all – the alphabet.

Alphabetic writing

The key difference between alphabetic systems of writing and those using some form of pictures is that, in the case of alphabets, the link with the real world has been lost completely. There is no connection between a letter and the sound it represents other than by convention.

The relationship is essentially arbitrary, that is, we could quite easily use another shape to represent a given sound provided everyone else agreed. Alphabets have no connection with things as such. What they do is to represent sound itself as a thing. Unlike other early writing systems, all the alphabets of the world – Hebrew, Ugaritic, Greek, Roman, Cyrillic, Arabic, Tamil, Malaysian, and Korean – are descended, however remotely, from one original script, invented by a Semitic people, or peoples, who lived in the Near East, along the eastern Mediterranean. The most direct descendants of this script are Hebrew and Arabic.

The history of the alphabet has been the consequence of adapting an already existing system to represent a different language. What the ancient Semites did was to take the picture signs circulating along the eastern Mediterranean in the period 1800 to 1300BC and use them, not to stand for an entire word, as previously, but for the first sound of the word. At the same time the picture gradually became more stylised and less recognisable as the depiction of a particular thing. Figure 3.8 shows the process by which scholars believe this happened.

The principle underlying the process can clearly be seen from the first example. The word *aleph* in Semitic script means 'ox yoke'. First of all, the word is represented by a drawing of an ox yoke. But over time it becomes stylised, and is used to represent the first sound of the

Ancient Egyptian Hiero- glyphics	Sinai Script	Meaning and Letter-Name in Semitic	Moabite Stone and Early Seals	Early Phoeni- cian	Western Greek	Early Latin	Oldest Indian
੪	੪	ox yoke: **aleph**	ⵎ	K,ⵘ	A,α	A	ⵊ
▢ ▭	▢▭ ◌	house: **beth**	𝄐	ⵛ	ß,B	B	▢
Y Y	Ꙟ	hook, nail: **wau**	Y	Y,Y	V,Y,Y	V	ⵙ
᳄᳄᳄	᳄᳄	water: **mēm**	ᵞ	⟨ ⟨	M,M	M	੪
ꙿ	ꙿ	snake, fish: **nūn**	Ɏ	⟨	N,N	N	⊥
⬬	⬬ ◯ ∮	eye: **'ain**	o	o	O	O	▷
ⵘ	ⵘ	head: **rēsh**	⟨	ⵛ	D,ⵛ,P	ⵛ R	⟩
	+	mark: **tau**	x †	+	T	T	⟨
	ᵕ	tooth: **shīn**	W	⌄⌄	ⵛⵛⵛ	ⵛS	⟨

FIGURE 3.8 EARLY HISTORY OF THE ALPHABET
Source: Firth, 1937

word. Similarly, with *beth* meaning 'house', and so on. The particular Semitic script which forms the basis of the modern alphabet was most likely Phoenician. Phoenicians lived in the fertile crescent, an area of land connecting the ancient Babylonian and Egyptian civilisations. Their script, as with all Semitic scripts, had one significant difference from modern ones. It only represented consonants, not vowels. This is still the case with Hebrew.[2] In these languages the letter *A* is considered a consonant; it represents a glottal stop (the sound London Cockneys produce in the middle of *butter* /bʌʔə/ (see Chapter 4)). In Semitic languages vowels provide only grammatical information, that is they indicate such properties as tense, aspect, and subject. They don't create new words, or lexemes. This is not the case in most other languages. In English, for example, the different vowel sound in *bid* from *bed*, creates an entirely new word. English is similar in this respect to Classical Greek, where difference in vowel sounds was also crucially important in distinguishing words.

It was the Greeks who took the final step of extending the alphabet to include vowels. Around 750BC they used the 22 graphic signs invented by the Phoenicians and applied them to their own language. Many of the signs fitted directly and came to be our consonants. Others, however, didn't, because they represented Semitic sounds not present in Greek. Instead the Greeks used them to represent the all-important vowel sounds. The uniqueness of the alphabet lies in the fact that a relatively small number of letters can be used to represent an almost infinite number of words. Greek writing depended for its achievement on the invention of the alphabet. It is not simply the expressive powers and easy convenience of the alphabet which enabled this, however. The alphabet is analytic in its approach to the spoken language. It breaks up the stream of sound into small units of sound, or phonemes. As Ong points out, it analyses 'sound more abstractly into purely spatial components' (1982: 90). It is largely to Greek habits of analytic thought and philosophic enquiry that we owe the western tradition of empirical science.[3] Scripts not only make us aware of the visual form of ideas and thoughts, they also, through the particular way they represent spoken language, provide a model for human thought itself. After the Greeks, western cultures learnt to approach nature in the way in which the orthography of the alphabet required them to approach language. It is surely no accident that the verb 'to see' has become, in so many languages, a metaphor for knowledge and understanding.

Today, a good many different scripts exist around the world. Most are alphabetic in character, but some, like the Chinese, retain a pictographic heritage. Such non-phonetic forms are capable of great beauty. Learning and drawing them involves time and ability. But to compensate, such a script can be very useful in a situation where speakers have strongly marked dialectal differences. It is also the case that Chinese has a good many monosyllabic homophones (words which have an identical pronunciation), and for which an alphabetic representation would not be helpful. Chinese represents an alternative, logographic, way of writing, which, as we have seen, is of great antiquity. It's as well to bear in mind that Chinese literary and cultural achievements are as old and significant as those of the Greeks. But their habit of mind, and outlook on life, historically, has been very different. Lloyd (1990), in an interesting comparison of the two cultures, points out just how different. Whereas the Greeks pursued logic, proof and formal evidence, the Chinese explored correlations, parallelisms and complementarities. Their orthography is aesthetic and holistic. The drawing of a word can represent all of it not just a segment. Intriguingly their orthography is matched to a different world outlook.

Even so, it will be interesting to see to what extent the progress of the alphabet, an essentially more democratic and less elitist form, will affect Chinese orthography. With the emergence of a main dialect in China one of the principal arguments for a logographic script diminishes. Elsewhere in the world, the other main alternative to alphabetic scripts is the syllabary. Syllabaries are also of ancient origin. Some scholars consider that the ancient Phoenician script was essentially a syllabary since the consonant letters were pronounced with an accompanying vowel sound. In which case we would have an interesting line of development from pictograms to phonograms, logograms, syllabaries, and the alphabet. The most widely known modern syllabary is the katakana syllabary used in Japanese. It's well suited to Japanese since the language has many syllable clusters consisting simply of a vowel and a consonant. So *America*, for instance which has four syllables, is represented by just four symbols. On the face of it this seems a simpler way of writing since it requires fewer symbols per word. In fact Japanese has 75 separate symbols. It's only possible to use it at all because Japanese syllable clusters are simple. It would be impossible in a language like English, for example, which has a complex syllable structure.

The truth is that no orthographic system is without its problems. Anyone learning the English alphabet knows just how difficult the

---

Varieties of fish

The writer Bernard Shaw famously suggested that the word *fish* could be spelt *ghoti* in English, following the correspondences below:

gh as in *tough*

o as in *women*

ti as in *nation*

However, this is to ignore the pronunciation rules of English: *gh*, for example, is never pronounced as *f* when it occurs at the start of a word.

---

spelling system is. The ideal of an alphabet is that one symbol represents one sound. But changes in the pronunciation of words make this impossible. No alphabet can hope to remain totally phonetic. Every so often spelling reformers come along with the intention of making orthographies more logical, but given the mutability of sound, and the diverse accents around the world among speakers of individual languages, it is a forlorn task. All the alphabets in use around the world have their own idiosyncrasies as well as their own special delights. It's in the nature of things this should be so. As Samuel Johnson, the eighteenth-century lexicographer, observed in his *Dictionary of The English Language* ([1759] in Bronson (ed.) 1958): 'Sounds are too volatile and subtile for legal restraints: to enchain syllables, and to lash the wind are equally the undertakings of pride unwilling to measure its desires by its strength.'

Conclusion

The argument in this chapter, as I am sure you will have noticed, has proceeded backwards rather than forwards. It started with our contemporary experience of language in the advanced electronic forms with which we have become familiar, and than travelled back in time to the invention of print, before ending up with the development of writing. This has been deliberate for two reasons: first, because it allows us, from our vantage point in the twenty-first century, to appreciate the extent to which language has rested for its development on technology, whether the pen, the printing press, the television set, or the computer.

Clearly, there has only been sufficient space to touch on these, let alone the other inventions used by language, the typewriter, the telephone, the radio, and so on. Nevertheless, the relationship between language and technology is both crucial and endlessly fascinating, and something I have been anxious to stress. But second, it has enabled me to focus on what has been the key theme of this chapter, namely, the interrelationship of the spoken and the written word. Speech and writing, I have argued, are the two principal media of language. All that technology provides us with are so many different channels for their circulation within communities. I say 'all', but with such provision, not only are the expressive possibilities of language extended, but our social, cultural, and human possibilities too. We live at a time when the boundaries between spoken and written forms have become progressively blurred. Like other distinctions in our world, those of class, rank, gender, and race, the divide between orality and literacy has become difficult to maintain in its traditional form. It may be that we are moving towards more complex linguistic media which will benefit from the advantages of both. It has become fashionable in western democracies to talk about opportunity, achievement, personal fulfilment. These are the modern pieties, as opposed to the older ones of duty, respect, and restraint. Whether they are any better is an open question. All we can say is that arguments about language are never just that. At bottom they are about how we position ourselves and those around us in the world in which we live. To that extent, the virtual person with whom we started, and whom we allow so easily into our homes, comes, like the supernatural visitants of old, with a message. It is one we are still unravelling.

Notes

1 The difficulty may be reflected in the fact that, as David Crystal points out, 'in early Greek and in Egyptian the same word was used for both "write" and "draw"' (1987: 196).

2 Modern Hebrew sometimes uses a system of vowel 'points', dots and dashes below or above the consonant letter to show the following vowel.

3 This is not to ignore the contribution made by Arab scholars, particularly in the fields of mathematics and medicine.

4 We Are What We Speak
Language and Society

> In our social relations, the race is not
> to the swift but to the verbal
>
> STEVEN PINKER (*The Language Instinct*, 1994)

The problem of silence

In one of his *Rambler* essays, the writer Samuel Johnson describes taking a stagecoach journey in mid-eighteenth-century England:

> On the day of our departure, in the twilight of the morning I ascended the vehicle, with three men and two women my fellow travellers ... When the first ceremony was despatched, we sat silent for a long time, all employed in collecting importance into our faces and endeavouring to strike reverence and submission into our companions.

> It is always observable that silence propagates itself, and that the longer talk has been suspended, the more difficult it is to find anything to say. We began now to wish for conversation; but no one seemed inclined to descend from his dignity, or first to propose a topic of discourse. At last a corpulent gentleman, who had equipped himself for this expedition with a scarlet surtout, and a large hat with a broad lace, drew out his watch, looked on it in silence, and then held it dangling at his finger. This was, I suppose, understood by all the company as an invitation to ask the time of the day; but nobody appeared to heed his overture; and his desire to be talking so overcame his resentment, that he let us know of his own accord it was past five, and that in two hours we should be at breakfast.

> His condescension was thrown away, we continued all obdurate; the ladies held up their heads; I amused myself with watching their behaviour; and of the other two, one seemed to employ himself in counting the trees as we drove by them, the other drew his hat over his eyes, and counterfeited a slumber. The man of benevolence, to shew that he was not depressed by our neglect, hummed a tune and beat time upon his snuff-box. (Johnson, in Bronson (ed.)1958: 163–4)

The problem which Johnson describes so vividly is a common enough one. Most of us at some point have been closeted with people we don't know in a confined space and felt the intolerable strain of silence. We don't ordinarily talk to total strangers. This is partly to respect their privacy, but, more importantly, to protect our own. Talking involves a risk. With tried and trusted partners that risk is lessened, but with strangers anything is possible. And yet closeted with people for any length of time it seems unfriendly, possibly even hostile, to stay completely silent. We need to reassure ourselves that the person sitting opposite us in the otherwise empty railway compartment is well disposed enough towards us not to be troublesome, while letting them know we share their feelings. But how do we begin? Nothing is truer than Johnson's observation that 'silence propagates itself'.

Fortunately language comes to our aid in such circumstances. All cultures have developed utterances and exchanges which enable speakers to negotiate situations of brief, but unavoidable intimacy. They are referred to as **phatic** language. The word 'phatic' comes from Greek and means 'utterance'; it's the same root from which we get 'emphatic'. So really this is speech for its own sake. As we noted in Chapter 1, the concept of 'phatic language', or 'phatic communion', originated with Malinowski, the anthropologist, who was struck by how much of what we say is essentially formulaic and meaningless. He did most of his research on the Pacific Islands and found the same was true of the languages there. Here is his description of the function of these exchanges:

> A mere phrase of politeness, in use as much among savage tribes as in a European drawing-room, fulfils a function to which the meaning of its words is almost completely irrelevant. Inquiries about health, comments on weather, affirmation of some supremely obvious state of things – all such are exchanged, not in order to inform, not in this case to connect people in action, certainly not in order to express any thought. It would be even incorrect, I think, to say that such words serve the purpose of establishing a common sentiment, for this is usually absent from such current phrases of intercourse; and where it purports to exist, as in expressions of sympathy, it is avowedly spurious on one side. What is the raison d'être, therefore, of such phrases as 'How do you do?', 'Ah, here you are', 'Where do you come from?', 'Nice day today' – all of which serve in one society or another as formulae of greeting or approach.
>
> I think that, in discussing the function of speech in mere sociabilities, we come to one of the bedrock aspects of human nature in society. There is in all human beings the well-known tendency to congregate, to be

together, to enjoy each other's company. Many instincts and innate trends, such as fear or pugnacity, all the types of social sentiments such as ambition, vanity, passion for power and wealth, are dependent upon and associated with the fundamental tendency which makes the presence of others a necessity for man. (from Quirk, 1962: 58)

Malinowski is suggesting that language acts as a form of social bonding; it is the adhesive which links people together. According to the psychiatrist Eric Berne (*Games People Play*, 1968), such language is the equivalent of 'stroking', and acts as an adult substitute for the considerable amount of cuddling which we receive as babies. Clearly it would be inappropriate to expect formulas which perform this function to be particularly sincere. Too many people are linguistic puritans and want everything to have a precise and clearly definable semantic meaning. But the point is that we need language at times to be imprecise and rather vague. Semantically empty language can none the less be socially useful. Greetings and leave-takings are often especially problematic. When you pass an acquaintance in the street by chance you can't ignore them because that would be rude, but at the same time you may not wish to start a lengthy conversation. Both parties need a set of ready-made phrases to negotiate the encounter without either being offended. So it might run:

Hello. How are you?
OK but I can't take this heat. What about you?
Oh, bearing up.
I know how you feel.

No one expects in reply to *How are you?* a detailed medical history. Phrases like these are the verbal equivalent of waving. They are also subject to fashion. *Have a nice day* is now well established, but when it was first used in England many people responded like the American humorist, S.J. Perelman, *I'll have any kind of day I want*, but it's not really so different from the more traditional, *Have a good time.* In the south of England the usual greeting is *Alright?* And fairly popular is *Take care.* The phatic use of language is mainly spoken, but there are some written equivalents. The most obvious examples are the conventionalised phrases for starting and ending letters: *Dear Sir/Madam ... Yours faithfully, sincerely, truly.* In an

> *A bore is a man who, when you ask him how he is, tells you*
>
> BERT LESTON TAYLOR in The *So-called Human Race*

episode of the British satirical series *Monty Python*, John Cleese played a senior civil servant investigating a subordinate over allegations of homosexuality. The evidence for the allegation lay in the letters he had written: what did he mean by addressing a man as *Dear* or declaring his faithfulness and sincerity, and what of *Yours truly* or even more incriminating, just *Yours*.

> *'What ho!' I said. 'What ho!' said Motty. 'What ho! What ho!' 'What ho! What ho!' After that it seemed rather difficult to go on with the conversation.*
>
> P.G. WODEHOUSE in *My Man Jeeves*

Phatic language, then, fulfils important contact uses; it helps us negotiate the start and end of exchanges whether in spoken or written form. Failure to observe these social courtesies can cause considerable embarrassment and even bad feeling. On the other hand, however, an entire conversation made up of ritualised exchanges would be tedious. Rather like finding oneself inside a play by Harold Pinter who, more than any other twentieth-century playwright, puts us in mind of the novelist George Meredith's remark that 'speech is the small change of silence'. Here is an extract from a short scene by Pinter called *Last to Go* in which an old newspaper seller is chatting to a barman. He has just told the barman that he has sold his last copy of the *Evening News:*

BARMAN:	'Evening News,' was it?
MAN:	Yes.
Pause	
	Sometimes it's the 'Star' is the last to go.
BARMAN:	Ah.
MAN:	Or the ... whatsisname.
BARMAN:	'Standard'.
MAN:	Yes.
Pause	
	All I had left tonight was the 'Evening News'.
Pause	
BARMAN:	Then that went, did it?
MAN:	Yes.
Pause	
	Like a shot.
Pause	
BARMAN:	You didn't have any left, eh?
MAN:	No. Not after I sold that one.
Pause	

(Pinter, 1968: 129–30)

Where other dramatists construct scenes around significant and telling dialogue, Pinter offers seemingly bland statements that carry no weight. Underlying the technique is his preoccupation with the failure of people to make relationships and our obsession with hiding behind repetitive phrases. In a sense, Pinter's plays dramatise the silence behind the words.

But while silence is a problem to be negotiated in any communicative situation, the nature of the difficulty varies between cultures. Ways of speaking can differ considerably from one society to another. In many western societies, for example, it is common for members to operate a 'no gap, no overlap' rule in conversational turn taking. If two people start to talk at the same time one will normally give way to the other so as not to overlap. Violations are usually a sign that some form of heated exchange is taking place. On the other hand, if a lull occurs in the conversation exceeding a few seconds someone will usually start talking to avoid the discomfort experienced by Johnson's stagecoach passengers.

But the 'no gap, no overlap' rule is not a universal rule of communication. In the Caribbean, for instance, it is thoroughly acceptable for two speakers to talk simultaneously. And at the other extreme, there are groups of American Indians where it is common for a speaker to wait several minutes before answering a question or taking a turn. This seems also to be the case among the Lapps of northern Sweden. The linguist Reisman tells the following story about his experiences in a Lapp community:

> We spent some days in a borrowed sod house in the village of Rensjoen … Our neighbors would drop in on us every morning just to check that things were all right. We would offer coffee. After several minutes of silence the offer would be accepted. We would tentatively ask a question. More silence, then a 'yes' or a 'no'. Then a long wait. After five or ten minutes we would ask another. Same pause, same 'yes' or 'no'. Another ten minutes, etc. Each visit lasted approximately an hour – all of us sitting formally. During that time there would be six or seven exchanges. Then our guest would leave to repeat the performance the next day. (cited in Fasold, 1990: 41)

Differences such as these make it clear that all societies have their own rules, or conventions, about how language is used in social interaction. Knowing these conventions is important in interpreting human behaviour and understanding correctly the significance of what is said to us. If we telephoned someone in Japan, for instance, we might be perturbed to be greeted with total silence. But, as Peter Trudgill (1983) points out, many people in Japan expect the caller to speak first. There

---

Information concealment in Malagasy

In Malagasy, a rural area of Madagscar, it is considered socially inappropriate to provide too much information to a listener. Malagasy villages are
small, and, as a consequence, everybody knows everyone else's business.
In such a setting, holding onto information becomes a way of both maintaining privacy and also a degree of privileged status. To an outsider this
can be irritating and appear insufficiently co-operative [see Chapter 2].
The verb *misy*, for example, literally means 'exist cry', or 'there is crying'. To
make this comprehensible in English we have to put in a subject and say
Someone is crying. Even then it could only be used in circumstances where
the identity of the person crying was unknown to us. This is not the case
in Malagasy, however. Malagasy also makes considerable use of the generic
expression *alona*, meaning 'person'. The linguists Ochs and Keenan, who
undertook this study of Malagasy speech habits, record hearing a woman
use it in reference to her husband sleeping, asking *Is the person sleeping?*
Not, as we would expect *Is my husband sleeping?*

FASOLD, 1990: 53–60

---

is in fact a wide diversity of telephone behaviour around the world. In
France it's quite normal for callers to apologise for the intrusion and to
identify themselves before asking to speak to someone, whereas American and British callers behave differently. A British caller might simply
ask for someone and if they're not there ring off, only at the last
minute possibly giving his/her name. Similarly, there are differing conventions about the order of talk and how to address someone – title,
first name, or surname. There are even conventions about the volume
of talk. In England, for example, conversations in public places are
usually subdued to avoid other groups overhearing, whereas in
America public conversations can easily be overheard by others unless
there is some special need for privacy.

The study of language in relation to these and other social and cultural variables is referred to by linguists as the **ethnography of communication.** The acknowledged 'father' of this aspect of linguistics is
Dell Hymes who defined it in the following way: 'The ethnography of
speaking is concerned with the situation and uses, the patterns and
functions, of speaking as an activity in its own right' (Hymes, 1962,
1968: 101). This is a very broad area of study which, according to

Hymes, includes not only the social conventions of language use but the functions and purposes it fulfils as well. Clearly there are any number of possible uses of language, from ordering a cup of tea, to reciting a poem. But, if we think of function on a more general level, it is possible to distinguish at least seven basic language functions, including the phatic function, with which we began:

Language functions

- To release nervous/physical energy (physiological function)

- For purposes of sociability (phatic function)

- To provide a record (recording function)

- To identify and classify things (identifying function)

- As an instrument of thought (reasoning function)

- As a means of communicating
  ideas and feelings (communicating function)

- To give delight (pleasure function)

Speech communities

With such a large, ill-defined, area of study, the problem is 'Where to start?' Ethnographers usually begin by identifying 'speech communities'. This is a concept which arises naturally from the view of language as a social phenomenon, subject to codes of conduct and behaviour like any other. Just as we exist within social, educational, and cultural groupings, so we also belong within communities which have shared rules for speaking. The difficulty ethnographers face, however, is in defining what exactly a speech community is. One way might be to try and identify a set of rules which speakers of particular communities obey. But in practice this is too rigid. English and French speakers, for example, share a number of conversational rules, such as the 'no gap, no overlap' rule, but in other ways their usage is significantly different. French speakers, for instance, characteristically accompany their speech with gestures and hand movements in situations which, to an English speaker, would seem inappropriate. And, in addition, there is the obvious fact that French and English are entirely different languages.

This has led many linguists to argue that speech communities must share not only rules for speaking but also one linguistic variety as well. The term 'linguistic variety' is narrower than just 'language'. British and American speakers share the same language but speak different varieties: British English, and American English respectively. And just to complicate matters further, within both countries there are different dialects, or regional varieties. Specifying a linguistic variety then effectively pushes the argument further back, because now we are asking 'What is a linguistic variety?' as well as 'What is a speech community?' The problem is not as great as it may appear, however. First, the term language variety is a useful one simply because of its generosity. We can understand it to mean a particular form of the language, whether a national or regional dialect, or a stylistic variety, shared by speakers in a particular social situation. In this way it can refer to the language used by courtroom lawyers in America just as easily as the Black Country dialect of the British Midlands. And second, speakers do not belong to a single speech community. We live within overlapping speech communities each with its own particular rules of communication. A convict, for example, might be an inmate of a particular prison, a white person, a British speaker from the north of England, and a member of a western, European society all at the same time. All of these are speech communities in the sense that there are shared rules, or conventions, which operate among those who belong to them. Part of our communicative competence as users of language is in negotiating these. Discussing a novel over the kitchen table with a friend is significantly different from doing so in the formal educational setting of a seminar. Becoming part of such a seminar group means joining a new speech community, with rules about when and how to speak. It becomes more complex if, in turn, this speech community overlaps with others in being white, middle class, and southern, whereas we are black, working class, and northern.

I have opted for a loose definition of a speech community as a grouping of people who share a language variety, and who have rules in common about how it is used, recognising that any single individual will necessarily belong to more than one community. Fasold (1990) gives the analogy of someone being in the kitchen, on the ground floor and in the house, all at the same time. Just so, we can regard individual communities as constituents of larger, higher order communities. What this means is that any utterance will contain within it elements of the speech communities from which it has originated. The ethnographer is a linguist trained to identify the particular components

"I can't put it into layman's language for you.
I don't know any layman's language."

which are salient in the social use of language. Dell Hymes (1972), who pioneered this kind of investigation, identified eight groups of components, which for ease of remembering, he labelled with one of the letters of the word 'speaking'. What these components do is set out the parameters within which the various speech communities we all belong to can be described:

S: Situation

This is composed of the **setting** and the **scene**. The setting is about the physical circumstances in which communication takes place including location, venue and time. Location covers geographical setting – city, country, continent – venue covers place – on top of a bus, in a court-room, in church – and time specifies date and period of the day. Scene is a more complex component. It's about the psychological setting, that is the kind of cultural speech event which is taking place, a proposal of marriage, a political rally, and so on. Scene and setting interact to comprise the social context for language interactions. So an exchange in church would vary according to whether the participants were chatting on the back row or getting married, and in the case of the latter, whether the marriage was Mormon or Anglican.

P: Participants

These are usually referred to as the **addressor** and **addressee**, that is, the person(s) initiating the communication, and the person(s) constituting the audience. Obviously in a conversation these roles are interchangeable. Two factors are important here: first, the particular profiles of the participants – age, sex, class, ethnicity – and second, the relationship, if any, between them. Linguists refer to the latter of these as **tenor**. Establishing the precise tenor of a relationship is crucial to understanding the style of language available to participants. Personal tenor captures the relationship at an intimate level – friends, strangers, relatives, and so on – while functional tenor describes it at an official one. Ethnographers are concerned here with factors such as status, class, rank and social roles. A doctor talking to a patient, for example, a boss to an employee, or a captain to a sergeant would be influenced by these factors in their choice of language. Complexities arise (complex tenor) when functional and personal tenor overlap – an employee who is married to his or her boss, for instance.

It may seem as though the terms 'addressor' and 'addressee' are simply fancy ways of talking about the 'speaker' and the 'listener'. And in most cases, it is true, these roles are indistinguishable. But there are occasions when it is useful to distinguish them. Someone repeating the words of another, for instance. This most frequently happens when a piece of written language, a speech, or dialogue in a play is delivered by a speaker other than the author, or addressor. A good deal of television advertising uses speakers in this way. In similar manner the person hearing, or receiving, a particular message may not be its intended target, or addressee. Overhearing a conversation or glancing idly at the television screen may put one into the role of a recipient rather than an addressee. Speakers and recipients, then, are secondary, rather than primary participants, although, as we have said, the roles may merge in practice. We have only to think of how the voice of the narrator in a novel may merge with that of the author.

E: Ends

Ends indicates a broad category which takes account both of the **outcomes** and the **goals** of social interaction. Outcomes can be understood as the cultural purposes of the event. So, for example, a wedding has as one of its outcomes the legal, and in some cases religious, binding together of two participants. A bargaining event, on the other hand, has the orderly exchange of goods between participants as its outcome. Goals are the personal purposes or intentions of the participants. In the case of bargaining we usually expect the seller to try and get the highest price, and the buyer, the lowest. For those getting married, however, their goals would normally include a public declaration of their love for each other.

A: Act sequence

This group of components focuses on the **message** aspect of communication. It's the domain of ethnography which links most closely with **discourse analysis** and **speech act theory** (see Chapter 2). Message content plays an important part here. This often relates to a particular topic area, the weather, sport, politics, cars and so on. All of these have their own vocabularies and their own topic structures. We don't normally hear politics or religion discussed in the same manner or language as sport, although it is not impossible. Content, then, is a constraint on form. But it works the other way round as well, because in addition to the distinctive lexical and syntactic content of these topics, they can all serve as subjects in a wide range of speech acts – warnings, information, enquiries, assertions, and so forth. An important part of communicating is working out what particular action is being performed through language. The precise way in which these acts are performed will vary from culture to culture, as we saw in the example of the Malagasy village, where the giving of information is handled quite differently from western-European cultures. Knowing the precise form of such acts, how to ask questions of one's boss as opposed to one's children, giving street directions, expressing a point of view, is an essential part of our communicative competence (see Chapter 2). We have to know what choices are available to us from a repertoire of culturally acceptable linguistic forms.

K: Key

Key refers to the spirit in which a speech act is performed, whether it is humorous, perfunctory, serious, or painstaking. In many cases there are conventional links between keys and other components such as setting and participants. We would expect a funeral to be solemn, for example, and a comedian to be funny. Having said that, more complex effects of communication are frequently created by a mismatch between the content and the expected key. This is typically the case with sarcasm. In many instances the clue to the key of a speech act is intonation. This is why key is generally harder to determine in written rather than spoken communication, and why, when writing an important letter, we struggle to find the right form of words to convey our meaning.

I: Instrumentalities

Instrumentalities covers two aspects of speaking: first the **channel** of speech, and second, the form or **medium**. By channel is meant the way a message travels from one person to another, that is by telephone, television, face-to-face, letter, fax, and so forth. And, as with the other components, channels can be simple or complex. A face-to-face discussion, for instance, may take place over the radio or the television, in which case we have one channel embedded in another. As we are all too well aware, channels do exert an influence over the style of language we adopt. Messages can also be transmitted by less conventional means of course. Flags, smoke, drums can equally be used as channels. As can our bodies, in the case of sign language.

The forms, or mediums, of speech are the codes we adopt for sending messages. The most significant code is language, although there are others. Gestures, for example, can be considered a non-linguistic code, the meaning of which will crucially depend on setting and scene. Language itself has two main subdivisions – an oral, and a written medium. And within these are various sub-codes. The different accents, dialects, and registers (see Chapter 2), which are available to us are all linguistic sub-codes, features of which are either more or less appropriate to speaking as opposed to writing. And there are a range of associated codes, semaphore, smoke signals, morse code and so on.

N: Norms

Norms have to do with our cultural expectations about the amount, style, and form of speech required in any given situation. As we have already seen, there are considerable differences around the world in how people are expected to converse depending on what kind of speech community they predominantly belong to. All things considered, Americans will tend to speak more volubly, avoiding silences, than inhabitants of northern Sweden. Very often, being aware of these differences is important in understanding correctly what is going on. Fasold (1990) quotes an example from the linguist Gumperz in which this is the case. It concerns a West Indian bus driver in London whose routine was to greet passengers with the request *exact change please*. If any passenger couldn't comply with this request he would repeat it, leaving a gap between *change* and *please*, and emphasising *please* with a higher pitch. To native English speakers, the intonation pattern here, or to use Hymes's mnemonic, the key, would suggest rudeness, since it is excessively direct and implies the passenger is too stupid to have listened properly. But according to Gumperz, in West Indian speech, the norms of intonation are different. Speaking in this manner is a way of being extra polite by isolating the politeness word *please* for special emphasis. In other words, there is no hidden message here. Native English speakers would need to adopt a more roundabout formula to achieve a similar effect. Something like *I'm sorry but I do need the exact change*. Such misconceptions are frequently the breeding ground for prejudice.

G: Genres

Genres are the linguistic modes in which messages are couched. We can regard these loosely as categories, such as poems, letters, adverts, lectures, sermons, and so on. All of these adopt certain conventions, some of which govern lay-out and structure, and others content and style. Everything we say or write is affected in some way by the expectations which attach to such genres. Even casual conversation. Genres characteristically contain formulas which immediately alert us to the kind of message to expect. Poems will frequently have rhythm and rhyme and be set out in lines, conversations will start with a greeting and end with a farewell, and if we read or hear the words *Have you tried the new ...* ? we know someone is trying to sell us something. As with the other components distinguished by Hymes, all genres will

consist of a variety of sub-genres. There are different kinds of conversations, including discussions and consultations and different types of
letters, love letters, business letters, even radio letters, as in 'Letter
from America'.

Hymes's classification of the ingredients in the social use of language is just one way of organising what is inevitably a large number of
variables. Its usefulness lies in the way it enables us to give a global
account of speech parameters. And, as we have seen, it can be extended
to written language as well.

Sociolinguistics

The ethnography of communication is just one branch of a broad field
of language study called sociolinguistics, a word coined from a blend of
sociology and linguistics. Sociolinguists are concerned with what has
been called 'socially constituted' language, that is, with the way language is constructed by, and in turn helps to construct, society. As such
it is a relative newcomer to the linguistic fold. It wasn't until the early
1960s, largely as a result of the pioneering work of William Labov in
America, and Peter Trudgill in Britain, that it developed into a recognised branch of language study. Before then there had been a long
tradition of studying dialects, usually in remote rural areas, as part of
language surveys, but with an agenda largely dictated by concerns to
record and preserve the historical features of languages. This kind of
dialectology was inherently conservative and formed part of larger,
comparative, language studies pursued under the discipline of
philology. Labov was one of the first linguists to turn his attention
away from rural, to urban, subjects, in an attempt to analyse the contemporary features of American speech. The popularity of sociolinguistics has grown considerably in recent years, largely as a reaction
to the more 'armchair' methods of formal Chomskyan linguistics.
While Chomsky and his followers tend to examine 'idealised' samples
of speech in which utterances are complete, in a standard form of the
language, and free from performance errors (see Chapter 5), sociolinguists are more interested in 'real' speech, within and among communities. Their overriding concern is with the way language varies
according to the social context in which it is used and the social group
to which it belongs. Willam Labov terms it 'secular linguistics'.

The 'hard edge' of sociolinguistics is concerned with the study of
accent and dialect, although there is much else in the subject besides.

We can define accent as 'a set of pronunciation features which identify where a person is from, geographically, or socially' (in other words it relates solely to auditory effects) and dialect as 'a set of syntactic and lexical features which identify where a person is from, geographically, or socially' (that is, it relates to grammar and vocabulary). Having said that, however, it is sometimes the case that 'dialect' is used loosely to include accent. This is because speakers who use what is called a 'non-standard' dialect will characteristically use an accompanying 'non-standard' accent. Accents and dialects are emotive subjects. Many people will reject the idea that their speech is subject to either of these factors. And indeed, in the popular mind, accents and dialects are what other people have. This is because language use is bound up with social prestige. Every language has evolved forms both of pronunciation and grammar which are considered prestigious to a greater or lesser extent. But social judgements about language are not the same as linguistic ones. From a language point of view no one dialect or accent is any more 'correct' than another, although they may be socially more useful and acceptable (see Chapter 5). Some languages have solved the problem of acceptability by developing two very different varieties, each with a different range of social function and each available to any speaker in the speech community. If you are in Greece, for example, you might well find native users of the language writing in one form, 'Katharevousa', but speaking another, 'dhimotki'. Such a situation is **diglossic**. It's usually the case that one form, sometimes called 'high', is used for the more serious purposes of education, politics and commerce, and the other, or 'low' variety, for domestic or informal settings. But while the 'high' is more prestigious, the 'low' is thoroughly acceptable in the contexts in which it is used. Diglossic situations can also be found in Egypt, where both classical Arabic, and colloquial Arabic are used, and in Switzerland, where speakers use High German and Swiss German. Historically, it is likely that the Romance languages, such as French, Spanish and Italian, arose from diglossic situations in which a high Latin was used in serious contexts, and a Latin vernacular, for everyday speech. Similar situations exist today in communities in the Caribbean where both a standard variety of English and a pidginised form exist side by side.

In England, however, dialectal varieties are not truly diglossic. In the first place they are predominantly regional in character whereas diglossic varieties aren't, and second, non-standard forms are clearly stigmatised in a way which prevents them being regarded as acceptable alternatives. At the same time non-standard forms are increasingly being used in informal situations both in Britain and America. A few years ago Ronald Reagan tried to rally the voters in his presidential campaign with the slogan *You ain't seen nuthin yet*, a ploy which was seen by cynics as a deliberate attempt to woo the black vote. While it is true that usages such as these remain the exception rather than the rule in serious contexts, nevertheless, on a more everyday level many of us will learn dialect-switching, or code-switching. This involves alternating between a regional or urban dialect and a standard one according to the formality of the situation. So we might, for example, speak local dialect to friends but not when being interviewed for a job. To a large extent the stigmatisation of non-standard dialect, particularly in Britain, is the result of our preoccupation with class. Saying *We done it* instead of *We did it*, using multiple negatives, or leaving 'ly' off manner adverbs, as in *She played beautiful* are popularly thought the consequence of poor education and identified with low social status. And it is true that a correlation does exist here. But that is quite different from saying that non-standard English is 'bad', or poorly learned English. Historically speaking, the basis of what is now standard English was the local dialect of the region bounded by Oxford, Cambridge and London. Its elevation has been the consequence of a number of social and cultural factors but these shouldn't hide from us the fact that any other variety could equally have achieved the same normative status if circumstances had been different. As the linguist Dennis Freeborn (1992: 95) points out, we have only to consider what might have occurred if York had become the capital of England rather than London.

But, of course, it didn't, and, in any case, there are great advantages to having a standard variety of a language, providing we understand 'standard' descriptively, as in 'standard shoe size' rather than qualitatively. The claim to 'standardness' by any language variety is based on two interrelated facts: first, that it is the variety of the language which is taught, and second, that it is also the medium of teaching, that is, other subjects are taught using it. This in turn is only possible because, unlike most other dialects, it is a written variety. Indeed, the need for standardness comes largely from the pressure exerted on language by the spread of literacy and the growth of printing. As a consequence, a standard variety is codified in dictionaries and grammars, and subject to what linguists call **minimum variation of form** and **maximum variation of function**. This means that syntactic variation and orthographic variation are limited (there is usually only one way to spell a word, for example), while at the same time the variety can be used in a wide range of contexts – the law, medicine, the church, politics, and so on. By contrast, other dialects are restricted in function and have no fixed orthographic form. Because of this they don't develop the same range of registers. Standard English has a number of different altern-ative words and expressions depending on how formal a situation is. So a *constable* might be a *bobby*, a *copper* or a *pig*. Not only that, most of our swear words *bloody*, *fuck*, and so on, are standard English and used regularly by those who would never dream of saying *We was going down the road*. By contrast, non-standard dialects usually only have one register and an impoverished range of functions. In many respects it is a 'restricted code'. It doesn't travel well. We wouldn't use it, for example, with foreigners. For that, we should normally employ the more 'elaborate' code of the standard variety.

We might wonder, then, why non-standard dialects continue to flourish as they do. If standard varieties are more versatile and more prestigious we should expect other varieties to wither away. And in the case of traditional dialects, this is so. All over England, as rural com-munities disappear, dialect words and constructions are disappearing with them. But, by contrast, modern dialect forms are on the increase. That is to say, very few people nowadays, apart from a few ageing inhabitants of the south-west of England, would say *Hoo inno comin*, whereas, a significant number of native speakers would say *She ain't comin* (cited in Trudgill, 1990: 5). So common are some of these forms that they are spread across many regional dialects and are rapidly being perceived as non-regional by users. Their popu-larity has to do with a phenomenon known as **covert prestige**. This is a term used by sociolinguists to describe the way in which non-standard forms are positively valued by speakers. Some communities clearly value such forms as a means of reinforcing group solidarity and local identity, even though this is not always a matter of conscious awareness.

Evidence of covert prestige has usually come from what is termed 'under-reporting', a classic instance of which is detailed in Peter Trudgill's 'Norfolk study'. As part of his analysis of Norfolk dialect Trudgill asked informants to take part in a self-evaluation test in

> 'Malloy on no occasion never said to me "Here y'are, touch for that."'
> 'That's a double negative,' noted the assistant manager as Yosser made a gesture to indicate the passing of money. 'Yeah, well, there's two of you, isn't there?' retorted Yosser.
>
> ALAN BLEASDALE in
> Boys from the Blackstuff

which they reported on what they believed themselves to be saying, which he then compared with what they actually did say. Using a range of linguistic variables he was able to show that perceptions of speech habits were often at variance with actual usage. Trudgill was preoccupied with analysing accent, rather than dialect, variation but his findings are equally good for both. In the case of **yod dropping**, for instance (the dropping of the 'y' sound before 'oo' in words such as *beauty* and *tune*), as many as 40 per cent of informants claimed to use the non-standard form (*booty, toon*) when in fact the tape recording showed them using the standard form. Even allowing for the influence of tape recorders on linguistic behaviour this represents a remarkable disparity. The conclusion which Trudgill drew from this is that 'Speakers ... report themselves as using the form at which they are aiming and which has favourable connotations for them, rather than the form which they actually use' (1983: 91). Interestingly, Trudgill discovered that under-reporting was more common among male speakers, a finding which correlates with the frequently observed phenomenon that women value standard forms of speech more highly than men. 'A large number of male speakers,' Trudgill concluded, 'it seems, are more concerned with acquiring *covert prestige* than with obtaining social status (as this is more usually defined). For Norwich men (and we can perhaps assume, for men elsewhere) working-class speech is statusful and prestigious' (p. 92).

Major differences between standard and non-standard dialects

Standard	Non-standard
National	Regional
Written	Rarely written
Codified (dictionaries and grammars)	Less codified
Overt prestige	Covert prestige
Less variable in form	More variable in form
Functional diversity	Little functional range
Taught	Not taught
Not paired with an accent	Paired with an accent

Linguistic variables

The usual way in which sociolinguists study accents and dialects is by random sampling of the population. In classic cases, like those undertaken in New York by Labov, or in Norwich, by Trudgill, a number of linguistic variables are selected and sections of the population, known as 'informants', are tested to see the frequency with which they produce them. Linguistic variables are different forms of pronunciation, vocabulary, or syntax, which speakers will adopt in ordinary usage. The results are then set against social indices which group informants into classes based on factors such as education, money, occupation and so forth. On the basis of such data it is possible to chart the spread of innovations in accents and dialects regionally. One complicating factor, however, is that people do not consistently produce a particular accent or dialect feature. As we have already observed, they vary their speech according to the formality or informality of the situation, a phenomenon known as **style-shifting**. So tests have to take into account stylistic factors as well as social ones. Interestingly, the findings which have emerged from such studies show that some variables are more subject to stylistic variation than others. What appears to happen is that people monitor their production of a variable they are particularly conscious of, while those they are less conscious of they ignore. The first kind of variable is termed a **marker** and the second an **indicator**. Most innovations start off as indicators, with certain social groups unconsciously producing them; a good example is 'h' dropping (as in *'e 'it the ball*). If successful they become adopted more widely by other groups for whom they become markers. In other words, they become used stylistically. If you listen to the speech of the current British Prime Minister, Tony Blair, you will hear his pronunciation alter quite considerably when speaking informally. There are many more glottal stops, for example (the insertion of what sounds, to listeners, like a grunt either medially or finally in words such as *butter* or *but*).[1] It is true that, as yet, he doesn't employ the glottal stop word medially (he doesn't say *b 'uh' er*) but it has crept into word final position with increasing frequency. For many Londoners, glottal stops are a feature which they produce unconsciously as part of their normal speech. It's an indicator, along with other features of what is commonly known as 'Estuary English', arguably the most productive variety of English in England today. For Tony Blair, however, the glottal stop is a marker, something he can turn on and off as the occasion requires. This is an example of **change from below**, that is, from below conscious awareness. Like most Prime Ministers before him, Tony Blair speaks a variety of English known as **received pronunciation** (rp). It's a variety which has emerged from a long history of dominance in our national life by the public schools and the Universities of Oxford and Cambridge. With the change in social attitudes which has occurred in the late twentieth century, however, such an accent has increasingly been perceived as over refined and socially remote. This has had the effect of changing rp quite significantly in the past thirty years or so. Even an ultra conservative speaker, such as Margaret Thatcher, altered her pronunciation during her years in office, and reportedly had elocution lessons to help her sound less 'posh'. A good way of hearing the difference between conservative and modern rp is to compare the speech of the Queen with that of her Prime Minister. Her consonants and vowels, as one would expect, are still in many respects pre-war. But then, of course, she always speaks formally.

Probably the most well-known study of linguistic variables is William Labov's study of the use of (r) in New York speech, carried out in the 1960s.[2] (r) is a consonant which has grown gradually weaker in standard English speech over the centuries. In Old English it was a strong sound, probably a tongue tipped trill, a kind of rolled 'r'. But like many 'vulnerable' sounds, that is, sounds at risk of disappearing, it involves a very muscular movement of the tongue. As one of the

---

Estuary English

A blend of London speech with received pronunciation distinguished by:

(i) Replacement of /t/ medially and word finally with a glottal stop /ʔ/ as in butter /bʌʔə/ and but /bʌʔ/

(ii) Vocalisation of /l/ (that is, making it into a vowel) where it occurs after a vowel or word finally, as in milk /miʊk/ and school /skuʊ/

(iii) Yod coalescence – using a 'ch' sound rather than a 't' + 'y' sound at the start of words like Tuesday and tune. The pronunciation .becomes something like choosday and choon. A similar thing happens with the sounds at the start of duke and dune, which become juke and june

(iv) Fronting of the 'th' sound to 'f' or 'v' , as in three ['free'] and brother ['bruvver']

(some commentators confine (iv) to Cockney English)

factors in sound changes is economy of effort it isn't surprising that the tendency to relax the tongue has produced a weaker 'r'. From the mid-eighteenth century onwards the sound began to disappear entirely from British English speech in unstressed positions. So that, while speakers would still sound their 'r's before a vowel, as in rat and trap, they stopped sounding them after a vowel, for example sort, poor. Instead, the vowels preceding 'r' lengthened or became diphthongs as in *here* (/ɪə/), *there* (/eə/), and *cure* (/uə/). Non-prevocalic 'r', that is, 'r' which is not before a vowel, vanished from the most prestigious varieties of British English. It lingers on in the south-west and parts of the north and is a dominant feature of Scottish, but the popular mind largely associates the sound with remote rural areas where 'quaint' speech and 'quaint' habits are still thought to continue (so the rolled 'r' of the Devonshire cider drinkers).

Such is the not the case in America, however, where non-prevocalic 'r', in General American speech is still a prestigious feature. Dropping one's 'r's there is a little like dropping 'h's in British English. Its absence is typical of less regarded accents, in particular, Black and Southern American English. And also of much New York speech. What is true of London is also true of New York, that many of the city's inhabitants don't like the dominant accent. For them 'r' is a linguistic variable. Labov's study was the first of its kind to show how pronunciation is linked not only to social aspirations but also social context. In this his method was quite original. Instead of visiting prospective informants in their homes and interviewing them, he collected his data from them unawares and without the use of recording instruments. Labov selected three department stores, ranked according to their prestige, in terms of location, goods and prices: Saks, the highest ranking, on Fifth Avenue, Macy's the middle ranking, on Sixth Avenue, and Klein's the lowest ranking, not far from the Lower East Side. An interviewer would enter each store and ask an employee for directions to a particular department located on the fourth floor. On receiving the answer *the fourth floor* the interviewer would lean forward and say *Excuse me.* The answer would then normally be repeated but more carefully. A similar scenario was rehearsed on the fourth floor itself, only the question here would be *What floor is this?*

On the basis of his evidence Labov was able to correlate the incidence of non-prevocalic 'r' against a range of variables: the prestige of the stores, casual as against careful speech, preconsonantal as opposed to word final position. Not surprisingly, the incidence of non-prevocalic 'r' was higher in Saks than Macy's and lowest of all in

Klein's. It was also higher in all stores in careful rather than casual speech. But interestingly, the difference was less marked in Saks where assistants' casual speech matched their emphatic speech more closely. The conclusion that Labov drew from this was that Saks' employees had greater linguistic security than in Macy's or Klein's. In these stores 'r' pronunciation was the norm at which employees aimed, but not the one they used most often. His findings bore out an observation of the sociologist C. Wright Mills that salespeople tend to borrow prestige from their customers. 'It appears,' concluded Labov, 'that a person's own occupation is more closely related with his linguistic behaviour – for those working actively – than any other single social characteristic' (cited in Coupland and Jaworski, 1997: 170). The findings are also supported by 'accommodation theory' (see Chapter 2) developed by the linguist Howard Giles, according to which speakers will tend to moderate their speech in the direction of those they are talking to. This may take the form of reducing the use of less socially acceptable modes of speech in the presence of speakers of higher prestige varieties. In the case of Saks, the customers who frequented the store had a higher proportion of such speakers than did the other stores.

Labov's methodology was one way of overcoming a besetting problem for the sociolinguist, known as the 'observer's paradox'. Formulated by Labov himself, this famously states that 'The aim of linguistic research in the community must be to find out how people talk when they are not being systematically observed; yet we can only obtain this data by systematic observation' (cited in Freeborn, 1986: 146). Most people will alter their speech if they know they are being observed, so rendering any analysis of their actual usage very difficult. The obvious solution would be not to tell informants and simply tape them without their knowledge. But for most researchers such a practice is unethical. Other possibilities include taking advantage of natural breaks, such as interruptions, or a break for tea, and leaving the tape recorder running, or asking people to talk about some event in their lives which might engender strong feelings and enable them to forget about being recorded. Even so, a researcher might have to wait a long time before the particular dialectal feature being observed appeared sufficiently to be analysed. This is one of the reasons why many contemporary researchers favour a method known as 'participant observation' which involves the researcher becoming attached to a particular group and observing their linguistic behaviour over a considerable length of time. The results of such research are often more accurate and revealing than those produced by random sampling, but the activity itself is time consuming and the range of people observed inevitably more limited.

Another possibility is to analyse the speech of people recorded for some purpose other than a linguistic one. One of the most fascinating of such analyses is Trudgill's study of the pronunciation patterns of British pop singers in the 1960s and 70s. Trudgill set himself the task of exploring why the pronunciation of British singers of this period differed so markedly from their normal spoken accents. Modified accents of some sort have been current in popular music for some time but in the mid-century these modifications became noticeably more widespread and more uniform. In particular, British pop singers became markedly more 'American' in pronunciation, adopting such features as:

- Pronunciation of 't' in words such as *better* to sound like 'bedder'

- Use of short 'a' in words such as *half* and *can't* ('haff', 'cant')

- Pronunciation of non-preovocalic 'r' in words such as *girl* and *more*

- Use of 'long a' in words with diphthong 'eye' in words such as *life* and *my*

- Pronunciation of *love* and *done* as 'lurve' and 'durn'

- Use of a 'long a' vowel sound in words such as *body* and *top* ('bardy', 'tarp').

These tendencies can all be found in American accents and, as Trudgill observes, 'are stereotypically associated by the British with American pronunciation' (Trudgill, 1983: 253). We could say that British singers of the period were seeking to accommodate to the pronunciation of their transatlantic cousins, except that accommodation theory is generally restricted to conversational situations. More helpful, Trudgill suggests, is the theory of linguistic behaviour associated with the linguist Le Page, who argues that speakers have a tendency to modify their pronunciation in order to 'resemble as closely as possible those of the group or groups with which from time to time we [speakers] wish to identify ...' (p. 253). The attempt by British performers to identify with American singers is perfectly explicable given the cultural domination of America in the field of popular music in the 1950s. More interesting, however, is the fact that the attempt was not entirely successful. It appears that many American listeners did not perceive British singers as sounding American at all. Individual singers were not discriminating enough in their use of pronunciation features to sound American. This is a problem with all stereotyping – we have only to think of American actors trying to adopt a Cockney accent. In this particular case, what British pop singers were unaware of was that their American models, singers such as Bob Dylan and Elvis Presley, were themselves identifying with a particular local variety of American speech used by Southern and/or Black singers. The origins of much popular music lie in the American South, and Presley was a Southerner himself. However, Southern speech, whether Black or White, is typically 'r-less', that is, speakers do not sound their 'r's in words like *girl* and *more*. In this respect the pronunciation is not stereotypically American and more in keeping with mainstream British accents. So we have the peculiarity of a singer like Cliff Richard inserting non-prevocalic 'r' into his pronunciation in order to sound more like Elvis Presley, while at the same time, Presley was deleting his, to sound more like a Southerner. In addition, British singers tended to do what most people do when linguistically insecure in an adoptive accent, that is, hypercorrect. Many of the Beatles' songs, as well as those of Cliff Richard, show them inserting 'r's where Americans wouldn't. So, for example while typical American speech has an 'r' in *sore* it doesn't in *saw*. None the less, Paul McCartney in 'Till there was you', inserts an 'r' in the line *I never saw them at all.*

From these, and other, inconsistencies, Trudgill, concluded that British pop singers in the early 1960s were only partially successful, both in determining the model group with which they sought to identify, and in working out the pronunciation rules they were following. Such middling success hardly seems to have mattered, however, because, by the end of the decade, British pop music, largely as a consequence of the Beatles' success, had 'acquired a validity of its own' and could afford to shed some of its quasi American features. Analysing albums in the next decade Trudgill shows a significant decrease in the use of such features. Correspondingly there is an attempt by some groups to sound more 'British'. This was particularly the case with 'punk rock' and 'new wave' music for which the intended audience was British urban working-class youth. Typically with such bands the model pronunciation being aimed at was London speech (that is, Estuary English). So glottal stops, fronting of 'th' and vocalisation of /l/ became more frequent. It perhaps would be nice to say that after flirting with an adoptive American identity, British pop music eventually assumed a unique British working-class one. But this would be too easy. The reality is that both models remained in competition throughout the 1970s, and beyond, with many groups alternating pronunciations even within the same recording. What seems to have emerged, however, was a greater freedom for British singers in their choice of singing style once the strength of the 'American norm' had weakened, a change which continued to have repercussions in the 1990s.

Dialect mapping

Once sociolinguists have isolated the important linguistic variables which serve to distinguish one accent or dialect from another, and assessed their incidence against relevant social indices of class, occupation, education, and so forth, their next task is to map their occurrence geographically. It is on the basis of such mappings that we can talk about groupings of certain features as constituting a particular dialect. And it's here that the concept of dialect becomes a little fuzzy. In practice it is often difficult to draw a precise boundary round a particular dialect area. Although, for example, it's possible to speak of Norfolk dialect and Suffolk dialect, there is no clear linguistic break between them. Travelling from one region to the other it becomes clear that many of the linguistic characteristics which make up these dialects change gradually. There's no sudden change at the county boundary. Moreover, it could be argued that there is more than one Norfolk dialect in that differences occur between eastern and southern parts of the county. It would be more accurate to say, in such circumstances, that there is a **dialect-continuum.**

Dialect mapping is done by means of **isoglosses.** These are lines drawn on a map to mark the boundary of an area in which a particular

---

A problem isomeme

In parts of the north of England *while* can mean 'until', as distinct from the rest of the country, where it means 'during'. A difference which could have had catastrophic consequences for drivers approaching the railway crossing which bore the sign:

WAIT WHILE LIGHTS FLASH

Cited in FREEBORN (1986)

FIGURE 4.1   CHILDREN'S TRUCE TERMS
Source: Trudgill, 1990: 119

linguistic feature is used. A number of isoglosses falling in one place suggests the existence of a dialect boundary. There are various types of isoglosses depending on the feature in question: an **isophone** marks the limit of a pronunciation feature; an **isomorph** the limit of a morphological feature (see earlier discussion); an **isolex** the limit of a lexical, or vocabulary item; and an **isomeme** the limit of a semantic feature (when the same words have different meanings in different areas). Figure 4.1 shows the distribution of children's truce terms in Britain.

But if the distinction between individual dialects is not always easy to determine, neither is the exact distinction between the terms 'dialect' and 'language'. At first sight this might seem obvious in that dialects are simply subdivisions of languages, but the issue is not so clear cut. Normally, speakers of different dialects can understand each other, whereas those of different languages can't, that is, dialects are mutually intelligible. This criterion isn't always sufficient, however. Along the Dutch–German border, for instance, the dialects of both languages are so similar that speakers can often understand each other fairly well; much better in fact than speakers from this area of Germany can understand a Swiss or Austrian speaker of German. Nevertheless, we still class Dutch and German as different languages, not dialects. These kinds of comparisons force us to acknowledge that linguistic criteria alone are not enough to distinguish dialects from languages. Also important are cultural, political, and historical factors. The most we can say is that languages in general are autonomous. In other words, they are independent, standardised linguistic forms with a life of their own. This applies to both German and Dutch. Dialects, on the other hand, are heteronomous, or subordinate, varieties. So different dialect users of German will nevertheless look to German as their standard language and will read and write in German. Similarly, Dutch speakers, of whatever dialect, will look to Dutch, not German, as their source of authoritative usage.

Language and discrimination

All societies suffer from inequality. This seems to be a fact of their organisation. The hierarchical character of social structure means that some people are inevitably more highly valued than others and, as a consequence, often more highly rewarded. This wouldn't matter in itself if those in such positions were always wiser or more virtuous than the rest of us. But this is not always the case. People are valued on the basis of all kinds of variable criteria, because they are white rather than black, thin rather than fat, abled rather than disabled, wealthy rather than poor, young rather than old, pretty rather than plain, straight rather than gay, and male rather than female. Many of these discriminations are reflected in the way in which we use language. Because words are laden with connotations they mirror fairly accurately the state of our prejudices and preferences. I used the term *gay* above, but how different would your reaction have been if I had used *queer* instead? Over the past decade or so we have become particularly sensitive to the way language can either encourage or discourage negative attitudes towards those who are disadvantaged, or simply different.

Language should treat everybody equally. So far so good, most of us would say. We have no problem in agreeing that vocabulary items which abuse a person's race, sexual orientation, or religion have no place in ordinary discourse, although to what extent their use should be legislated against, as opposed to simply discouraged, is a matter for debate. But to what extent can language change the way people feel and think about each other? Does the search for a more caring vocabulary really reflect a more humane society, or is it an instance of our inability to face up to the more disturbing facts of existence, an indication of our love of euphemisms in the manner of those Victorians who shied away from *die* in favour of *passed away* and *fell asleep*, or, allegedly, covered up the legs of tables and chairs in case they caused offence in mixed company? Is anything gained by describing short people as *vertically challenged*, or fat people as *horizontally challenged*? Probably not.

As for the term *disabled*, exchanging it for *differently abled* seems over-anxious to deny the existence of impairment. But apart from this, the besetting problem with attempts to manipulate language in this way is that changing a word does not of itself eliminate the prejudice which may attach to it. Referring to people who are neither pretty nor handsome as *aesthetically challenged*, or to those with mental handicaps as people with *learning difficulties* may appear to neutralise bias, but experience suggests that eventually it transfers itself to the new form. As the Director of the British charity Mencap said in 1992 when changes were first proposed in terminology: 'A change in name is not going to make any difference to the problems people face. The general public – the people whose attitudes we need to change – do not recognise "learning difficulty" as mental handicap. It is only a matter of time before even the most right-on expression becomes a term of abuse. It has been the same since people talked about village idiots, and "learning difficulties" is no exception. Children are already calling each other LDs as an insult' (cited in Crystal, 1995: 177).

> *I used to think I was poor. Then they told me I wasn't poor. I was needy. They told me it was self-defeating to think of myself as needy, I was deprived. Then they told me under-privileged was over-used, I was disadvantaged. I still don't have a dime. But I have a great vocabulary.*
>
> JULES FEIFFER
> (cartoon caption 1956, cited in Crystal, 2000)

And yet language surely does matter, if only because having to think about the words and expressions we use makes us question the hidden assumptions they contain. Setting aside some of the puritanical extremes of 'political correctness' which would have us avoid *black* in words such as *blackboard* and reduce all difference to varieties of 'challenge', there is arguably a virtue in confronting linguistic representations which, however unconsciously employed, are prejudicial to members of the community. The case for this is most convincingly seen in the work that has been carried out on language and gender.

Men and women speaking

Most languages differentiate in some way between language used by and about women, and language used by and about men. However, the nature and degree of such differentiation varies considerably. Since the work of the American linguist Ann Bodine, it has become common to distinguish between 'sex exclusive' and 'sex preferential' differentiation. The first kind is often found in traditional tribal languages where men and women sometimes have a range of different vocabularies and even grammatical structures. The linguist Mary Talbot quotes, as an extreme example, the language of the Carib Indians who, when first encountered in the seventeenth century, were thought almost to have separate languages for the sexes:

> The men have a great many expressions peculiar to them, which the women understand but never pronounce themselves. On the other hand, the women have words and phrases which the men never use, or they would be laughed to scorn. Thus it happens that in their conversations it often seems as if the women had another language than the men. (cited in Jespersen, 1922: 237)

As Talbot observes 'This linguistic situation is more likely in stable, conservative cultures, where male and female roles are not flexible' (1998: 5). As soon as social roles become more mobile within a society, language forms cease to be sex exclusive. This is currently the case in Japan. Japanese has a range of words for the first person pronoun *I*, depending on whether the speaker is male or female. The formal pronouns *watashi* and *watakushi* can be used by both sexes, but in informal speech *atashi* is used only by women, and *boku* by men. However, it is reported that young girls in Japanese High Schools are increasingly using the male form *boku* 'because if they use *atashi* they cannot compete with the boys'.

Sex-exclusive differentiation is unusual in European languages. We rarely find words or forms that are restricted to male or female use. Sex preferential differentiation, on the other hand, is common, if not the norm. All western languages have preferred forms of gender-related speech. What these seem to reflect, in most cases, is the long history of male dominance, politically and culturally. The first linguist of any prominence to write about this phenomenon in any detail was Robin Lakoff in *Language and Woman's Place* (1975). Her material was largely impressionistic and confined to the language used by women in Middle

America, but her findings have had a broader resonance worldwide. Lakoff looked both at language used to describe women, and language typically used by women. One of the things she drew attention to was the lack of symmetry between the terms *woman* and *man*. *Woman* she argued had unfavourable connotations, similar to terms like *Jew*, or *Negro*, which made its use socially problematic and impelled people to use the euphemism *lady*, with its suggestions of gentility and elegance. In so doing an important aspect of femaleness was denied and stigmatised, namely, sexuality. Ladies are not perceived as having bodies, or as working, except in a part-time, or leisure capacity. A *lady doctor*, or *lady poet*, implies the activity is not entirely serious. As other commentators have also observed, this lack of symmetry extends to other pairings in which the male term has a higher status and where the female frequently has unfavourable, often sexual, connotations: *wizard/witch*, *governor/governess*, *master/mistress*, *sir/madam*, *bachelor/spinster*.

An additional feature of some male terms is that they are conventionally used for general reference where the sex of the person being referred is either uncertain or irrelevant. So we have phrases such as *the history of mankind*, *the man in the street*, *the working man*, *the descent of man* in which the term *man* is intended to include women as well. But the difficulty here is that the same term is also frequently used to refer to men exclusively. How can we be sure that the generic meaning doesn't retain an underlying sense of maleness, almost as if women were a sub-species of men?[3] If we take the well known logical syllogism about Socrates and substitute Sophia the result is odd even though the terms men and man here are meant to stand for 'human being(s)':

All men are mortal
Socrates [Sophia] is a man
Therefore, Socrates [Sophia] is mortal. (cited in Fasold, 1990: 112)

Matters are similarly problematic for generic 'he'. This is a particular difficulty which afflicts English due to its lack of a generic pronoun in the third person singular present tense. Languages differ considerably in the extent to which they incorporate gender into their pronoun systems. Some have a worse problem than English. French, for example, has separate third-person plurals as well, while Japanese distinguishes in both the first and second person. One can't help but feel that Finnish, in which all pronouns are gender neutral, has adopted the best solution. The general rule, in those languages where a distinction is made, is for the male pronoun to operate as the default term, that is,

Gender games

A number of riddles focus on our tendency to associate certain occupations with a particular sex:, as in the following, 'A man and his father were involved in a crash. The father was killed, but the boy was badly injured. As the attendants wheeled him into the operating theatre, the surgeon looked at him and said "Oh no, it's my son". What relation was the surgeon to the boy?'

if a person's sex is not known, or irrelevant, we use *he*. Or at least we did. It has become clear, as a consequence of substantial research, that it has the effect of excluding women. When people are asked whether sentences such as *When a botanist is in the field, he is usually working* could refer to a woman they say 'no', in large numbers, despite the fact that *he* is being used generically since the sex of the botanist is not given. Ralph Fasold (1990) reports the error rate here among a mixed group of American students on whom this experiment was tried as more than 90 per cent. In order to factor out the possibility that some respondents were basing their answers on the hypothesis that botanists were likely to be male, the same group were tested on their response to the sentence when the pronoun was eliminated – *A botanist in the field is usually working.* The error rate on this occasion dropped to 43 per cent. This leaves some 50 per cent of responses in which the group appear to have been influenced by the non-generic sense of *he*.

Because of the problems associated with the generic use of masculine forms most public writing tends to avoid them, although finding alternatives is not always easy. Also decreasing in use are the so-called 'female' morphemes, the *ess* and *ette* suffixes which stuck on the end of *manager, poet*, and *usher* indicate the person to be a woman, and in so doing characteristically confer maleness on the root word, as if managers, poets, and ushers were invariably male. Indeed, once one looks at the use of English, instances of discrimination in favour of men can be found almost everywhere. Most pairings, for example begin with the male term: *male and female, boys and girls, husband and wife, Jack and Jill, man and wife, Dear Sir or Madam, his and hers, men and women*.[4] There are more insulting animal comparisons directed at women: *bitch, cow, shrew, crow, vixen, dog*. And, historically, they have been subject to a much richer vocabulary of abuse, characteristically focusing on sexuality or appearance; *slut, slattern, trollop* and so forth.

The linguist Schultz (1975) lists more than 500 English slang terms for 'prostitute', but only 65 for 'whoremonger'.

As well as language about women, Lakoff also discussed language used by women. She argued that women use language expressive of uncertainty, lack of confidence, and excessive deference or politeness. Among other features she identified the following as particularly associated with female speech:

- *Tag questions:* questions tagged onto an utterance such as *don't we? haven't you?* which are sometimes used to gain approval or confirmation.

- *Rising intonation:* used to turn a statement into a question, so weakening the force of it. According to Lakoff, whereas men would tend to reply to the question *'When will dinner be ready?'* with a blunt statement *'Around six o'clock'*, women would moderate this with a querying tone *'Oh ... around six o'clock?'*

- *Super polite forms.* Women will tend to avoid directives such as *Please close the door* in favour of weaker, more self-effacing forms such as *Could you close the door please?* or *Would you mind closing the door please?* The characteristic of these forms is that they appear to offer the respondent the opportunity of refusing.

- *Hedges.* The use of 'filler' items like *you know, well, kind of,* which make assertions more tentative.

- *Expletives.* Women will tend to use fewer swear words than men and to avoid some of the stronger forms (for example, they rarely use the term *cunt*).

The overall picture which emerges from Lakoff's study is that women's speech is generally inferior to men's and reflects their sense of personal and social inferiority. A considerable degree of research has been undertaken since Lakoff's book which has helped both to qualify her findings and also to suggest a different context within which to view them. Paradoxically, while Lakoff drew attention to some of the differences between men's and women's speech she tended to assume that male speech was the norm from which women deviated. But it is not at all clear that women see communication in the same way as men. A later book by Jennifer Coates (*Women, Men, and Language*, 1986), for instance, suggests that women's speech is based on cooperation whereas men's is based on competition. If this is the case it could help to explain

---

Do you uptalk?

Uptalking is the colloquial term applied to the use of a rising inflection, or 'high rise terminals', at the end of statements, which has the effect of making them sound like questions. Uptalking is particularly common amongst young female speakers of English. Observers differ about the origin of this phenomenon, some ascribing it to the influence of Californian 'valley speak', some to Australian English, and others to Irish English.

---

some of the phenomena which Lakoff observed from a positive rather than a negative vantage point. To take the issue of tag questions, they are not in themselves necessarily an indication of tentativeness. They may equally be used cooperatively to invite participation and get a conversation going, or perhaps as Pamela Fishman suggests (1980, 1983), to compel attention from an inattentive male. Moreover, it is not true that women uniformly use them more than men. As Ralph Fasold (1990) argues, there is an assertive form of tag question which seems to be more typical of male speech. This has the effect of making the statement to which it is attached more insistent. Fasold quotes as examples some of the responses from a question and comment segment of a professional meeting in which only the men used tag questions:

You would miss it, wouldn't you?
They're going from a base of a so called standard, aren't they?

The first of these is close to a sarcastic use which research has shown is more typical of the speech of young British males:

Q: *Have you done your homework yet?*
A: *Like I've got time, haven't I?*

Simply counting the number of tag questions in samples of speech without considering their interactive use is of limited value. An interesting piece of research undertaken by Bent Preisler at Lancaster University supports this. He set out to observe the use of a variety of so-called 'tentative markers' – modal verbs, hedges, such as *possibly* and *perhaps*, together with tag questions – in male and female speech. His starting hypothesis was that the factor determining the use of these markers was not the sex of the speaker but their conversational dominance. More dominant speakers would use them less, and vice versa. However, his observations of mixed group conversations indicated that while dominance was an issue, far more important was the sex of the speaker. Even in conversations where women were more dominant than men they used more tentative markers. Clearly, these markers were not being used because speakers felt insecure or inferior but because women had different conversational goals than men.

Findings like these have been strengthened by research into patterns of interruption and silence in cross-sex conversations. Candace West and Don Zimmerman (1983) found that of the 48 interruptions in 11 two-party conversations, 46 were by men. Equally striking was their analysis of silences. When a woman was developing a topic and came to a natural pause, the gap before her partner contributed was longer than if a man had been speaking. Moreover, the contribution was often a form of back-channelling of the 'um hmm' variety. Zimmerman and West interpreted this as an attempt at topic control by men. By offering minimal support to their partner's speech they guaranteed themselves the floor. Both Pamela Fishman (1980, 1983), and Leet-Pellegrini (1980), found similar evidence of

> *Women like silent men.*
> *They think they're listening.*
> MARCEL ACHARD
> (French playwright)

topic control in male speech in experiments conducted with cross-sex conversations. These were contrasting studies in style and form. Fishman's involved leaving a tape recorder running in the homes of three couples for several hours whereas Leet-Pellegrini's was a laboratory style investigation. College student volunteers were asked to discuss in same-sex and cross-sex dyads the effects of television violence on children. But a similar pattern of competitive talk among the men, and more supportive and collaborative strategies among women emerged from both studies. As Leet-Pellegrini comments 'Whereas the name of the man's game appears to be "Have I won?" the name of the woman's game is "Have I been sufficiently helpful?"' (cited in Fasold, 1990: 111).

The gender pattern

The consistent finding which has arisen from the study of the way in which men and women use language is that women tend to employ more prestigious forms of speech than men. In other words, they speak in a way that is considered more socially 'correct'. This applies world-wide, across national, regional, class and ethnic boundaries. Labov found it to be true of New York black speakers, and the linguist G. Sankoff of speakers of Montreal French. Exceptions are occasionally encountered – women speakers in some traditional African communities where there is less chance for them to learn, or use, prestigious national or regional languages than men may as a consequence employ more non-standard variables – but in general the remarkable thing about, what is called, the 'gender pattern' is the regularity with which it is confirmed by researchers.

A variety of reasons has been advanced to explain this phenomenon: that women are more careful in their speech because of their child rearing role; that they are less socially secure in most societies and need to signal their status linguistically; that unlike men they are not normally rated by their occupation but by their appearance; that non-standard speech has connotations of masculinity; that women are more genteel than men, and so on. Clearly some of these explanations overlap, and certainly all of them assume that societies are controlled by men. But they also tend to assume that it is women's speech which needs explaining rather than men's, as though speaking in a more standard fashion was somehow anomalous.

In more recent times a different approach to the 'gender pattern', arising from the work of Lesley Milroy in the 1980s, has yielded an alternative explanation. Milroy investigated the speech of three working-class neighbourhoods in Belfast. What she found suggested there was a close link between the social networks formed by the inhabitants and their style of speech. In Ballymacarrett, where the gender pattern was strongest, men had strong network ties: they were employed locally, many in the shipyard industry, frequently working alongside family and friends, with whom they spent their leisure time in local pubs and clubs. The women, by contrast, had looser social networks, mostly working outside the area, and not fraternising socially with work mates. Milroy speculated that network strength was a factor in the equation. In dense social networks peer pressure is strongest and resistance to standard forms of speech greatest. This was borne out by the situation in Clonard, one of the other areas investigated by Milroy, in which, significantly, the gender pattern was reversed. In Clonard women used more non-standard features than men. At the same time, this was an area of high male unemployment. Women were more likely to be working than men and to have strong social networks similar to their male counterparts in Ballymacarrett.

If the determining factor distinguishing male and female speech is the strength of the social networks to which the sexes belong it removes the burden of the argument from the fact of gender itself. Since the Belfast survey a number of sociolinguists have pursued the hypothesis that in western societies women tend to contract weaker social networks than men. Strong social networks thrive on covert prestige. In other words, they encourage forms of speech which are socially disfavoured, and even taboo in some circles. This works at all levels, whether the use of vernacular speech, or of non-standard dialectal variants. We all belong to different networks: family, friends, colleagues, neighbours, and so on. The points at which they overlap are those at which we are most likely to drop any linguistic guard we may have. Labov found that if he wanted to learn about the dialect of black teenage gangs it was necessary to talk to those at the centre of the gang where peer group pressure was strongest, not those on the periphery. If women are more likely to be marginalised in modern societies it would not be surprising if they succumbed less to this kind of pressure. In any event, even if social network theory provides only part of the answer to the 'gender pattern', it has the merit of removing from women's speech the strange charge that it is deviant merely by being more standard.

Conclusion

We have looked in this chapter at ways of categorising the social use of language, at terms such as 'dialect', 'speech community', 'register', 'language variety', and 'language' itself. One thing that is glaringly clear is that they are inevitably approximations of the true reality of speech. Once we probe any one of them this becomes apparent. Dialects, as we have seen, have no hard and fast boundary. We have to think of a configuration of dialectal features which changes subtly within and between regions. Similarly with speech communities and language varieties – even usages which we think of as discriminatory. If we could go far enough down we would be left with the individual speaker situated in a particular place and time. Everybody, as we noted in the first chapter, possesses their own idiolect, their own distinctive way of using the language, what we might call their linguistic fingerprint. It is this that we read good literature to experience. Much of the delight of prose fiction is in the creation of characters who have the illusion of being like us: unique. For we know, as users of the language, that any utterance only achieves its true reality in the person, situation, and time of its uttering. Language is inexhaustible simply because of this fact, and exploring language in its social dimension is just one of the ways of reminding ourselves of that.

Notes

1   The phonetic symbol for the glottal stop resembles a question mark /ʔ/. For some speakers it characteristically replaces the sound represented by the letter 't' where it occurs in the middle or at the end of a word.
2   Round brackets are characteristically used by linguists to identify variables.
3   This is more of a problem for modern English than Old English where *man* was nearly always used generically. The term for 'man' in Old English was 'wer' as in werewolf (manwolf).
4   An exception to this rule is bride and groom, a reflection perhaps of the idea that a wedding is popularly regarded as the 'bride's day'.

5 The Finite Instrument
The Design and Structure of Language

Language is a finite instrument crudely
applied to an infinity of ideas

Tom Stoppard (*Jumpers*, 1972)

The structure instinct

One of the paradoxes about language is that it rests on a complex set of rules which are mastered effortlessly and, to a large extent, unconsciously by native speakers. Ask most people what the rules are for forming a question or issuing orders and they will probably stare blankly back at you. And yet they have no difficulty in actually performing any of these operations. This is not the case with most other rule-governed activities. It's difficult to imagine someone being able to play chess, for example, without being able to say what the rules are. The structure of language is distinctive in being invisible to us. We negotiate its intricacies almost as naturally as our bodies do walking or running.

In Chapter 1 we called this unconscious knowledge competence. Competence is a cognitive, or mental, ability which allows us to endow what we hear and read with meaning, and in turn, to produce meaningful patterns for others. These two skills are not inevitably linked in human learning. We can recognise quite sophisticated melodies in music without being able to sing or reproduce them on an instrument. In the case of language, however, productive and receptive skills are cognitively closer. If we can hear something we can normally, barring a speech defect, say it, although we might not do so as proficiently. In most people production skills generally lag behind those of reception. Just think how difficult it is to reproduce an accent which you can none the less distinguish very clearly. Similarly, young children characteristically hear and understand a greater range of sounds than they can make. The problem here, however, is not so much mental as physical. In the case of children, their speech organs are insufficiently developed to enable them to make the sound, while with adults, all we need to reproduce an accent is sufficient exposure to it. The difficulty, in linguistic terms, is one of **performance** rather than competence.

Performance and competence capture two essential dimensions of language which underlie its structure. All language has both a concrete and an abstract dimension. As we observed in Chapter 1, if this were not the case it would never have emerged from the basic calling system of our primate relatives. As a simple illustration of this consider how it is that native speakers are all able to identify individual sounds within the stream of noise we term 'speech'. In physical terms speech is a very messy process. We tend to think that we speak in distinct sounds joined together as in a chain. But that is an idealisation. The reality is far different. When we hear the sounds in cat, for example, we don't process them individually and add them together. We hear the sounds as a meaningful sequence. They are **smeared** across each other. The 'c' runs into the 'a' which runs into the 't'. This process is known as **coarticulation**. Not only that, but the pronunciation of individual sounds differs according to the sounds which accompany them. The 'c' in *cat* is very different from the 'c' in *cool*. If you start to say *cat* and switch to *cool*, this quickly becomes apparent. *Cool* is unpronounceable with the 'c' of *cat*. And yet we hear them as the same. The segmentation which we impose on what we hear is a mental process and, as such, quite different from the physical reality. We can manage this because we possess an abstract idea or mental image of individual speech sounds. Linguists call these **phonemes**. As human beings we are looking for structure. Arguably this is one of the definitions of being human: we are structure creating animals. Or again, think of the experience of listening to something in a language you know with something in one you do not. In the latter case you have no idea where words begin or end, or even what constitutes a word. Indeed, listening to a foreign language can be an unsettling experience because it seems to be just a meaningless babble with no discernible pattern and no natural boundaries except in the occasional pause for breath. This, of course, is how we sound to foreigners. The problem does not lie with our, or their, hearing: it is not a performance problem. The real difficulty is that the patterns, or mental shapes, created by the sounds within the system of the particular language are not discernible to us. As a consequence we are unable to connect the sounds to the words. Once we know the shapes we experience the language differently. This ability of sounds to function as carriers of meaning we referred to in

Chapter 1 as **duality of patterning**, where we saw it as one of the special characteristics of human language.

The point is, then, that the boundaries between sounds, and, as a consequence, words, in a language are in the ear of the listener. There's a humorous poem by Eugene Field, called 'A Play on Words', which draws attention to this. Perhaps you can make sense of the following lines. The solution is immediately below, if you can't:

Assert ten barren love day made
Dan wood her hart buy nigh tan day;
But wen knee begged she'd marry hymn,
The crewel bell may dancer neigh. (cited in Aitchison, 1987: 134–5)

Standard written version:

A certain baron loved a maid
And wooed her heart by night and day;
But when he begged she'd marry him,
The cruel belle made answer nay.

It would be perfectly possible, given the spelling system of English, for this verse to sound to a native English speaker as Field represents it. The fact that native users wouldn't hear it like that is because they confer meaning on what they hear. They know first of all, that certain sounds make up certain words. But it's more than that. Being able to recognise the word boundaries isn't simply a matter of knowing what words there are in a language. All the words in Field's poem are English words, although not always spelt conventionally; it's just that they don't make sense in those sequences. 'Assert ten barren' is not a meaningful sequence in English. Word recognition depends not only on sound, or **phonetic** knowledge, but on **grammatical** knowledge too. It is this which enables the mechanical skill of hearing to become transformed by the mental skill of understanding.

Grammatical knowledge

Many people popularly think of grammar as a fixed code of dos and don'ts about language, such as 'never start a sentence with a conjunction' (*and, but, also*), 'never use a split infinitive' (*To boldly go*, instead of *To go boldly*), or 'never use a double negative (*I haven't got **no** money*). But these are merely conventions, adopted, for the most part, in the eighteenth century when some writers became exercised about the need to prescribe rules for what was considered correct usage. The majority of these are matters of taste, like a preference for wearing jeans and trainers as opposed to a suit and shoes. Taste is a social phenomenon, important enough in its way, but not constitutive either of being clothed or speaking grammatically. The linguist Noam Chomsky drew an important distinction between an utterance being **acceptable** and being **well-formed**. We tend to blur the two and as a consequence erect our own tastes into prejudices. The difference, however, is seminal. Acceptability is a social judgement, well-formedness a linguistic one. For example, our immediate reaction to the utterance *It ain't no cat can't get in no coop* would probably be to consider it completely ungrammatical. To begin with it has two sets of double negatives – *n't … no, n't … no*, not to mention the non-standard word *ain't*. But if we understand the second negative of each pair as reinforcing the first, it becomes a more emphatic way of saying *There isn't a cat that can't get in a coop*. This is an example of Black English, one feature of which is its vigorous style of expression. In fact, the double negative used to be a feature of English up until the eighteenth century when it began to disappear. We find it regularly in Middle English, as in this example from Chaucer (*But now can **no** man se **none** elves more* – 'But now no one can see no more elves'). What has happened over the centuries is that speakers have weakened the negative to a single item in the standard version of the language. Interestingly, the reverse is the case in French where the negative normally has two particles *ne* plus *pas* or *rien*. To use a single negative in French is to speak non-standardly.

What can we deduce from these examples? Simply this: an *utterance is grammatical, and, consequently well-formed if it follows a rule.* In the case of the double negative there are two rules, one for standard, and the other for non-standard, speakers. The acceptability, or otherwise, of either utterance is dependent on the social circumstances surrounding their usage, but it doesn't affect their well-formedness. Just occasionally a usage may be ill-formed even though it does appear to follow a rule. Young children, for instance, often over-extend the rule for forming the past tense in English by adding the regular 'ed' suffix onto verbs which are irregular. So we get *bringed* instead of *brought*. Misapplication of a rule is a minor infringement of grammaticality which will quickly be corrected when the child is sufficiently exposed to the well-formed item. But in some cases misapplication can lead to a modification in the language itself. The verb *thrive* used to have a past tense *throve*, after the pattern of *strive/strove*, but extension of the regular suffix has now given us *thrived*. This process of regularisation has happened to a number of formerly irregular verbs in English. Native speakers do not say *glode* or *chode* for the past tenses of *glide* or *chide*, although they may still say *smote* for the past tense of *smite*.

All of which makes clear an important point about grammar which is that it is never static. It grows with use. This is true for all languages. Grammar is organic. It resembles a living thing in its ability to produce fresh matter apparently without end. What people term 'rules' are not so much laws, as linguistic patterns of behaviour governing the operation of a language. Every speaker of a language contributes to these, for not only do we speak our native language, but in a more subtle sense, it speaks through us. Rules are open to interpretation and negotiation, whereas laws, being immutable, are not. It is, for example, a rule of English that intransitive verbs do not take an object. So *fall* and *die* are intransitive – you can't *fall* or *die* something. Equally so, according to this account, is the verb *disappear*. *He disappeared* is well-formed, whereas *he disappeared him* isn't. But to an increasingly large number of people it is thoroughly grammatical. In some parts of the world to *disappear* someone is to make them vanish, usually in highly suspicious circumstances. It's a usage which has been popularised by the media, in particular the American film industry. And if we look at *fall*, it's possible in African English for that to be used transitively. A Nigerian, for example, can say *Don't fall me down*, meaning 'Don't cause me to fall over'. British speakers, on the other hand, would have to say *Don't push/knock me over*, but the meaning here is subtly different. Innovations like these are important because they make us look more closely at the rules of a language to see how they can be modified to accommodate the new evidence. And what we begin to discover when we look more closely at verbs is that being transitive or intransitive is an operation potentially open to the great majority, and possibly all, of them. In other words, rather than classify them into transitive and intransitive, it's better to talk of transitive and intransitive uses. Those which we class as intransitive are simply the ones for which we have not yet discovered a transitive use. In the case of *disappear* we now have. The sinister process by which some governments cause people to disappear without trace has led to the verb developing a transitive sense. And just as some verbs can extend their grammatical range, others may contract theirs. Today, the verb *like* is only used transitively: the sentence *I like* is incomplete – we must like something or someone. In Shakespeare's time, however, it was quite normal for the verb *like* to be used without an object. In his preface to the *Devil is an Ass*, the seventeenth-century playwright Ben Jonson writes, 'If this play do not like, the Devil is in it'. The verb *like* is being used here with our modern sense of 'please', a sense it has since lost. Because of this the intransitive construction is no longer usable.

People who study language like to compare it to a game, usually a board game because there are pieces which can be moved around, and usually chess, because it's arguably the most complex of the board games. It's quite a good analogy because, as we noted in Chapter 1, in chess each piece moves in a specified way, but its power to do so at any particular moment in the game depends on the place it occupies on the board and its relationship to the other pieces. Similarly with words. Verbs, nouns, and adjectives all have specified ways of behaving. We can't, for example, put a noun into the past tense – only verbs permit that manoeuvre. But within that restriction, the freedom which individual verbs, nouns, and adjectives have to move about in the language depends on the state of play at any given time. In the case of *disappear* an obstruction has currently been removed and its range increased, whereas with *like*, an obstruction has been imposed and its range limited. But, as we noticed earlier, there is one important difference between chess and language. If you want to learn how to play chess you study the book of rules and these tell you exactly what you can and can't do. This is not, of course, how native speakers learn to use their language. Since the work of the American linguist Noam Chomsky in the mid-twentieth century, it has become clear that children do not learn how to speak by copying adults. They do so by formulating rules for themselves, by actively constructing a grammar and modifying it in the light of contact with actual speakers. If this were not the case, using a language would simply be a matter of imitation rather than the constant innovation which it is in actuality. Studying the structure and design of a language, then, means studying how it is really used: the rule book exists inside every native speaker. For the professional linguist this poses a problem. It means that linguistic knowledge is not open to direct inspection: it is locked within our heads. All we have is the evidence of it in particular acts of communication. Inevitably, then, analysing a language involves working backwards from individual word strings to the hidden operational code, a bit like trying to establish the rules of chess from watching an actual game. This is exactly the process that Chomsky elaborates for studying language: linguists observe, describe, and explain.

The power of infinity

Of all the features which language shares with the game of chess perhaps the most important is its ability to reuse the same items over and over again in apparently endless combinations. In the words of William von Humboldt, a nineteenth-century pioneer of modern linguistics, language involves 'the infinite use of finite media'. A simple example of this is the alphabet. Many languages use an alphabet to represent speech. Despite their variation they are all based on the same principle of representing a speech sound by an individual letter. The orthographical, or spelling system of English, for example, uses an alphabet of 26 letters. Yet the remarkable thing about this system, as with all such alphabets, is that it is sufficient to represent a limitless number of words. It gains its productive power from the simple fact that the tokens it uses are symbolic. The representation is entirely conventional. Alphabets are founded on an arbitrary pairing of letter shape and sound. There is no reason, for instance, why the letter 'y' should represent the sound it does in English as opposed to any other sound. The connection is based on no natural resemblance. The great advantage of this is that it can be used to represent more than one entity. In the word *yacht*, for instance, 'y' is pronounced entirely differently from the 'y' in *boy*. Indeed, if we were to have a separate letter for every speech sound in English we should need many more than 26. Nor would it stop there. As we observed earlier, there are different kinds of 'c's in the words *cat* and *cool*. And beyond that, different accents and different European languages, all making use of the same alphabet.

The concept of arbitrariness is not an entirely comfortable one for people to live with. Most of us would rather think of letters and words as fixed entities, moored securely to a single meaning. From time to time people have endeavoured to make English more logical, either by tinkering with the alphabet or, more adventurously, by inventing a language on supposedly scientific principles, but they have all foundered on the rock of arbitrariness. It is this which makes possible the creativity of language. No alphabetic system founded on totally phonetic principles could ever be more than a linguistic fossil. As the writer Philip Howard comments:

> all such schemes of basing spelling simply on pronunciation are ... doomed to failure, because they attempt to substitute the tyranny of phonetics for our present haphazard democracy. English spelling conveys many more messages than simple pronunciation. If it were to cease to do so, the language would be greatly impoverished. (1986: 154)

Bishop Wilkins

One of the more ambitious attempts to create a language on scientific principles was undertaken by the seventeenth-century writer and philosopher, Bishop John Wilkins. In 1688 he elaborated a scheme for assigning a non-arbitrary name to everything. This worked by dividing the universe into categories, subcategories and sub-subcategories rather like a huge tree, and using vowels and consonants to indicate branches of the tree. So the name for dogs would be indicated by the word *zita* on the principle that *z* represented 'animals', *i* 'quadrupeds', *t* 'European canines', and *a* 'the species'.

The combinatorial basis of linguistic structure was captured in the early part of the twentieth century by the Swiss linguist, Ferdinand de Saussure (see Chapter 2). Saussure approached language as a self-enclosed system. Items are related to other items because they can either be substituted for, or combined with, them. He imagined linguistic structure as having two axes on which items could be sorted in these ways. The axis of substitution he termed **paradigmatic**, and that of combination he termed **syntagmatic** (Figure 5.1).

The usefulness of Saussure's structure is that paradigmatic and syntagmatic relations operate at all levels of language and help to provide criteria for the classification of items. Substitutability, for instance, is important in the classification of words into various categories such as 'noun', 'verb', 'adjective', 'pronoun', and so on. If we take the sentence *I like linguistics* as an example, each of the words can be exchanged

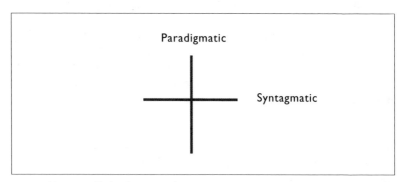

FIGURE 5.1 SAUSSURE'S MODEL OF LINGUISTIC STRUCTURE

with a number of others without changing the basic syntactic arrangement:

They	*love*	*art*
You	*hate*	*bread*
I	***like***	***linguistics***
We	*despise*	*him*
People	*adore*	*treats*

Interchangeability of this kind allows us to classify words which can substitute for *I* and *linguistics* as pronouns or nouns, and those which can substitute for *like* as verbs. Similarly, in the sound system of English, the sounds *b*, *k*, and *p* can all be substituted for the *f* in the context of *it*, as can a number of others:

b
k
f   *IT*
s
l

And we could perform similar substitutions for *i* and *t*. Indeed, it is on the basis of such possible substitutions that linguists are able to determine the distinctive speech sounds, or phonemes, of a language. Sets of paradigmatically related items are often referred to as **systems**, so we can talk about the 'consonant system', or the 'pronoun system' of a language.

Paradigmatic relations are only one side of the coin, however, because clearly we cannot put any pronoun or noun in front of *like*, nor any consonant before *it*. There are other constraints operating on these items which narrow down the options available. Making certain substitutions will affect the rest of the string, whether of words or sounds. We cannot, for example, simply exchange *He* for *I* in *I like linguistics* without altering the following verb to *likes*. This is because it is a rule of standard English that this particular pronoun must be followed by a form of the verb carrying the inflection 's'.

Neither are we free to change the sequence of the items in any way we want to. There are certain permitted orders to their arrangement. All of these constraints are what is meant by syntagmatic relations. A syntagm is simply a sequence of items. Every language has its own method of sequencing. English, like 75 per cent of the world's languages characteristically has a subject/verb/object order. All the sen-

---

OSV

Object/subject/verb languages are very uncommon. The most well known example is Japanese. Less common occurrences can be found in South American languages. In English, the construction is used in American-Jewish speech, itself influenced by Yiddish, as a form of emphasis: 'Hamburgers you like, bagels you don't.' As observers have pointed out, it is the favoured style of the Jedi Master in *The Return of the Jedi*: 'Strong with the force you are.'

---

tences above are of this kind. This isn't to say that English doesn't permit other arrangements on occasions, clearly it does, but this is the **unmarked** or normal pattern. Some languages, about 10–15 per cent, use a verb/subject/object order. Welsh is one of these. Our sentence in Welsh would be the equivalent of *Like I linguistics*. And a few languages, mainly found in the Amazon basin, have an object/verb/subject structure: *Linguistics like I.*

Once we understand the sequencing arrangements of a language we are close to understanding its grammar. So, for example, identifying all the possible syntagmatic relations which a sound unit, or phoneme, is capable of entering into in a particular language would provide us with a key to the possible words which could be formed using that phoneme. The study of permitted or non-permitted sequences of phonemes in a language is called **phonotactics**. We know, for example, that English does not permit syllable beginnings, or endings, in which /t/ is followed by /b/. So we could never find a word *tbat* or *tatb*. Similarly with other levels, such as phrases and clauses. While the grammar of a language will allow considerable freedom in the movement of items in order to make something thematically more important, there is a limit to such rearrangement. We can't move an item to any position. In the phrase *the table* which consists of a determiner and a noun, we can put a variety of items between *the* and *table*, but we are not permitted to reverse them *table the*.[1] The study of this grammatical sequencing is termed **syntax**, and as with phonotactics, identifying the syntagmatic relations which a word can enter into would provide us with a key to the constructions which could be formed using it.

We need, however, to register an important qualification here. Saussure's framework could lull us into the idea that language is simply a vast engine for producing endless sequences of words according to a pre-set pattern. All we have to do is program it and it will run itself. But we know that language is not like that. If we take the example we have been using, *I like linguistics*, and follow the instruction 'substitute any noun or pronoun for I', we shall come up with some very weird possibilities. This rule would allow *Sincerity likes linguistics* or *My birth likes linguistics*, which are clearly not permissible to most of us even though the subjects in both cases are nouns. Abstract qualities cannot be said to like things, and neither can events, even in fairy stories or dreams. Only objects with some degree of consciousness can be said to have the capacity for liking. However, this is not such a straightforward matter. The linguist George Lakoff reports that among the Papagos islanders, events and properties are assumed to have mental powers (cited in Radford, 1988: 11). In other words, the concept of 'sincerity' or 'birth' being endowed with the power to like would not be inconceivable. These sequences might thus be perfectly normal to an English-speaking Papagos islander. This alerts us to an important point about linguistic structure: a sequence can be semantically odd and yet syntactically well-formed. In other words, we are led to the strange conclusion that *My birth likes linguistics* is syntactically fine, even though for the vast majority of people it is nonsense.

The modular system

What Saussure's account of language leads to is a view of language processing which has been developed most influentially by American linguists. This is to see linguistic abilities as parcelled out in various areas, or modules of the mind. The module that is responsible for syntax enables us to create endless strings of well-formed combinations following very general rules of sequencing. The instruction to change *like* to *likes* after the third-person singular pronoun is one of these, as is the ban on following /t/ with/b/. In addition, however, we also possess a mental dictionary, or **lexicon**. This module provides us with information about individual items. It's here that words are classified into nouns, verbs, adjectives, and so on. When we construct a sequence we draw words from the lexicon and put them into an available slot. But the lexical component of our language also informs us about the meanings of words, and about which sequences make sense and are consequently acceptable. This semantic ingredient has access to the real world but is mediated by our culture. It's here that a good deal of the creativity within language takes place. Changes are occurring in individual entries all the time, allowing us to say things which were previously unsayable. The semantic constraints on sequences are called **selection restrictions**. This means that items in a language select the other items which accompany them. Verbs, for example, are commonly said to select their subjects and objects. The verb *eat*, for instance, will select a noun which is animate as its subject. This will allow us to say *He/the cat/the man is eating a banana*, but not *The stone/the peanut is eating a banana*. Similarly, the object of *eat* has to be edible, so that we can't eat a brick or a house. Nouns will also select dependent items with which they are compatible. This is especially the case with adjective combinations; so we find *tall trees* and *tall people*, but not **tall cushions* or **tall ants*.[1] At least, most of the time we don't. Given a few seconds we could all probably think of exceptions. We might complain about an onerous job *eating our time*, or read a children's story which distinguishes between *tall* and *short* ants, for example, without feeling that any of these usages were unacceptable. Indeed, much of the appeal of innovative, especially figurative usages, is in the way they force us to lift selection restrictions to express meanings which are emerging into consciousness. As we saw in Chapter 2, we have many more things to say than language will allow us to express. Semantic processes, such as transference, allow us to move words into slots they do not normally fill and create that frisson of recognition on which creative expression characteristically relies. It is because of this that we instantly accept Philip Larkin's use of the word *tall* in *The Whitsun Weddings* as he looks out of the train window on a hot afternoon and talks about the 'tall heat'.

The hierarchic principle

So far we have been considering the structure of language in terms of Saussure's grid pattern and the refinements we can make to it following more recent developments. But horizontal and vertical axes only tell us so much about the way language is organised. What they cannot show us, except in a very broad sense, is the relationship of the individual items to each other. Until we know that we can't judge how it is that certain items can be moved around while others can't. In the sequence *The cat sat on the mat*, for example, we can move *the cat*, *on the mat*, and *the mat*, but not *on the*, *the*, or *cat sat*. Certain words are glued together: if we disturb one we disturb the whole unit. This should give us a clue to how we form sequences. We don't form them in a simple linear fashion, that is, by thinking of a determiner – *the* – then selecting a word which can syntactically follow it, possibly an adjective, followed by a noun, then a verb, and so on. That would be rather like dressing ourselves by starting with our socks, then selecting our shoes to match, and working our way up our bodies to our hat. No doubt some people do dress like that, but it's hardly guaranteed to produce the desired effect. Most of us select the central items we want to wear and then choose the other bits and pieces to fit in.

In order to establish what the central items of a language are we need to discover its **constituents**. These are the building blocks out of which sequences are made. The concept of constituency owes its currency in language study to the linguist, Leonard Bloomfield (1933). He argued that any well-formed sequence can be described as a hierarchy of interlocking constituents. The most basic constituents are words but these don't stand alone. They belong within higher level categories of increasing complexity up to the rank of sentence. Starting from the top, a sentence can be analysed in terms of its **immediate constituents**, the largest building blocks, which can in turn be divided into further constituents, and so on, down to those at the ground level of words, or **ultimate constituents**. Items demonstrate their constituency by their ability either to be substituted with similar constituents, or redistributed to form other sentences. If we take a sentence like *The large Siamese cat jumped onto the table* we can show these hierarchical arrangements in the form of a **tree diagram** (Figure 5.2).

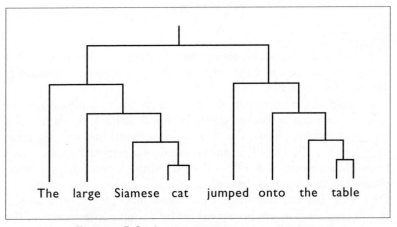

FIGURE 5.2 A TREE DIAGRAM OF A SENTENCE

This diagram shows us that the entire sentence is built out of two main blocks: *the large Siamese cat* and *jumped onto the table*. These are its immediate constituents. The first one has as its key word the noun *cat*, and is a **noun phrase**, while the key word in the second is a verb and is a **verb phrase**. We can say, then, at a simple level that a sentence consists of a noun phrase plus a verb phrase, or NP + VP. This basic rule allows us to generate a wide variety of similarly constructed sentences. Proceeding further, we can see that each of the phrases has its own immediate constituents. The noun phrase consists of a determiner *the* and an incomplete noun phrase *large Siamese cat*. If, following current linguistic analysis, we call this partial unit a **noun bar** then we can say a noun phrase consists of a determiner plus a noun bar: $NP \rightarrow DET + N^1$. However, the noun bar *large Siamese cat* has within it a smaller one, *Siamese cat*. So, extending the analysis, we can say that a noun bar is made up of a **modifier** (in this case an adjective, *large*) plus another noun bar (*Siamese cat*): $N^1 \rightarrow MOD + N^1$. There is clearly something a little odd about this rule since the two noun bars on each side of the equation appear to cancel themselves out. We can see why this is so if we continue the analysis further, because the smaller noun bar *Siamese cat* is composed of a modifier (another adjective, *Siamese*) and a noun (*cat*): $N^1 \rightarrow MOD + N$. The point about the noun bar rule, in other words, is that it's recursive. We can reduplicate it several times adding more and more modifiers and extending the phrase for example *The* + *lovely large grey Siamese cat*. The two rules can now be collapsed to show this:

$$N^1 \rightarrow MOD + \begin{Bmatrix} N \\ N^1 \end{Bmatrix}$$

The curly brackets indicate alternatives. The rule is now telling us that a noun bar can consist either of a modifier plus a noun or a modifier plus another noun bar.

Moving to the other side of the sentence, the verb phrase *jumped onto the table* can be broken down in similar fashion. It consists of a verb plus another phrase, this time a prepositional one *onto the table*, or $VP \rightarrow V + PP$. The PP, in turn consists of a preposition *onto* plus a noun phrase *the table*, or $PP \rightarrow P + NP$. At the lowest level, the noun phrase is made up of a determiner, *the* and a noun *table*, or $NP \rightarrow DET + N$. The fact that there is no intermediate phrase, or noun bar, in this construction can be catered for by a simple amendment of the noun phrase rule. Putting all the rules together gives us a simple grammar for generating sentences:

$$S \rightarrow NP + VP$$
$$NP \rightarrow DET + \begin{Bmatrix} N \\ N^1 \end{Bmatrix}$$
$$N^1 \rightarrow MOD + \begin{Bmatrix} N \\ N^1 \end{Bmatrix}$$
$$VP \rightarrow V + PP$$
$$PP \rightarrow P + NP$$

These rules can be made more powerful by amending them to include more possibilities. Some verbs, for instance, such as *kick* have to be followed by a noun phrase rather than a prepositional one – *kick **the ball*** – while others require nothing at all, just the verb, for example *fall.* If we put round brackets, instead of curly ones, round NP and PP to indicate they are optional, it will allow us to generate more sentences:

$$VP \rightarrow V + (NP) + (PP)$$

This rule will now account for the following VPs:

> *falls*
> *drop the desk*
> *drop into his tea*
> *drop the desk onto his foot*

And by a simple manoeuvre we can manipulate the rules to allow complex sentences to be formed, that is, sentences which contain another one embedded in them, as in *I told John she was a rogue*:

> (*I told John* [*she was a rogue*])
> S1   S2

The rules for the verb phrase will now read: $VP \rightarrow V + (NP) + (PP) + (S)$. In addition to the other options the possibility now exists of another recursive pattern since we can go on embedding sentences endlessly as in *I told Jill that she should inform John that Brian leaked the story that Bill told me* and so on.

The kind of grammar which I have been describing is called a 'generative' grammar.[2] It's based on a foundational principle, which we discussed in Chapter 1, that language is a system of finite rules enabling the creation of limitless permutations. Well-formed sequences are made by assembling constituents in a hierarchical arrangement characterised by dependency. To capture this a familial metaphor is often used. The Sentence, or 'S' node, in Figure 5.3 is a mother with two daughters – an NP and a VP. These, in turn, have two daughters apiece; the NP has a DET and a Noun bar, while the VP has a Verb and a PP and so on down to the individual word categories. If two constituents share the same node they are said to be sisters. The great advantage of a tree diagram is that it shows the way power flows downwards from the topmost node. Each node dominates those below it. So, for example, S dominates all the constituents below it. But, because it is immediately closer to the nodes NP and VP, it is said to 'immediately' dominate them. Similarly, VP dominates everything below it, but immediately dominates V and PP. If we fill in the tree diagram with the full complement of nodes this should become clearer (Figure 5.3).

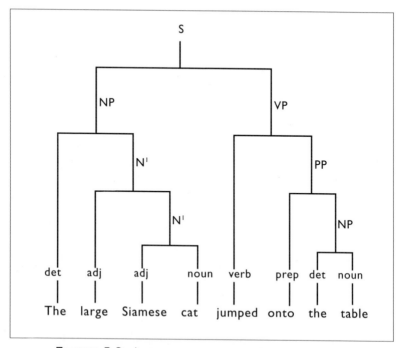

FIGURE 5.3 A TREE DIAGRAM OF CONSTITUENT NODES

We could now, if we wish, remove the individual words of the sentence and simply leave the grammatical tree in place. This is the tree without, if you like, its leaves. It is the skeleton, or scaffold, which forms part of the grammatical competence of native English speakers.

Language universals

The features we have been considering so far are basic to the design of all languages. All languages are combinatory systems, structured hierarchically, employing categories such as noun, verb, noun phrase, verb phrase, and sentence. These are sometimes described as **absolute universals**. But within these rather large boundaries there exist considerable variations both in form and substance. Although all languages have nouns and verbs, for example, they differ considerably in the way they treat them. Some languages, like Latin, will alter the shape of a noun if it is the object of the verb's action:

	*Caesar **puellam** adiuvit*
(literally)	Caesar girl helped
	Caesar helped the girl

	*Puella **Caesarem** adiuvit*
(literally)	Girl Caesar helped
	The girl helped Caesar

The little suffix *m/em* indicates that the noun is in the object **case**. Case is a property of all languages since they all have subjects and objects (the distinction between who did what to whom) but they don't necessarily distinguish between them in the way that Latin does. In English we normally know which is the object because of the word order: the object comes after the verb in an unmarked sequence. This hasn't always been so, however. Old English, or **Anglo-Saxon** was just like Latin in relying very heavily on grammatical changes to show the relationship of items. This meant that one could, on occasions, change the sequence of the words and still retain the same meaning, as in the following:

Se cyning meteth thone bischop – The king meets the bishop
Thone bischop meteth se cyning – The king meets the bishop

Case

Finnish probably holds the record for the most cases. It distinguishes 15 separate inflections: nominative (subject); genitive (of); accusative (object); inessive (in); elative (out of); illative (into); adessive (on); ablative (from); allative (to); essive (as); partitive (part of); translative (change to); abessive (without); instructive (by); and comitative (with).

The contrast with English is not so great if we bear in mind that many of these cases are expressed in English through its prepositional system, that is, *of* the dog, *in* the room, **out of** the frying pan, as opposed to Finnish, which chooses to express them by attaching small suffixes to the ends of nouns.

The clue to interpreting these sequences is that *se* and *thone* are different forms of the same linguistic item: they are varying forms of our modern word *the*. But unlike our modern equivalent it changes according to whether it is attached to the person performing the action or the person to whom it is performed. Such changes are known as **inflexions/inflections**. One of the great historical shifts which has occurred in English has been the loss of many of these inflections. Sometimes people say English doesn't have much grammar. Obviously this is not true. What they really mean is that English has few inflections compared to many other languages in the world.

Case is just one of several grammatical distinctions which languages characteristically make, although, as with case, they vary in the manner in which they make them. Others include **number** (singular, plural); **tense** (past, present, future); **mood** (orders, questions, statements); and **gender** (masculine, feminine). These are distinctions which are basic to making sense of the world so it is not surprising we should find them replicated in languages world-wide. But languages, like cars or types of furniture, differ considerably in their construction and the possibilities they afford their speakers. In English, for example, speakers mark the expression of time by inflecting verbs: *I love, I loved*. But in Japanese adjectives can perform a similar function, for example *shiroi* 'white', *shirokatta* 'was white', *shirokute* 'being white'. And in a North American Indian language called Potowatomi, the ending /pən/ which is used to express past time on verbs can also be used on nouns, for example /nosˑ/ (my father), /nospˑən/ (my dead father); /nčiman/ (my canoe), /nčimanpən/ (my former canoe) (Crystal, 1987: 92). A more interesting pattern of variation can be found with respect to number. English has a very reduced number system. The only contrast it allows is between 'one' and 'more than one'. If someone uses the pronoun *we* it is impossible to tell how many people are being referred to without knowing the context. And in the case of *you* we cannot even know whether it is singular or plural since English long ago lost the distinction in its second person. Some dialects retain the Irish word *youse* meaning 'you two' but it is not useable in the standard variety. Being able to distinguish number more precisely can be an advantage, however. In Melanesian, for example, it is possible to express a four way distinction: singular, dual, trial, and plural. The language also has a separate form for when *we* excludes, as opposed to includes, the hearer:

/ainjak/	I
/aijumrau/	we two (excl.)
/aijumtai/	we three (excl.)
/aijama/	we (excl.)
/akaijau/	we two (incl.)
/akataij/	we three (incl.)
/akaija/	we (incl.)
/aiek/	you (sing.)
/aijaurau/	you two
/aijautaij/	you three
/aijaua/	you (pl.) (Bloomfield, 1933: 257)

Clearly, languages have to weigh the advantage of keeping these and other distinctions against the extra burden they place on human memory. One of the reasons for the dominance of English among the world's languages has been because it has shed a considerable amount of, arguably, excess baggage. To a large extent this has been the indirect consequence of conquest. First came the Vikings in the eighth century and then the Normans in the eleventh, both with rival grammatical systems. Old English which was a highly inflected language with a variety of case endings and verb suffixes survived, not as we might think, by a series of compromises with the invaders, but by abandoning whole areas of overt grammar and developing a leaner, simpler model. A case in point is gender. Gender is a device frequently used by languages for grouping nouns into different kinds or species. The word is related to *genus* and *generic* and doesn't necessarily have anything to do with sex, although masculine/feminine distinctions are usually catered for. A New Guinean tribe, called Arapesh, for example, has 13 genders, most of which are phonological. Nouns are grouped according to whether they end in a particular syllable or phoneme, such as *ar* or *r*. More usually, languages have two or three genders. Old English, like modern German, had three: masculine, feminine, and neuter. French and Dutch have two. Over a period of time English lost its grammatical gender, so that we no longer have male and female nouns, as opposed to the European nations which do. One important reason for this has been the pressure exerted on English by other languages with rival systems. English probably began to lose its gender system quite early, but the process accelerated after the Norman conquest in 1066. Bilingual speakers were now faced with the problem of using and remembering two different gender systems, Old English and French. The French system, the language of government and the law, needed to be represented correctly. It was English which suffered, with speakers eventually dropping the system of grammatical gender entirely, keeping it only for contrasts of natural gender in the pronoun system.

The variety that exists among the world's languages is fascinating and could occupy us seemingly forever. But since the middle part of the twentieth century linguistics has been concerned to go beyond the study of individual languages in an effort to determine what, if any, are the universal properties of language. The generative theory of language proposed a single set of rules which would account for all the grammatical sentences in a language. It was both a short step, and a giant leap, from this to entertain the possibility of a **universal grammar** which

---

List of common universals

All languages:

1. have consonants and vowels
2. combine sounds into larger units
3. have nouns – words for people and objects
4. have verbs – words for actions
5. can combine words
6. can say who did what to whom
7. can negate utterances
8. can ask questions
9. involve structure dependence
10. involve recursion

after AITCHISON, 1996

would correspondingly apply to all languages everywhere. The difficulty with establishing such a grammar is with knowing how to proceed. One way is to collect as much data as possible from the world's languages and then try and distil a core of common properties. But because languages are so idiosyncratic all this method allows us to deduce are fairly broad principles of the kind we have already encountered.

Rather more precise information can be gleaned if we concentrate on relative, rather than absolute, universals. These are properties which are true of a majority of the world's languages, or at least those which have been studied. So, for example, in most languages grammatical subjects precede objects, and there are very few instances of languages without a nasal consonant. In themselves these are not greatly interesting. But they become more so, however, when they suggest the possibility of universal design features. Some linguists argue that language consists of a prototypical core of features not all of which are necessarily present in every actual instance. It is noticeable, for example, that although the inventory of speech sounds, or phonemes, in the world's languages differs widely, certain contrasts are recurrent and appear to be basic. The Czech linguist Roman Jakobson pointed out that the consonant system employed by languages contains as a minimum, an opposition between a nasal and an oral stop (for example *man-pan*), and an opposition between labial and dental consonants (*man-tan*, *pad-dad*). Similarly vowel systems tend to have a core minimum of [i], [u], [a]. These are the vowels in *deed*, *tool*, and *hat*. They are all formed at the extremes of the oral tract and are probably the sounds we can distinguish most clearly as humans.

Many of these core features suggest that a major constraint on any kind of universal grammar is the relative ease with which items can be processed by speakers and listeners. The preference for subject/object ordering fits in with a tendency by language users to package their utterances so that information which is less accessible comes towards the end. In the sentence *James fell down the hole* the starting point, or subject, 'James' is understood as already known to us. The information about what happened to him is entirely new. Were James a total stranger we should expect a different starting point, for example *A man called James fell down the hole*, in which 'James' becomes part of the new information and 'a man' is the understood, or given, starting point. A similar explanation can perhaps account for the fact that languages significantly prefer using suffixes to prefixes. In English, for example, all grammatical inflections go at the end of words, and so do all those items which create new nouns or adjectives: *employ + er >*

employer, clever + *ly* > *cleverly*. Word recognition takes place from the beginning of a word and prefixes slow down the process, although, as Jean Aitchison points out a few languages, such as Swahili and Welsh, regularly alter word beginnings and seem to manage alright.

Probably the most fertile activity of universal grammarians in recent years has been to establish links between languages of the kind 'If a language possesses feature x, then it will normally possess feature y'. These implicational chains suggest that languages do not vary in a random manner but tend to follow regular patterns of behaviour. The system of number which we looked at earlier is a case in point. The whole range of number: singular (one), plural (more than one), dual (two), trial (three), can be found in Melanesian and in-between we have languages with partial systems. But the extent of any individual system is predictable. If a language has a trial it will normally have a dual; if it has a dual it will have a plural; if a plural then a singular; and all languages have singulars:

Singular < plural < dual < trial

Similarly, languages can be grouped in terms of some of the syntactic relations they allow. One such is the use of relative clauses. Relative clauses are dependent on nouns or noun phrases. In English they are normally signalled by a WH- word (for example *which, who*). These WH- words or phrases are able to function either as the subject, the object, the indirect object, or the oblique object (sometimes 'oblique case') in clauses, as in the following:

*The woman **who** broke the bank at Monte Carlo was a professional gambler* ['who' as subject of 'broke the bank']

*The man spent the money **which** he had stolen* ['which' as direct object of 'he had stolen']

*The girl wrote to the gallery to **which** the picture belonged* ['which' as indirect object of 'the picture belonged']

*The army surrounded the house in **which** the terrorists lived* ['which' as oblique object of 'the terrorists lived']

Not all languages, however, have such a wide set of relative clauses. Those that don't follow an implicational chain similar to the one for number. It's called a 'noun phrase accessibility hierarchy':

If a language has oblique relative clauses then it will have indirect, direct, and subject ones.

If a language has indirect object relative clauses then it will also have object and subject ones.

If a language has object relative clauses then it will also have subject ones.

This can be expressed as follows: S > O > IO > OBL.

Linguistic universals and implicational chains can tell us something about the inner core of what a universal grammar might consist of, but we need some other mechanism to explain how as learners of a language we are able to generalise from this to the multitude of available languages. The answer which has been suggested capitalises on the idea of language as a genetic inheritance. Let's suppose that we are born knowing a few broad grammatical principles, for example, that words are arranged hierarchically in larger units or constituents to form well-formed strings. What we have to determine from the evidence we hear as children is which particular hierarchical pattern our language uses. Or, to put it another way, given that universally languages have phrases consisting of a main, or head word with various dependent words or complements, our task as learners is to decide whether the head comes first, before the complement, or after it. Interestingly, there seem among the world's languages to be only these two possibilities; a particular language is either head-first or head-last. English is a head-first type, as the following phrases illustrate:

(i) *Students of physics* (noun phrase)
(ii) *In the kitchen* (prepositional phrase)
(iii) *Go with him* (verb phrase)
(iv) *Keen on football* (adjective phrase)

In Korean, however, heads regularly come last. So in the last example the Korean equivalent would be *football on keen.*

According to this approach languages vary according to certain **parameters**. In theory there are numerous possibilities for the ordering of heads and complements but they don't seem to appear. Universal grammar permits only a binary set of possibilities. This considerably narrows the amount of structured grammatical learning children have to engage in to acquire their native language. Another advantage of this approach is that implicational linking sometimes means that acquiring one feature enables others to fall in behind. A good example of this is the **pro-drop** parameter. This accounts for a distinction between those languages which allow sentences to be formed without a subject, and those which do not. In Italian, *Parla Francese*, is a well-formed sentence, but the equivalent in English, *Speaks French*, isn't. The difference is that Italian allows for an understood subject, *he/she*, whereas English doesn't. Languages like Italian, which have subject-less sentences of this type, are called 'pro-drop' languages, and it has been found that they share a number of other characteristics, such as the ability to change the order of subject and verb – in Italian, *Falls the night* is just as acceptable as *The night falls*. What children appear to do according to this theory is to set the pro-drop parameter when they are acquiring their native language and then other characteristics which depend on this parameter either 'fall in' or 'fall out' as a consequence.

The **principles-and-parameters** theory as it is known is the most recent development in universal grammar. Its architect, Noam Chomsky, has used it to account for the well-known fact that learning a second language later in life is never so successful as the acquisition of a native variety. Once the mental switches which determine whether we are learning a head-first language or a head-last one, a pro-drop one or a non-pro-drop one, are thrown, then, so the argument goes, the grammatical co-ordinates of our mental apparatus are set accordingly. We become increasingly locked into the structure and design of our native language which eventually confirms its conquest by becoming invisible to us. It's a persuasive theory and one which looks set to become the dominant account of what a universal grammar might consist of.

Moving things around

You may have noticed that the majority of sentences we have been examining so far are all of a certain type. They are all complete with their subjects, verbs and objects in the correct place, and all in statement, or declarative, mode. Linguists call these **kernel** sentences and they usually form the basis of most linguistic enquiry into the nuts and bolts of syntactic form. But, of course, we manipulate sentences in all sorts of ways to form questions, give commands, make requests, and perform the many speech acts of which language is capable. In addition to a grammar which can tell us how items are sequentially related we need one which can tell us the rules for moving them around. Such a grammar would explain how the following sentences are linked to each other:

(i)   *The man kicked the ball.*
(ii) *The man hasn't kicked the ball.*
(iii) *Has the man kicked the ball?*
(iv) *The ball has been kicked by the man.*
(v)   *Which ball has the man kicked?*

There is clearly a semantic relatedness between these sentences. The person doing the kicking is always the same, as is the thing being kicked, but the subjects and objects are not always in the same order and the functions of the sentences are all different. The first one is an unmarked statement, (iii) and (v) are questions, (iv) is a construction known as **passive** and (ii) is a negative. A conventional constituent analysis would have to view them as being generated by separate grammars, since they are all differently constructed. But we can't have a situation where every new sentence type has its own grammar. Besides which, such an analysis would not capture our intuitive sense that their propositional core, who did what to whom, is the same.

A more productive approach is offered by a type of grammar known as **transformational grammar**. According to this, all of the sentences above derive from a common original, or deep structure, represented most nearly in the sentence *The man kicked the ball.* The propositional basis of this can be expressed following the conventions of a method called **logical form**, in the following manner:

Kick {*man, ball*}

This representation means that there is a verb *kick* which has as its subject *man*, and its object, *ball.* The advantage of representing the items in this way is that the deep structure is not language particular. To get from this abstract mental proposition, or **mentalese**, as Steven Pinker terms it, to our starting sentence we have to imagine a series of minor transformations involving the addition of tense to *kick* and determiners to *man* and *ball*, plus some reordering, which is language specific. To derive the passives, negatives and interrogatives above, however, would involve more complex transformations. The consequence of all this is to suggest that we all possess two grammars as part of our linguistic competence. First, a constituent structure grammar, which consists of the rules governing kernel sentence formation, and second, a transformational one which enables us to manipulate sentences to produce the full range of sentence types.

The great advance which this additional layer of grammar affords is that it can account for some of the anomalies which occur in sentences. Indeed, it was the presence of these which first alerted Chomsky, with whom transformational grammar is most closely linked, to the limitations of a purely surface description of sentences. He noticed that there were pairs of sentences, such as *John is eager to please* and *John is easy to please*, which had the same surface structure but which were entirely different sentences. In the first, *John*, is the one doing the pleasing, while in the second, he is the one being pleased. He saw that there were different structural relationships here which are masked by a simple description of surface forms. He argued that the sentences, although superficially similar, derived from two different deep structures which had disappeared in the process of transformation. Representing them in logical form makes them reappear:

John is eager to please
EAGER {JOHN} + PLEASE {JOHN, SOMEONE}

John is easy to please
EASY {JOHN} + PLEASE {SOMEONE, JOHN}

We can see that the significant difference between these two sentences lies in the second clause of each. In the first instance *John* is the underlying subject of *please* (this is indicated by its position within the brackets), whereas in the second *John* is the underlying object. The transformational rules of English allow the two clauses in each sentence to combine in ways which produce the same surface structure. None the less, our intuitive knowledge of their deep structures enables us to interpret them correctly. The deep/surface divide has also proved useful in providing an explanation of much sentence ambiguity. In *The police caught Gus in their panda car* the phrase *in their panda car* could be modifying either *the police* or *Gus*. Using a transformational approach we can see that there are two different deep structures possible here, masked again by a common surface structure.

Insights such as these into the relatedness of sentences have been greatly advanced by the concept of transformation. And at the same time the deep/surface distinction fits neatly with the notion of a universal grammar. Perhaps what children are born with is a knowledge of deep structure. Syntax acquisition then becomes a process of learning the particular transformational processes which individual languages permit. Despite its successes, however, transformational grammar has had its problems. Under its influence syntax became a highly elaborate study. Arguably, too elaborate. In its heyday, in the 1960s and 70s linguists began seeing transformations everywhere, with the consequence that the concept became troublesome. Seemingly quite small differences such as that between *Tom gave a sandwich to Jane* and *Tom gave Jane a sandwich* became the subject of intricate transformational rules. In recent years Chomsky has simplified the transformations and slimmed the processes down to just a few central operations. And the terms 'deep' and 'surface' have also been refined so that Chomsky now refers to 'D' structure and 'S' structure. This is to avoid the possible suggestions of 'profound' or 'complex' in 'deep' and those of 'superficial' or 'obvious' in 'surface'. Nevertheless, transformational grammar continues to be a fertile concept in modern linguistics and is the best explanation we have of how language works to provide the variety of forms available to us.

Communicative grammar

A grammar of a language consists of a set of rules for generating well-formed word sequences, whether these are phrases, clauses, or sentences. But as you have probably noticed, this begs the question of what counts as 'well-formed'. Who actually decides whether something is well-formed or not? People differ considerably in what they consider acceptable in a language and in many cases the rules recited to justify these differences are little more than historically, or socially acquired preferences. This is why linguists tend to deal with 'idealised' utterances, that is, with complete sentences unaffected by variations in local dialect, fashion, or individual taste.

Tidying up language in this way has its advantages and disadvantages. On the credit side it enables linguists to set aside individual usage and concentrate on the underlying structure of a language. Only in this way can the mental blueprint we all possess as native speakers be established. On the debit side, however, it ignores a lot of evidence about language use which is arguably very interesting. Most of us do not communicate in this idealised way all the time. Real speech is rather messy: we abbreviate our utterances, repeat ourselves, hesitate, and slip from formal language to slang without noticing it. Some of the rules governing these linguistic phenomena have to do with **discourse**, that is with the use of speech, and also writing, in social and communicative situations. We don't have the space to consider this topic in any great detail, but it is worth spending just a little time on discourse now because it impacts on our notion of grammar.

The key point to bear in mind is that grammar is affected by social and stylistic considerations. Take, for example, the concept of 'sentence'. Traditional definitions of sentences tend to describe them as grammatically complete units capable of standing on their own and semantically independent. This is true of many sentences, including the previous one. But it is clearly not so for all. As we have already commented, in real speech we often abbreviate utterances, most usually by eliding elements. The purpose of this is to maintain fluency and avoid pointless repetition as in the following exchange:

Q: *Where are you going?*
A: *To the pictures.*

Here the sequence *To the pictures* functions as a perfectly acceptable reply because the full meaning is recoverable from the context. The listener has access to the idealised form *I am going to the pictures,* so it doesn't need to be spelt out. **Sentence fragments** of this kind are frequent in speech and increasingly common in writing, too. They have always been a feature of novels and short stories, where their aim is to reproduce the utterance flavour of language, but they can also be found in advertisements and even public announcements. In Chapter 3, following the linguist Geoffrey Leech, who has observed the growing frequency of this style in late twentieth-century culture, we referred to it as **public colloquial**.

Sentences, then, are units of style as well as grammar. This raises the problem of how we can formally describe them in grammatical terms. How can we arrive at a description which takes account of both the fully independent kind and the sentence fragments? The most helpful way is to distinguish, as some grammars do, between **minor** and **major** sentences. Minor ones are incomplete in some way while major ones are complete. This is a useful terminological distinction which enables us for purposes of grammatical description to focus on the major variety. It also allows us to discern two sets of rules here; first, the grammatical rules which govern sentence formation, and second, **text formation rules**, which operate on sentences when they become part of connected discourse. Such rules govern the coherence and cohesion of discourse. We can also say, that in addition to being grammatically competent in a language, we need to be communicatively competent as well (see Chapter 2).

Part of this second type of competence consists also in knowing how to arrange sentences for their best effect. There is a good deal of evidence to indicate that sentences are basically designed to accommodate the needs of speakers and listeners. Analysing sentences with these in mind is the job of **functional grammarians**. We have already seen that in formal terms idealised major sentences consist of a noun phrase plus a verb phrase: S = NP + VP. The noun phrase is normally the subject and the verb phrase the remainder, in traditional grammar, the **predicate**. In functional terms this structure is described as **theme + rheme**, or alternatively, **topic + comment**, although these pairs are not always used in the same manner, as we shall see in a moment. The theme of a sentence is its first major constituent. This may be simply a word, *John has done his homework*, a phrase, *Our garden gate needs mending*, or a clause, *Going home, we saw a badger*. The theme is the starting point of the sentence – what it is principally going to be about. The linguist Michael Halliday refers to it as the 'psychological subject'. In many instances the theme is also the grammatical subject, but there are frequently cases where another element may be promoted to theme, as in the last example above. The effect of such promotion is to give extra prominence to some feature. This is particularly so where the movement is for stylistic effect. In the case of *Going home* the reduced clause evidently derives from a longer one in which it is non-thematic *While we were going home*. Its thematic status is a consequence of abbreviation. As we noticed in Chapter 2, the thematisation of *down* in *Down came the rain*, makes it more important that in its normal, word final, position – *The rain came down*. Linguists refer to such themes as **marked**. Sentences can also have more than one theme. Of necessity they must have a theme which functions as the topic – sentences have to be about something. But additionally, they may have textual, and/or interpersonal themes as well. Textual themes include conjunctive, or linking, items, such as *on the other hand*, *however*, and *now*, and interpersonal ones include *frankly* and *maybe*. In the following sentence we can find all three: *But* (textual) *surely* (interpersonal) *Sunday* (topical) *would be better*. The rheme, or comment, is simply the remainder of the clause after the theme. Its typical use is to expand on the theme and provide more information.

Theme and rheme overlap with another pair of terms, **given** and **new**. These relate specifically to the information structure of sentences. Any text/utterance is necessarily delivered in a linear fashion, and as such, we are forced as listeners/readers, to process it in a similar fashion. Because of this it is easier, as we have already noticed in the section on universal grammar, to process sequences in which the burden of new information comes towards the end of the sentence. We expect the starting point of the clause to present us with information which is largely given, that is, assumed to be known. This gives us time to prepare ourselves for the new, to come later. We are much more likely to say *There's a bird on the lawn*, than *A bird is on the lawn*. In this case the empty subject *there* prepares us for the receipt of information. The theme is usually the given part of the communication and the rheme, the new, although this is not always the case. Marked themes are typically those in which the new piece of information is given topical status by being put first as in *Down came the rain*, where the fact that it's raining is the given element and functions as the rheme, or comment. Sentences in which the new information falls at the end are said to have **end-focus**. The term **focus** is really another way of describing what is new. In that sense all sentences will have a focal point. In many cases this is picked out by intonation rather than word position, as in the following:

> *MAry did it*

Here *Mary* functions as both theme and focus. It's the first topical constituent and it's also providing us with new information – the stress pattern indicates this. The given information is contained in the rheme *did it*. This is clearly a marked utterance. Anyone hearing it would be expected to sit up and take notice. An unmarked version with *Mary* still the focus but no longer thematic would be *It was Mary who did it*.

Conclusion

Much of this chapter has been about grammar, or, more particularly, grammars, since, as we have seen, there are a variety of ways in which the structures of a language can be described, as well as simply different structures themselves. It's an irony of English etymology that the word *grammar* is closely related to *glamour*. *Glamour* is a Scottish word, a corruption of *grammar*, introduced into the language in the eighteenth century. The connection with its more sober parent rests in an ancient sense of 'learning'. *Glamour* was associated with necromancy and the black arts. It involved erudition of a quite different and altogether more superstitious kind. But in a curious way both *glamour* and *grammar* are historically linked to pursuits which recognise the power of language, and while few people today would consider grammar a glamorous subject, it's probably true to say, that for many linguists, it represents the pinnacle of linguistic enquiry. This is apparent in the way the term has expanded in meaning. Traditional usages confine the scope of grammar to syntax. To provide a grammar of a language is to list the rules for sentence formation, in the way we have been doing. Since then, however, and particularly in America, grammar has come to incorporate all rule-governed language processes, from pronunciation rules to those dictating the conduct of conversations. To accompany the expansion we have different kinds of grammars: functional, communicative, generative, transformational, descriptive, and so on. But basic to all of them is the concern to link the transitory and ephemeral reality of sound with the abstract, mental, world of meaning. The question which preoccupies linguists is this: 'what are the rules, phonetic, syntactic, and semantic, which allow us to manipulate air in such a way as to produce the wealth of utterances of which we are capable?' This is an enormous question, and one which still has to yield a definitive answer.

A number of times in this book I have likened language to chess. It's a useful comparison because it captures something of the endless fertility with which novel sequences can be created from a fixed number of elements. But, at the same time, it limits language to a purely mental activity. Language emerges from the whole self, not just a part of it. W.H. Auden tried to express something of this when he said, 'Every created thing has ways of pronouncing its ownhood'. A better comparison would be with music. Musicians sometimes say that the whole art of music is in learning how to make one note follow another. This is not so simple a matter as it may at first sound. The right notes played in sequence produce a melody, the wrong ones, discordance. Melodies are either well-formed or ill-formed. Like language, they involve 'the infinite use of finite media'. And, also like language, the rules for producing acceptable sequences are in a constant state of evolution as conventions change over time. Musicians talk of 'phrasing' and 'dynamics', of 'pace' and 'rhythm', all of which have a cross-over with language. In many respects the human voice is like a musical instrument, except the melody it produces consists of words rather than notes. Music has an easy advantage over language in that it doesn't need translating to communicate itself. In fact translation is impossible. Some writers argue that all art aspires to the quality of music because it seems to come to us context free, transcending national, political, and linguistic barriers. Whatever the truth of this, perhaps, following the analogy with music, we should look upon grammar as concerned with the harmonics of language, with the way one sound, one word, one sentence, follows another. By any account, this is a pursuit not without its own glamour.

Notes

1   The symbol * is used to indicate an unacceptable sequence.
2   The description is of necessity simplified. Anyone seeking a more comprehensive account should consult a recent discussion of syntactic theory, such as Geoffrey Poole's (2002) *Syntactic Theory*.

6 The Parent of Language
Language and Mind

Language ... springs out of the most retired, and inmost parts
of us, and is the Image of the Parent of it, the mind
BEN JONSON (*Timber: Or, Discoveries
made upon Men and Matter,* 1640)

Mind: The seat of a person's consciousness, thoughts, volitions,
and feelings; the system of cognitive and emotional
phenomena and powers that constitutes the subjective
being of a person.
Brain: The convoluted mass of nervous substance contained in
the skull of humans and other vertebrates.
Oxford English Dictionary

Mind over matter

Language is an operation performed by the mind. From a simple pragmatic viewpoint, it's a device for allowing minds to exchange ideas,
thoughts, feelings, via a code of sounds, or written symbols. Equally
importantly, it enables minds to communicate internally with themselves. Without language many of our thoughts would remain unfor-
mulated and, in an important sense, unthought. But how does the
mind do this? How does it manage to translate the silent world of our
unconscious into the form of words and then transmit it across to the
mind of another person?

Before we try and answer these questions we need to establish what
we mean by 'mind'. For many people it probably means much the
same thing as 'brain'. Indeed, in popular thought these terms are often
used interchangeably, but there is an important difference between
them, as the definitions above indicate. The brain is the physical organ
in our skulls which controls bodily behaviour and thought. Like any
other organ, its operations can be observed. Modern imaging tech-
niques allow us to see the electrical circuitry firing up when various
sensations are being experienced by the nervous system. The mind, on

the other hand, comprises the mental and emotional capabilities which make us human. In contrast with the brain, it's not a physical organ and not open to direct observation. It's the mind which makes decisions and has goals and intentions. When we misjudge someone or make a mistake, the error is a mental one, but we don't blame our brains. The mind is the nearest we can come to naming something which is uniquely us. People's brains may be similar but yet their minds are very different, much as twins may physically look alike and yet have separate personalities.

And yet our minds are clearly dependent on our brains. It's the brain which processes the thoughts and the feelings. Our heads house an incredible factory ceaselessly working to service our physical and mental needs. But however much we cut open the brain, or observe its workings electrochemically, we will never see a thought or a feeling. And we will never see a word or trace a sentence. It's a little bit like taking apart a television set in order to find the pictures and the people inside them. All we will find is circuitry. In an earlier age theologians were exercised with trying to find the exact location of the soul in the body. Similarly with the mind. In some way we don't yet fully understand, the brain creates the unique landscape of our individual minds. The boundary between the physical organ and its more abstract counterpart is represented by the different disciplines which study them. Neuroscience is principally concerned with the brain and its physical make-up. Psychology, on the other hand, is concerned with the mind and human behaviour. They are twin sides of the same coin, but the interconnecting links between them represent an ongoing challenge for the branches of linguistics known, respectively as **neurolinguistics** and **psycholinguistics**.

Language and the brain

Much of what we know about the way in which the brain processes language comes from the observation of stroke victims whose language abilities have been impaired. Probably the most famous of these observations was carried out by a nineteenth-century French neurologist, Paul Broca. Broca became very interested in the possibility that certain language functions could be localised in the brain and in 1861 he presented a paper based on the study of a patient who had suffered a severe stroke. This unfortunate man was known as 'Tan', or sometimes 'Tan Tan', because this was the only syllable he could utter. However, despite the fact that his speech production was so badly impaired, he could none the less understand what was said to him without any problem. After Tan's death Broca conducted a post-mortem and discovered a large lesion in the frontal left lobe of his brain. He concluded from this that speech production was handled by a relatively small area of the brain while a separate area was responsible for its reception. As a consequence of Broca's work, difficulties in speech production have since become known as **Broca's Aphasia** – from a Greek word meaning 'without the power of speech'. The speech of such sufferers is typically slow and effortful, although not usually so severe as that of Tan's.

Broca's findings seemed to be confirmed, 13 years later by the experiments of a German neurologist, Carl Wernicke, also working on stroke patients. In 1874 he presented information on two patients both of whom had severe speech impairments but who differed markedly from Tan in the nature of their disability. Unlike Tan they had no difficulty with producing language. They could speak fluently and apparently effortlessly, but their speech was full of odd, inappropriate, and sometimes made-up words. Not only that, but they had great difficulty with comprehending what was said to them. Their post-mortems revealed that while Broca's area, as it has come to be known, was relatively uninjured, there were lesions towards the back of the left hemisphere.

Wernicke himself produced an attractive explanation for the differing impairments. He noted that while his area was close to the part

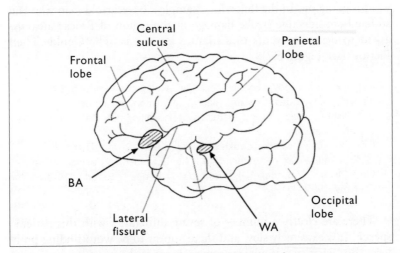

FIGURE 6.1 BROCA'S AND WERNICKE'S AREAS
Source: Radford, 1999: 14

of the brain responsible for hearing, Broca's was close to the part which controlled the motor functions of speech production (see Figure 6.1). From this Werrnicke hypothesised that his area stored the auditory memories of words while Broca's area stored memories of how to pronounce them. Superficially this seemed to explain why Wernicke's patients could speak fluently but with little understanding of meaning, as opposed to Broca's who could understand alright but had difficulty speaking. But since the mid-twentieth century it has become clear that this explanation is insufficient. And for two related reasons. First, while the speech of Wernicke's aphasics is fluent, it is also often nonsense. According to Wernicke's theory this is because the loss of auditory memory disables patients from locating the right words, forcing them to rely on inappropriate or invented ones. But this is to simplify how words are stored in the brain. We now know that words are filed in more sophisticated ways than simply their sounds. The problem seems to be more with word selection rather than pronunciation memory. Moreover, as we shall see in a moment, patients' memory loss doesn't affect all words equally. And second, experiments with Broca's aphasics have shown that, contrary to received opinion, they have difficulty not just with production but also with comprehension.

Rather than separating production from comprehension as older accounts of aphasias used to do, a more helpful approach is to consider the precise linguistic nature of the conditions. One of the usual tests given to aphasics is to show them a picture and ask them to describe what is going on. In the following example a 64-year-old man who had suffered considerable stroke damage in the region of Broca's area was asked to describe events in a picture known as 'The Cookie Theft Picture' (see Figure 6.2):

> Kid...kk..can...candy...cookie...caandy...well I don't know but it's writ...easy does it...slam...early...fall...men...many no... girl. Dishes...soap...soap...water...water...falling pah that's all ...dish...that's all.
> Cookies...can...candy...cookies cookies...he...down...That's all.
> Girl...slipping water...water...and it hurts...much to do..Her...clean
> Up...Dishes...up there...I think that's doing it. (cited in Obler and Gjerlow, 1999: 41)

There are clearly a number of severe difficulties with this patient's speech. It is extremely slow and there appear to be word finding problems. But what stands out, overwhelmingly, is the impoverished grammatical structure. As Obler and Gjerlow point out, there are a few

FIGURE 6.2 COOKIE THEFT PICTURE

Source: Produced by Goodglass, H. and Kaplan, E. (1983) as part of the 'Boston Diagnostic Aphasia Examination' published by The Psychological Corporation

stock phrases repeated smoothly, for example *easy does it, that's all,* and *I don't know,* but for the most part the words do not link together. The commonest items are nouns, *candy, cookie, dishes, soap, water,* and so on, and verbs, *fall, slipping, clean up* and *hurts.* What are missing are the grammatical, or function, words which glue items together in sequences. There are no determiners – *a, the* – very few prepositions – *in, out, to* – or auxiliary verbs – *am, was, have, had* and so on. And even though there are a couple of pronouns, their use is variably correct. *Her... clean up ... dishes,* wrongly uses the object pronoun *her* instead of the subject form *she.* If we put the utterance in its correct form, *She is cleaning up the dishes,* we can see just how much grammatical information is absent.

Language deficiencies of this kind are referred to as **agrammatism** – loss of grammar – and sufferers are called **agrammatics.** In English the most familiar feature of agrammatism is loss of function words, but it may take a different form in other languages where the reliance on function words is not so great. In these languages, Italian, for example, there are other kinds of grammatical errors, for example erroneous verb inflections, or gender markings. But the general story is the same. Broca's aphasics seem to suffer from some impairment of their syntactic ability.

It's this which slows down their speech and results in their almost tele-graphic style of utterance. And, interestingly, it also impairs comprehen-sion. For while the understanding of Broca's aphasics is better than that of Wernicke's, it none the less can let them down on occasions. As Ray Jackendoff (1993) reports, if Broca's aphasics are shown two pictures, one of a boy hitting a girl, and the other of a girl hitting a boy, and then asked to say which picture goes with the following sentences, they get the right answer with (a) but choose randomly with (b):

(a) *The boy hit the girl*
(b) *The boy was hit by the girl*

The problem seems to lie in (b) with the functional words *was* and *by*. Normal users of the language will intuitively know that the passive sen-tence derives from an active original, *The girl hit the boy*. Broca's apha-sics, on the other hand, although registering the presence of *was* and *by*, are confused about what function they perform. Similarly. they have difficulty distinguishing between sentences such as (c) and (d),

(c) *He showed her baby the pictures.* (Who saw the pictures? The baby did)
(d) *He showed her the baby pictures.* (Who saw the pictures? She did)

To Broca's aphasics both of these sentences have the form of (e)

(e) *He showed her baby pictures*

in which the meaning is ambiguous, that is, *He showed pictures of the baby to her* or *He showed pictures to her baby*. The difficulty here would seem to be in processing the determiner *the*.

By contrast with Broca's aphasics, sufferers from Wernicke's aphasia have no difficulty with function words. They speak quickly and confi-dently and may at first hearing sound normal. But only superficially so. The problem with their speech is that it lacks meaningful content. While there are plenty of determiners, pronouns, auxiliary verbs and prepositions, the lexical content, that is, verbs, nouns and adjectives, is severely impoverished. Here is an excerpt from the speech of a 75-year-old man with Wernicke's aphasia:

> Is this some of the work that we work as we did before? ... All right ...
> From when wine [why] I'm here. What's wrong with me because I ...

was myself until the taenz took something about the time between me and my regular time in that time and they took the time in that time here and that's when the time took around here and saw me around in it it's started with me no time and then I bekan [began] work of nothing else that's the way the doctor find me that way. (cited in Obler and Gjerlow, 1999: 43)

This is largely uninterpretable. The word *time* is repeated seven times, *took* three times, and *work* three times. So desperate is the man for vocabulary that he even invents a word *taenz*. And yet if we took some of the sequences and simply changed the vocabulary it could make sense:

What's wrong with me because I ... was myself until the taenz took something about the time between me and my regular time (original version)

What's wrong with me, because I was myself, until the stroke affected something, about the time between getting up and my regular bath (conjectural intended version)

Unlike the speech of Broca's aphasics, there is a grammatical or syntactic framework here, of sorts, but the slots for the content words appear to be filled quite arbitrarily. If Wernicke's aphasics have difficulty accessing such items it would explain why they have such poor understanding of what is said to them. Most of us can usually fathom messages of the telegraphic kind, in which the grammatical bits are missing. *Home tonight, Marion,* is fairly transparent. By contrast, *I shall be ...* provides us with the skeleton but not the flesh.

Evidence such as this suggests that separate parts of the brain are responsible for storing different vocabulary items. This has been supported by recent experiments on the brains of sufferers from epilepsy, conducted while patients are fully conscious. It should be pointed out that these are only possible because there are no pain receptors in the brain, so patients feel nothing. In these experiments patients are shown pictures and asked to talk about them while, simultaneously, electrodes are applied to different parts of the cerebral cortex. The results indicate that not only do words appear to be distributed about the brain according to their word class, but that types of words seem to be stored separately: nouns for wild animals are filed separately from those for flowers, for example. All of which has vastly complicated the picture emerging from the two classical aphasias. Much more of the brain than was at first envisaged is involved in language production and reception.

At the same time, however, the common occurrence of non-fluent and fluent aphasias, as Broca's and Wernicke's conditions are commonly known, suggests that there is a categorial difference in brain function involved. In other words, that what is at issue here, more than simply linking bits of the brain with items from our mental lexicon, is different kinds of language competence.

In 1941, and again in 1968, the linguist Roman Jacobson linked aphasia with Ferdinand de Saussure's notion of language as a combinatorial system. We considered this in Chapter 5. As we saw there, Saussure distinguished between two dimensions of language: the paradigmatic, and the syntagmatic. Words are syntagmatically related to each other in that they can occur next to each other in word strings, as in *He walked*, or *John ate*, as opposed to *He it*, *John me*, where they can't. And they are paradigmatically related to each other in so far as they can substitute for one another: so, in the case of *He walked* we could substitute either the pronoun or the verb, for example *I walked*, *He strolled*, and similarly with *John ate* – *He ate*, *John drank*. There are two interrelated competencies here. One is the ability to select equivalent items from our mental lexicon, that is, to know the range of words which can substitute for given items. And the other is the ability to sequence them acceptably. Fluent aphasics, the kind associated with damage to Wernicke's area, have problems with paradigmatic competence. They misselect words. The disturbance here is to the semantic system. This is important because such aphasics will usually get the word class right; they won't substitute a determiner for a noun, only another noun. At the same time they have little difficulty in stringing the apparently arbitrary selection of words together in a fluent manner. In other words, their syntactic component appears to be functioning reasonably well. On the other hand, the problems of non-fluent aphasics are syntagmatically related. Patients with this impairment have difficulty constructing words into sentences. So while their semantic understanding is relatively intact, their understanding of syntactic relationships, of inflectional systems and the like, is deficient, as is their competence in using functional vocabulary items.

Left-hemisphere dominance

All the language areas which we have been discussing so far are situated in the left hemisphere of the brain. Why this should be so is still something of a mystery. The brain is essentially symmetrical in structure. As

---

Conduction aphasia

A third form of aphasia which, like Wernicke's, involves problems with selection. But in this case the misselection is targeted at phonemes rather than whole words. Conduction aphasics characteristically substitute the wrong phoneme and will frequently make successive attempts to pronounce a word correctly, as in the case of a patient trying to pronounce the word *whistle* – *tris* … *chi* … *twissle*. Unlike Wernicke's aphasics their mispronunciations cause them anxiety. They also show a marked inability to repeat words. The vulnerable area is thought to be the section of the cortex between Wernicke's and Broca's area, responsible for conducting information between them. Thus the name of this language impairment.

---

with many other organs it has two of everything, except that, unlike the other duplicates, the two parts function differently. Strange as it may seem, the left side of the brain controls the right side of the body, while the right side of the brain controls the left. Moreover, both hemispheres have developed small differences, which mean that although structurally symmetrical, they are functionally asymmetric. In particular, it is the left side which is programmed for language. The dominance of this side linguistically has been demonstrated by a number of tests. One of the clearest demonstrations has resulted from the Wada test. This involves a patient being injected with an anaesthetic called sodium amytal into one side of the brain. If it is injected into the language hemisphere the patient is soon unable to speak for several minutes, after which s/he becomes aphasic. Injecting the drug into the right hemisphere, however, has no similar effects on speech. Equally conclusive are the observed effects on epileptics who have undergone an operation to sever the two hemispheres in order to control seizures. As Ray Jackendoff (1993) reports, if such people are shown a salacious picture visible only to their left visual field. they will giggle and blush in recognition. But when asked what they can see will reply 'nothing'. What seems to be happening is that, while the right-hand side of the brain is processing the visual information correctly, it is unable, because of the separation of the two hemispheres, to pass it on to the language centres in the left. The patient is in the peculiar position of having experiences which s/he is unable to talk about.

But it would be wrong to conclude from this that the brain's right hemisphere plays no part in linguistic development at all. Numerous experiments in recent years have demonstrated quite the contrary. We now know that patients with damage to their right hemisphere may also suffer language impairment. More tellingly, children who are born with a left-hemisphere deficit are still able to acquire language pretty well. How can we explain this, given the overwhelming evidence for the linguistic dominance of the left-hand side of the brain? The best, and most recent, guess involves thinking of the brain as a large corporation in which an enormous array of tasks have to be regularly performed. Like any organisation faced with such a situation the readiest way is to develop centres of excellence, with a backup in case, for any reason, they should fail. Similarly with the brain. Genetically it is symmetrical, but during its evolution the brain has developed small asymmetries to cope with specialised functions. In the case of language, the left side has evolved just enough of an advantage to make it more efficient for the brain to concentrate its linguistic centres there. The outcome of this has been the inhibition of the right side's ability to process language in favour of the left's. In the case of children who lack a left hemisphere, however, no such inhibition occurs and the right side kicks in as a backup. But it is only able to do this while the brain is still forming. Once the critical period for language development is over, the right side is no longer able to take over the left's ability. Backups are, after all, expensive to maintain, particularly if they are needed for other functions. This is still only a guess, but if true it may explain why children who are forced to rely wholly on their right hemispheres often appear to retain some language difficulties. In evolutionary terms, the left still retains a slight advantage. Equally significant, it would account for the ability of left-handed people to recover more quickly from aphasias than right-handed. Such people have less asymmetry in brain function and therefore less inhibition of right-hemisphere language activity.

This leaves the question of what part the right side plays in those with unimpaired language function. There is now a growing body of evidence which suggests that this side is important in what is generally called the **pragmatic** level of language use. This has to do with our ability to communicate effectively and to understand subtlety and nuance in language. Patients with right-hemisphere damage, characteristically have difficulties judging the appropriateness of discourse, in knowing, for example, that the conventional relationship between a boss and an employee makes it inappropriate for the employee to say *I've postponed our meeting* as opposed to the more deferential *Is it possible for us to meet later?* Grice's maxims of cooperation (see Chapter 2), which most normal speakers take for granted in speech, and which control the orderliness, quantity, relevance, and accuracy of most conversational exchanges, are far harder for patients with right-hemisphere impairment to negotiate. One of the conventions of discourse is that referents indicated by *he*, *she*, or *it*, in our speech are fully recoverable, either from the situation, or from what we say. Young children often forget to do this, and so do those with damage to the right hemisphere. Unlike children, however, they also have difficulty responding to the emotional context of information. In an interesting experiment a group of patients, some of whom were normal, and others with damage either to the right or left side of the brain, were shown a series of pictures designed to elicit an emotional response, for example, a girl seeing a dog run over. Subsequently they were shown pictures showing a non-emotional event (for example how to fry an egg) and then asked to talk about the two series. What the experimenters found was that, while sufferers from right-side damage produced as much language in talking about the pictures as those with left-side damage, their ability to talk about the emotional significance of the first set was markedly impaired (Bloom et al., 1992).

If we put these findings alongside other evidence a consistent picture begins to emerge about the involvement of the right hemisphere in language production and comprehension. It has long been known that patients with right-side impairment generally seem to care less about themselves and their appearance. They are more likely to speak with little expression in their voices and may make inappropriate, sometimes rude, remarks or interrupt other speakers. Speaking expressively has a lot to do with intonation. On many occasions we are only able to judge whether an utterance is a statement or a question by the falling and rising of someone's voice. This seems, as far as we can judge, to be the responsibility of the right hemisphere. When people are presented with two emotionally intoned sentences they are far quicker at determining whether they are the same or different when presented to the left, as opposed to the right, ear. Interestingly, patients with right-brain damage also have difficulty appreciating sarcasm and humour and often interpret metaphorical expressions literally. When presented with expressions using words capable of more than one meaning (for example *blue*, the colour, and *blue*, meaning sad), for example, right-brain-damaged subjects will more often than not select the literal meaning (Gardner et al., 1994). This is a significant finding because it suggests that some lexical knowledge is processed by the right hemisphere. It looks as though being able to understand certain semantic distinctions, at least in context, involves our right side. Tests of verbal fluency appear to confirm this. Patients with right-brain damage find it easier to activate vocabulary in terms of formal links – beginning with the same sound, or belonging to the same word class – than they do using semantic information – belonging to the same meaning category (for example animals, furniture). They also experience difficulty in understanding the ambiguity of such sentences as *The boy hit the man with the cane* where it is necessary to see that the phrase *with the cane* can either modify *the man* or *hit* (Schneiderman and Saddy, 1988).

Taken together, the array of linguistic difficulties experienced by right-brain-damaged patients suggests that while the left hemisphere is largely responsible for the formal properties of language, phonology and syntax (our 'linguistic competence'), the right has a greater responsibility for contextualising language use (our 'communicative competence'). If we connect these difficulties with problems of socialising, which right-brain-damaged people often experience, then it is likely that what we are talking about here is some impairment of a more general cognitive competence. One possible explanation for this is that sufferers have an impaired ability to think about what is in the mind of people they are talking to. In other words, that their 'Theory of Mind', the development of which, as we saw in Chapter 1, is crucial to the development of full adulthood, has been affected by injury. In the final analysis, however, we have to bear in mind that much of the brain's working is still a mystery to us. Although it's convenient to talk of areas and hemispheres, the brain is not compartmentalised in the way this might indicate. Jean Aitchison (1996) suggests thinking of language in the brain as like a restaurant. There are separate areas for cooking and eating food, but, in addition, food is constantly in circulation in the hands of waiters. More than ever before, neurolinguists are concentrating on the messengers, the couriers who link the various parts of the brain together. Perhaps language is circulating all the time in our brains like blood around our bodies. We still need to understand what makes it flow and how it is controlled.

The mind's language processor

Understanding aphasia has enabled us to comprehend a little better the highly complex process of language production and comprehension. But something is still missing. As we noted at the beginning, no matter how much we search inside the brain we will never find language. All we can do is trace the effects of brain interference on language competence. That is effectively what all the experiments on aphasics are about. But which bit of the wiring is responsible for the syntactic knowledge, or the phonological, or the semantic, is something we have to infer. The language which whizzes round our brains is in code. We can't identify a bit of neural firing with a word or grammatical function. If we think back to the television analogy used earlier, something very similar happens there. An electromagnetic impulse enters the set carrying both vision and sound images in encrypted form. Inside the set is a device with separate compartments for turning the signal back again so that we can see and hear exactly what is happening hundreds, and even thousands, of miles away. Separate bits of the device deal with sound as opposed to vision, as we know from the fact that we can turn one or the other off. And within vision we can alter the brightness, colour, contrast, and even speed. But while all these functions have their own separate compartments, they have, eventually, to be coordinated. When we watch the programme everything has to be synchronised to occur at the same time and in the same space.

A similar device must exist within our heads, although considerably more advanced, for translating between sound waves and thoughts. Because this is what essentially language does. When speech sounds reach the brain various processors get to work analysing the acoustic signal into its component parts. These consist of *who* is speaking (voice recognition), *what* is being said (language perception), and *how* it is being said (intonation and stress pattern). Just as with the television analogy, these appear to be handled by different modules in the brain. We know this, again, from work with stroke victims, some of whom can tell who is speaking to them, or respond to tone of voice, without knowing what is being said, and vice versa. And, indeed, most of us can recognise voices and emotional tones in foreign films even when we don't know the language. All of this information is important in translating the acoustic signal into thought, but key to it is the device concerned with language perception. Our phonological processor is busy distinguishing the speech sounds from the frequencies which comprise the sound waves. Just how it does this is still uncertain. Some linguists argue that the neural firings which pass the signal through the auditory nerve are similar to those which activate the vocal tract in speech production. Consequently, we recognise a sound because it utilises the same processes as those involved in producing it. Others regard the processor as a scanning device which matches the incoming sounds to patterns stored in our mental vocabularies, or lexicons, and provides a best fit. These views are not mutually exclusive – there is no reason why we shouldn't use more than one process – although of the two, the second is more persuasive. But one thing is clear, the phonological processor is not simply passively registering sounds. The end product of its labour is not just a string of speech sounds, but a word. To perform this feat it must know both the sounds which make up the hearer's language and the permissible patterns which it allows. Figure 6.3 shows part of this process.

This diagram conflates both language production and reception because our phonological processor has both to initiate speech and interpret it. The bottom half shows the processes involved in production. When we talk we have to convert the words we are using into a set of instructions for making the appropriate speech sounds. These instructions then pass to our vocal tract and result in us moving our lips and tongue in the directions and shapes necessary for us to speak. Conversely, when we are listening to someone, we have to convert the frequencies from the acoustic signal back into words. The top half of the diagram shows that. Perception of voice tone and voice recognition are situated outside the language box itself since, as we have seen, it is possible to recognise someone's voice and the intonational pattern they

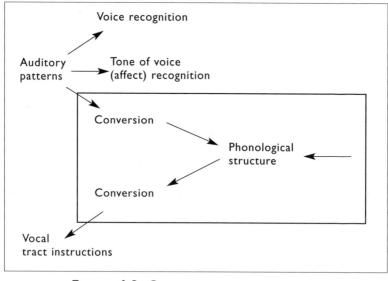

FIGURE 6.3 OUR PHONOLOGICAL PROCESSOR
Source: Jackendoff, 1993[1]

are using without knowing what is being said. This is not to say that this information is irrelevant. Clearly it isn't, because a full, context-rich, interpretation of speech will include knowing who is doing the talking, as well as the manner in which it is being said. But in the process of identifying the actual words, such information needs to be filtered out. This becomes all the more interesting if, as we have supposed, the contextualising activity is the responsibility of the brain's right hemisphere, and the more purely linguistic, that of the left.

The phonological processor, then, enables us to build up speech sounds into words, so that we can identify what is said to us, as well as communicate successfully ourselves. But there is more to language than this. In addition to identifying the right words we have to be able to assemble them in well-formed strings, or patterns. To do that we need access to more information. The phonological structure may correctly identify an incoming word, for example *table*, but whether it's being used as a noun, as in *Put it on the table*, or as a verb, *We'll table it at our next meeting*, is outside its province. That bit of the analysis involves being able to analyse the syntax of the sequence. In this particular instance, native speakers of English know that the determiner *the* is always followed by a noun. Clearly, then, the first sentence has to be interpreted with *table* acting as a noun. In the second case, however, *table* is not preceded by a determiner, a good sign that it can't be a noun, since as a noun it belongs to a subspecies of the class which requires a determiner in the singular. Here, speakers draw on their knowledge that verbs have subjects. In unmarked sentences these occur immediately before the verb and usually take the form of a noun or pronoun, as here. This is just a tiny sample of the syntactic information on which native speakers rely in correctly assigning words to their appropriate functions within sentences. We could add on the identification of plurals, present and past tense, and intermediate structures, such as phrases and clauses. To perform this extra level of analysis, we have to imagine another processor acting on the output of the phonological one (see Figure 6.4).

As in the previous diagram, the process is two way because syntactic analysis is a process we perform in speaking as well as listening. Before uttering the words in their appropriate sound forms we have to decide on their syntactic arrangement.

At first sight this might seem the end of the story. Once we have the words and a correct ordering of them we have language. But what about meaning? This is a much more tricky ingredient of language processing. To some extent meaning is involved in varying degrees all along

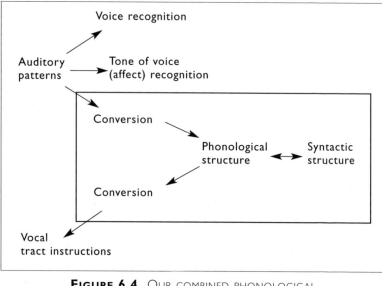

FIGURE 6.4 Our combined phonological
and syntactic processor
Source: Jackendoff, 1993

the line. Words, after all, are meaningful units. On the other hand, we can be trained to recognise words in a language, and even pronounce them without knowing what they mean. Our phonological processor has to have the concept of 'word' in its system, but doesn't necessarily have to know what individual words mean. Superficially things seem more straightforward at the syntactic level. As we have seen, arranging words into well-formed patterns is done on the basis of word classification – nouns go into certain slots, verbs, adjectives, into others. But what determines a word's classification? Most of us have been brought up on the idea that words are classified on the basis of their meaning: nouns are naming words, verbs doing words, adjectives describing words, and so on. But there is a lot of evidence to suggest that classifying words into 'parts of speech' has more to do with the demands of syntax than any expectation of meaning. The word *hunting*, for example, is usually classified as a verb, the present participle of the verb *hunt*. It quite clearly seems to be a 'doing' word. But in the following pair of sentences *hunting* is variably a verb and a noun:

(i) *I go hunting* (verb)
(ii) *Hunting is wrong* (noun)

The fact that *hunting* is a noun in (ii) can be shown by the possibility of preceding it by a determiner *All hunting is wrong*. This is not possible in (i) **I go all hunting*.[2] At the same time, *hunting* is not any less of a 'doing' word in (ii) than in (i). Nor, on the other hand, is it any less of a 'naming' word in (i) than in (ii), since in both sentences an activity is being named. Once we pursue, with any rigour, the distinction between nouns and verbs on semantic grounds, it vanishes before our eyes. Examples such as this permeate language use. Adjectives are popularly said to indicate properties, or attributes, yet *redness* only ever performs as a noun in English. We are driven to the conclusion that it is not what words *mean*, which determines their classification, but how they *behave*. Sentences require subjects, a slot which cannot be filled by verbs. Similarly, they require a predicator, a slot which cannot be filled by a noun. In (i) above, *hunting* is part of the predicator *go hunting*, whereas in (ii) it is the subject of the sentence.

Our syntax processor, then, operates according to the structural rules of the language we are speaking, and it is these which determine how individual words are classified. This explains why nouns in some languages are verbs in others, and vice versa. Similarly, it explains why we can create well-formed sentences which are nonsense, as in *My cat is a dog*. Of course, once generated, we set to work to make sense out of them, and it's not too difficult to ascribe a contextual meaning in this case (for example *The animal you are calling 'my cat' is not really a cat but a dog*). Our natural instinct is to look for meaning. But the important thing is that our syntax processor can generate sequences simply on the basis of how words behave without any thought to their content. The world of thought or meaning must, to some extent, exist separately from language. If this were not the case it would be impossible to translate from one language to another. Ideas can't be synony-

---

'Colourless green ideas sleep furiously'

Probably the most famous example of a supposedly meaningless sentence. It was formulated by Chomsky to illustrate the autonomous working of syntax. Since then, many people have claimed to find a meaning in it. And, indeed, queerer lines occur regularly in poetry. Chomsky's purpose, however, was not to defy human ingenuity, but to illustrate how easy it is to ignore meaning and still construct syntactically well-formed sentences.

mous with the words or structures used to express them. Obviously this doesn't mean that languages are exactly equivalent. Translators often bemoan the fact that some words don't have precise equivalents in the language into which they are translating. But this doesn't necessarily mean that speakers are incapable of having the same thoughts, simply that languages differ in their expressive possibilities. Not too much otherwise translation would be impossible. But, for the most part, using a foreign language means accepting that the same idea can be expressed by different words differently arranged. In English, for example, adjectives normally precede the noun they modify, whereas in French it is usually the reverse, as in, *le chat noir – the cat black* ('the black cat').

In order to complete our picture of the mental apparatus involved in the production and reception of language we need to add on a further dimension to our diagram. Both the starting point and the end result of both processes has to be a thought, whether in the mind of the speaker or the listener (Figure 6.5). The distinctiveness of 'thought' as a faculty is indicated in the diagram by its non-inclusion in the language area. But this presents us with a conundrum, because if thoughts or ideas are not dependent on language, what is it that language allows us to do that we couldn't do in its absence, and, more intriguingly,

---

Sapir–Whorf hypothesis

A celebrated hypothesis first put forward by the American linguist Edward Sapir (1881–1939), and later taken up, and developed by his student, Benjamin Lee Whorf (1897–1941). According to this view, the way in which we conceptualise the world depends on the particular language we speak. As Whorf puts it,

> We dissect nature along lines laid down by our native language.

He argued that the Hopis, a tribe of American Indians, had a different way of conceiving time than Europeans as a consequence of differences in their language. Since then, his research has been challenged, most publicly by Steven Pinker (1994). The consequence of Whorf's views would seem to be a kind of linguistic determinism, that is, certain thoughts and perceptions would be denied us unless our language allowed them. Most linguists now accept a softer version of the hypothesis in which language 'influences' thought, rather than determines it.

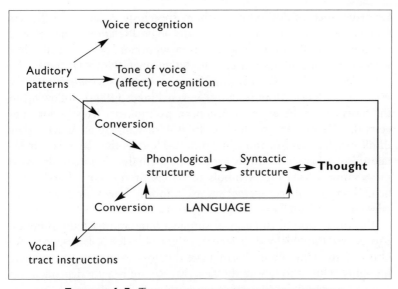

FIGURE 6.5 THE COMPLETE LANGUAGE PROCESSOR
Source: Jackendoff, 1993

what exists of thought prior to language? This is a difficult area to speculate about because, as we noted in Chapter 1, most of our thinking is performed in language. Most, but not all. The qualification is important here, because if we define thinking as the creation and manipulation of ideas then day-dreaming could quite easily be seen as a form of it. Day-dreaming involves the use of pre-linguistic images which are, typically, the visualisation of ideas. A recent advertisement by the publisher Collins confidently states, 'If you don't know the word, you can't think the thought'. But this is patently an over-statement. I can think the thought of going to the shops simply by imagining myself walking there. I don't need any accompanying words. Collins are perpetuating an idea, given currency in George Orwell's novel *Nineteen Eighty Four* in which Big Brother attempts to abolish the ideas of 'freedom' and 'equality' by abolishing the words (see Chapter 1). The ideas become unthinkable without the words. But does this necessarily follow? It all depends on how far we consider language to be a distinct faculty, quite separate from the general ability to think. And although the jury is still out on that one, it's fair to say that most linguists are coming round to the idea that it is. Evidence for this comes from research on two groups of people: first, those who have very little or no language, such as deaf adults without speech, who can none the less understand mathematical processes and logical relations; and second, severely mentally subnormal children who can speak fluently, but without making much sense. Jean Aitchison (1996: 41) quotes the example of Marta: *She was thinking it's no regular school. It was just good old no buses.* More recently, Steven Pinker (1994), following in the footsteps of the eminent American psychologist Jerry Fodor, suggests that 'people do not think in English or Chinese or Apache; they think in a language of thought' (p. 81). He calls this 'language' **mentalese** (see Chapter 5). To its exponents, mentalese is a logically based programme which uses symbols to represent concepts. For Pinker, being linguistically competent means 'knowing how to translate mentalese into strings of words and vice versa'.

But the notion of language as simply a translation activity is not an entirely comfortable one. It repeats a very old idea of language as the 'dress of thought', as if all language did was to express pre-existing thoughts. This is to ignore the fact that we are heavily dependent on language not only for the expression of thought but also for the process of thinking itself. What language does, supremely, is to make thought conscious to the mind. Images do this in part, but there is a limit to how much thinking we can do in images. Language brings thought into the daylight, and in so doing enables us to control and develop it more fully. I may have the notions of 'freedom' and 'equality' without the words but I can't think through the concepts in their absence. Or to use my day-dreaming example, I may imagine the idea of going to the shops, but as soon as I begin to consider the pros and cons of such a trip I need language. This is because words are able to organise and analyse thoughts as well as generate fresh ones. As we saw in Chapter 1, the ability of language to do this represented an important stage in the evolution of becoming fully human. An illustration of the fertility of language in this respect is given by the linguist, Randolph Quirk :

> Most of us can remember passing through stages like the following. Let us suppose we have attained, in early childhood, the distinction between 'round' and 'square'. Later on, 'round' is further broken down into 'circular' and 'oval', and it becomes easier to see this 'obvious' difference between shapes when we have acquired the relevant labels. But then we come to metaphorical extensions of the terms. We grope towards a criticism of arguments and learn to follow a line of reasoning; we learn to exercise doubt or be convinced according to how the argument goes. Some arguments may strike us as unsatisfactory, yet they have nothing in common except their tendency to give us a vague lack of conviction and

some discomfort. Then we hear someone discussing a line of argument and we catch the word 'circular' being used. At once everything lights up, and we know what is meant; the idea 'clicks', as we say. There is of course nothing about an argument which resembles the shape of a circle, and we may never have thought of 'circle' except in terms of visual shapes. Yet in a flash we see the *analogy* that the *metaphor* presents, and thereafter we are able to spot this type of fallacious argument more speedily, now that we have this linguistic means of identifying it. (Quirk, 1962: 55)

Quirk's illustration of the creative way in which language and thought interact should make us pause in our mental modelling. While the processor concept seems in many ways to fit with our experience of language it leaves a number of questions unanswered. How, for example, do we account for the place of non-linguistic knowledge in the interpretation of utterances? As Brown and Miller point out (1991), if we came across the following sentence,

The telephone dial was made of marzipan

we should know this was no ordinary telephone precisely because in the real world telephones are not made of this. Such knowledge cannot be said to be linguistic in origin. Looking up the word *telephone* in a dictionary wouldn't tell us anything about what the object was made of. It's something we have acquired as part of our general knowledge. And at what point does out knowledge about *who* is talking to us, and the intonation pattern being used – those things we have suggested are right-hemisphere responsibilities – come into play?

Another difficulty with our model is that it presumes that the processes are performed in a linear order. In other words, that we first of all identify the speech sounds then identify the words then the sentence types before finally deciding on the meaning. But is that really how we interpret utterances? Most of us probably feel that the processes are simultaneous. That's partly because of the speed with which they are performed. On average adult native speakers of a language can produce more than 150 words a minute – about one word every half second. If we take into account that we probably know about 30,000 words then we are having to make choices at a phenomenal rate. And it's equally true for listeners. Not surprisingly, linguists are divided over how our processors actually accomplish these extraordinarily complex tasks in such a short space. One view is that processing is indeed done in sequence with all decisions of a certain type being taken before decisions of the next type. This means that information which may be available on the basis of later decisions cannot inform earlier decisions. Known as the **serial-autonomous** model of processing, it visualises the individual stages of processing as completely discrete. When we hear a sentence with the word *tables* in it, for instance, the syntactic, semantic and contextual information which would tell us whether it is being used as a verb or a noun cannot be accessed until it has first of all been identified as a word. On the face of it this would seem common sense. But, on the other hand, we don't normally encounter words in isolation. If we hear the sentence *Can you bring the tables?* we are surely primed by the context, both linguistic and extra-linguistic to expect *tables* to be a noun. This would involve seeing the various processors acting not serially, but in parallel. In other words, as soon as we encounter language all our processors get to work: they don't form an orderly queue but work in tandem to interpret the utterance. Not only that but they pass information freely between each other.

Supporters of the **parallel-interactive** model, as it is called, cite a number of experiments in support of their model. When, for instance, people are asked to press a buzzer every time they hear a certain word, for example *party*, they do so more quickly when it is part of a well-formed and meaningful sentence than otherwise, which seems to indicate that grammatical and semantic considerations do play a part in word recognition. At the same time, supporters of the queuing model can also cite experiments in their favour. These again involve word recognition and response times. Subjects are shown a sentence such as *The young woman worked in a bank.* Immediately afterwards various words are flashed on a screen and they have to press a buzzer when they recognise them. If the word *money* is flashed the response time is very quick. Understandably so, because it's clearly associated in meaning with *bank*. The word *bank* **primes** us to expect a word linked to it. Correspondingly, if a word totally unrelated is flashed on the screen, for example *village*, the response time is slower. The interesting thing is what happens when *river* is flashed up. The parallel-interactive theory would predict a much slower time since this meaning of bank is irrelevant here. But this appears not to be the case. Both senses of the word seem to be primed, even though, from the context we should expect only one.

Most current accounts of processing try and combine features of both theoretical models. And perhaps this is the way forward. Rather than thinking of our processors as either a series of separate dominoes or as an organised team, we should see them as having a federal rela-

tionship in which a measure of autonomy and dependence are inseparably part of their constitution. One thing is clear, however. Both in
our planning and interpretation of language we are looking for structures, at whatever level. The evidence for this is substantial and comes,
not so much from our success at communication, but our failures.

Garden paths and other distractions

Garden-path sentences are sentences in which the hearer/reader is
misled about the direction in which the sequence is going. The usual
experience of most people on encountering them is complete bewil-
derment. The sentence seemed to make sense and now it doesn't, as
for example:

The body slipped into the river froze

Despite its oddity this sentence is perfectly grammatical. All we have to
do is insert the auxiliary verb *was* and the relative pronoun *which* to
make this apparent,

The body which was slipped into the river froze

The problem is really caused by the elision of these elements from the
final sentence. What they would tell us, were they present, is that *the
body* is not the subject of *slipped* but its logical object. Without them
our processor interprets the sentence as a simple one which is complete after *slipped* only to discover that this isn't the case. We are
impatient to determine meaning. So impatient that we can't wait till
the end of a sentence before interpreting it. When we process sentences we are looking to close the phrases and clauses as soon as possible. Our minds are programmed to look for subjects, main verbs and
objects quickly so we can understand the utterance and move on.
Garden-path sentences, however, defeat that objective and force us to
go back and reprocess them.

    Similar findings emerge from what are known as 'click' studies.
These are, quite simply, experiments in which recorded sentences are
played to people with clicks, or beeps superimposed on them. They are
then asked to say at what point in the sentence the clicks occur. This is
a difficult task since it involves the subject listening for two things at
the same time: the sequence of words and the clicks. Not surprisingly,

they make mistakes. But the interesting thing is that the mistakes are not random. Subjects will tend to hear the clicks close to clause boundaries, even when they aren't. So, for example, if the sentence *The man who nobody likes is leaving soon* is played with the click occurring between *man* and *who* listeners will get it right every time because *who nobody likes* is a relative clause which can be syntactically marked off from the rest of the sentence *The man [who nobody likes] is leaving soon.* However, if the click is placed elsewhere as in,

The + man who nobody likes is leaving soon

Or

The man who + nobody likes is leaving soon (cited in Radford, 1999: 396)

subjects will still tend to hear the click occurring very near or even on the clause boundary. Results like these suggest to linguists 'that the clause is the major sentence processing unit' (Radford: 396). In other words, that we are segmenting the sound signal into syntactic units almost immediately and homing in on the major structural boundaries.

As well as mistakes in receiving language, we also make mistakes in producing it. Speech errors, or 'slips of the tongue' as they are popularly called, are very important to linguists in revealing how our minds process language. They typically occur when our minds are under pressure, either because we are nervous or because we are having to speak quickly. As a consequence, the normal ordering of sounds, syllables, or words, gets mixed up. But although we call them 'slips of the tongue' it's not our tongues which are at fault. What we are experiencing is some interference with our language processing. To understand how this happens we need to remind ourselves of something considered in Chapter 2, namely that words consist of a sound shape matched with a concept. So, for example, the word *table* is made up of a series of sounds linked together and at the same time it expresses a concept 'table'. It's this combination, of course, which makes it a word in the first place. Both of these aspects also can have an independent existence – the pronunciation, and even spelling, of *table* might change over time, as indeed it has, without the concept altering. And, conversely, the concept might change without the pronunciation altering at all. This fits nicely with the modern linguistic view that the sound *table* and the concept 'table' have no necessary link, the relationship is fundamentally arbitrary and conventional. The natural corollary of this is that concepts and sounds are stored in different parts of our minds.

Once a concept is primed, or activated, it calls up its corresponding sound pattern. Normally, that is, because most of us at some time have had the experience of knowing what we want to say but not being able to find the right words. But given that we do find them, they don't necessarily come in the right order immediately. The sounds of *bike* may be called up at the same time, or even before, *take* in the sentence *Take my bike*, leading us to transpose one of the sounds, *Bake my bike*. Transpositions characteristically occur in places where the words have a similarity of sound. In this instance, *take* and *bike* are half rhymes. A similar kind of error occurs in reversals, where the initial sounds of adjacent syllables are reversed, as in *parcark* (carpark). Here again we have a half rhyme. These are mistakes, then, which occur at the sound, or phonetic level, of word assembly.

Word mistakes can also occur at the conceptual level, for example, when we select the wrong word, as in *He's a tall man* (short), or *Cover your face* (eyes). These sorts of substitutions nearly always consist of items which have a sense relation to the target word (see Chapter 2), either in being an antonym – tall/short – or a meronym (eyes are part of one's face). If we think of concepts being stored in semantic networks in the mind then it's easy to imagine a primed word also priming one of its relations. And because the relation is the last to be primed it's ready to be inserted into the wrong slot. Blends also seem to be conceptual in origin (*which* + *what* > *whatch*; *ghastly* + *grizzly* > *ghrastly*). Unlike substitutions, however, the words involved are invariably similar in meaning. People never seem to blend antonyms (*hot* + *cold* > **hold*).[2] And they are also often similar in sound, although not always. Arguably what happens here is that two related concepts are primed, both of which could equally fill the sentence slot available. Rather than choose between them, the mind tries to combine them

---

Tips of the slung

The Rev. William Spooner (1844–1930), dean and warden of New College Oxford, was reputed to have made many verbal slips. Among other errors attributed to him, are the following toast to Queen Victoria *Three cheers for our queer old dean*, and a tribute to the British farmers as *Noble tons of soil*. The frequency of these slips gave rise to the term 'Spoonerism'. Spooner seems, by all accounts, to have been an extremely clever man whose brain was more agile than his tongue.

both, a temptation all the greater if there are similarities in sound as well as concept. So we come out with embarrassing slips such as *I missed the lection today* (*lecture* + *lesson* > *lection*).

Language acquisition

All the studies we have looked at assume as their starting point that our minds are programmed for language. In other words, that we possess what linguists call, a 'mental grammar', that is, a set of principles for producing and receiving language in a structured and orderly manner. This is a cornerstone of modern linguistic study. Unlike the school grammars we encounter in books, mental grammar is largely unconscious. We are not aware of how we process language, any more than we are aware of the set of instructions needed to make our legs move. But this raises a problem, because if it is unconscious, how are we to investigate it? For many linguists, the principal testing ground for theories about mental grammar lies in the way in which children acquire language.

Two things have intrigued researchers over the years about children's language acquisition. First, the speed with which they learn to speak their native language. By the age of five most normal children understand the fundamental principles of language and are amazingly fluent. And second, their ability to accomplish this feat without being taught. We have only to think how difficult and time consuming it is as an adult to learn a language to appreciate this achievement. In their early years children seem to have a remarkable facility just to pick up language. Evidence of this exists in abundance. Children of immigrants to a new country invariably learn to speak the language more fluently than their parents. Adults will often retain an accent and be more hesitant speakers, despite years of exposure to the new language, but their children will assimilate relatively easily and, in many cases, become linguistically indistinguishable from the native inhabitants.

This belies the idea, if we harboured it, that parents teach us how to speak. For the most part parental instruction in language is confined to naming things: *That's a shoe. Can you say 'shoe' Sally?* It would be rare to find a parent teaching a child the use and meaning of *with* or *could*. And unproductive too. Because an understanding of such words involves an understanding of grammar. Most people who have attempted to 'correct' an infant's grammar will know how impossible it is. There is a well known illustration of this recorded by the linguist David McNeill:

CHILD: Nobody don't like me.
MOTHER: No, say 'nobody likes me.'
CHILD: Nobody don't like me.

(eight repetitions of this dialogue)

MOTHER: No, now listen carefully; say nobody likes me.
CHILD: Oh! Nobody don't likes me. (cited in Jackendoff, 1993: 22)

All adults can really do in the early stages of language learning is to provide children with examples of sentence patterns. It's up to the child to work out for himself/herself the principles on which those patterns are based. And if we consider just how messy and reduced actual speech is (what linguists call 'poverty of stimulus'), this is even more remarkable. The major relationships of subject to objects, and verbs to their complements, are never explained to us in childhood: we just acquire them. To take an early example from Chomsky, we have no difficulty in understanding the difference between *John is eager to please* and *John is easy to please* despite the fact that no one has ever explained it to us. Neither has anyone needed to teach us the working of the reflexive pronoun *herself* in the very different sentences, *Jane wrote to Mary about herself,* and *Jane asked Mary about herself.*

Clearly, we could say that children are just very good at learning things in general. And there is some truth in that. But there are also plenty of things they are slow at, including learning to share with others, telling the time, and tying their shoelaces. And not all of language learning comes easily either: the process of learning to read and write is painstaking and not generally complete until age eleven. The most current explanation of children's facility at language learning is the **Genetic Hypothesis**. This supposes that children are born with an innate ability to acquire language much as they are born with an innate ability to walk. In other words, that the human brain is physically organised, as a consequence of biological evolution, to think linguistically. If this is the case it helps to explain why all children go through the same stages of acquisition, providing they receive the right stimulus from their surroundings. Our brains are not fully formed at birth. The neural structure of the brain still has to develop the myelin sheaths which insulate the neurons electrically from each other. As our brains develop so does our capacity for language. We are timetabled to talk just as our adult teeth are timetabled to replace our baby teeth.

But there is a caveat to this. Our adult teeth will emerge without the intervention of anyone else. This is not true of language, however, because language is an inherently social, interactive, ability. A child left entirely on its own will not acquire language. There have been several cases of 'wild children' which have demonstrated this. One of the most recent is the case of 'Genie', a 13-year-old child, discovered in 1970, who had been subject to the most appalling treatment by her family, locked in a small room and never spoken to. Not surprisingly she had virtually no language, and although with kindness and training she subsequently improved, her language ability never went higher than the level of a two-and-a-half-year old, although her general mental ability was higher. So language acquisition requires both an innate language endowment and an external stimulus, or language input. In this sense we are the products of nature and nurture.

But attractive as this hypothesis is, what concrete evidence is there that we are born equipped for language? Difficult as it is to interrogate adults it surely must be impossible with infants. None the less, some of the most startling evidence comes from experiments conducted with children in the first few months of life. We now know that infants can discriminate many subtle distinctions between speech sounds, some of which are hard even for adults to distinguish. The technique used to elicit this evidence is called **high amplitude sucking**. The infant is given a pacifier to suck on, connected to a sound system. Each time the child sucks a noise is generated. The effect of this is to make the child suck faster until s/he gets bored and begins to slow down. The experimenter then changes the sound. If the baby renews the sucking it's a good indication that s/he has detected the change and is showing a revived interest. Using this technique researchers have been able to show that infants can distinguish between the sounds /b/ and /p/ in the syllables /ba/ and /pa/. When we consider that these sounds are different only in one respect, that is, the vibrating of the vocal cords, or voicing in the case of /b/ (see Chapter 1), this is a significant achievement. Even so it could still be argued that the child might have learned this from hearing people speak around him/her. More surprising is the evidence from this technique that children can discriminate between speech sounds they could not previously have heard. One experiment involved playing two very similar speech sounds from the Czech language [ʒa] and [r̝a] to Canadian infants. Interestingly, the children were able to tell them apart just as easily as /b/ and /p/ whereas the adults to whom these sounds were played were not. This finding has been replicated in other studies. English infants between six and eight months have been found to discriminate between sounds used in Hindi but not in English. As children move towards year one, however, and the production of their first words, their performance declines towards that of adults.

All of this suggests that children are born with the ability to differ-entiate between the major sound contrasts on which the world's lan-guages depend. In other words, they have an ability to acquire any language. As they begin to focus on those which are relevant to their own language, however, this ability atrophies until only the more obvious contrasts from other languages are detectable. There would be no point, after all, in the brain maintaining a facility that is going to have limited use. If this evidence is to be credited, and the regularity with which it is replicated suggests it should, then it means that children are born possessing, at least in part, the concept of the **phoneme** (see Chapter 5). This is the first item of **universal grammar** and on its foundation is erected the entire edifice of language. Not only that, but it seems clear that babies are clued into their detective work even in the womb. Four-day-old infants can distinguish their own mother's voice from that of others and can tell utterances in their maternal language from those of another language. Right from the start of life our linguistic knowledge is intimately relational.

The first year

Babies are noisy things; they emerge into the outside world crying, much to the consternation of their parents. In the main these cries are **vegetative sounds** which reflect the baby's biological state. They signify either wind, hunger, or the passing of a motion. While such primitive vocal sounds have little to do with language, none the less the baby is exercising its lungs and learning to control its air flow and produce rhythmic sounds. After a few weeks babies enter the **cooing** stage. They now begin to make more settled and musical sounds, quieter and low pitched consisting of a vowel sometimes preceded by a back con-sonant (typically, *oo* or *goo*). This stage usually lasts for a couple of months, during which most babies are learning to control their tongues, and as they do so strings of cooing noises begin to emerge in a form of **vocal play**. Between about four and six months we start hearing the first syllable-like noises (*ba ga*). The baby is now ready for what most parents will recognise as the **babbling stage**. These involve syllabic sequences, at first repetitious, *bababa*, and from about nine months becoming more varied, with syllables joined together in a kind of proto-speech, or **scribble talk** (*badaga, babu*) as the baby tries to imitate adult sounds. An important component of such 'talk' is the production of adult-like intonation patterns. All of this culminates at around 12–15 months in the production of the magical first word (*gone, dada, teddy*).

The regular occurrence of this canonical first year, like the child's first smile, is a good indication, as we have suggested already, that language is maturationally controlled. But this still leaves the mystery of where and how the leap into language occurs. For, however we consider it, there is a marked difference between a simple string of sounds and a word. To understand this mystery we need to bear in mind, first, that babies understand more language than they are capable of producing. This is clear from the experiments referred to above, and it is true in general in the early years of acquisition. And second, most parents are actively encouraging their children to talk, right from birth. They characteristically imagine the sounds their children are making to be words and engage in mock conversations with them. This is a two-way process. Research has shown that adults respond more to babies who produce speechlike sounds, rating them as cuddlier or nicer, while, correspondingly, a baby will produce more speech-like sounds in response to adult encouragement.

This lays the groundwork for sounds to acquire meaning. But this is not enough on its own. At some point the child makes the important discovery that certain sound sequences can have a specific effect on an adult. Then, and only then, sounds cease to be mere noises and become signals. Of course, to a fond parent all baby noises are signals,

---

The 'fis' phenomenon

An observed phenomenon of young children's speech which indicates their ability to identify sounds they cannot pronounce themselves clearly. The classic demonstration of this, recorded by the linguists Berko and Brown, concerns identification of the word *fish* in adult speech:

> One of us, for instance, spoke to a child who called his plastic fish a *fis*. In imitation of the child's pronunciation, the observer said: 'This is your *fis*?' 'No,' said the child, 'my *fis*.' He continued to reject the adult's imitation until he was told, 'That is your fish.' 'Yes,' he said, 'my *fis*.'

BERKO AND BROWN (1960: 531)

even at birth, but it takes some time for the infant to cotton on to this. Once it does we see the emergence of **intentional communication**. This realisation usually coincides with the development of gestures, such as pointing at, or touching, a toy, rather than stretching or trying to grab it. Such gestures are inherently symbolic. A dog or cat, for example, will look at the end of the finger being pointed, not the object. Symbolic gesturing usually begins towards the end of the first year. Soon afterwards, the child realises that it can simply make the sound without the accompanying gesture to get what it wants. Once this happens it rapidly develops what the linguist Michael Halliday (1985) calls **proto-language**. This consists of a range of invented sounds, unique to the child, which s/he has discovered can influence a parent. As we saw in Chapter 1, Halliday investigated the speech of his infant son Nigel and found that he had many different sounds, most of which could be linked to adult meanings; *na* meant 'Give me that', *yi* 'Yes I want that thing there', while other syllabic utterances meant 'I'm here', 'Let's look at this', and 'That's funny'.

But proto-language, while a significant step forward for the developing infant, is pretty limited in what it can convey. It's impossible to mean more than one thing at a time, for example, or to refer to things not present, or in the past. Even more limiting is the fact that it can usually be comprehended by only two people: the child and a parent. At around one year old the child leaves proto-language and moves into

---

Proto-language

Halliday identified seven main functions which he argued proto-language fulfilled:

i.   Instrumental: 'I want'

ii. Regulatory: 'Do as I tell you'

iii. Interactional: 'Me and you'

iv. Personal: 'Here I come'

v.   Heuristic: 'Tell me why'

vi. Imaginative: 'Let's pretend'

vii. Informative: 'I've got something to tell you'

According to Halliday the more specific linguistic functions, v, vi, and vii, develop later than the rest.

language proper. S/he leaves behind a system in which meaning and sound are directly related, for one which is mediated by an intervening layer of words (see Chapter 1). Words involve recycling a relatively small number of sounds to make an almost limitless number of words. To do that one must have a grammar. It's this leap into grammar which is unique to humans and which most children make effortlessly as they enter their second year.

The growth of language

Most of the single word utterances which children say at around 12 months consist of nouns, with verbs trailing second. This fits in with what we observed in Chapter 1 as probably the most primitive function of language: naming. But it is clear, even so, that children often mean far more by their single word utterances than the simple act of naming. The child who looks at her mother and says *shoes* has in mind an entire action: *I want my shoes* or possibly *Those are my shoes.* It's usually the parent's job to interpret these utterances and expand them into full sentences. As

> *A child when it begins to speak, learns what it is that it knows.*
>
> JOHN HALL WHEELOCK
> *A True Poem is a Way of Knowing,* 1963

we noted in Chapter 1, single words which stand for larger units in this way are termed **holophrases**. Typically, children will also under-extend a meaning at this stage, using *shoes* to mean only their own but not anybody else's. The linguists Herbert and Eva Clark (1977) report a child as using *car* at the age of nine months only for cars moving outside on the street but not for cars standing still, or in pictures, or in which she rode herself. Also frequent is the counterpart of under-extension, that is, over-extension, in which children refer to all animals as *dogs* or all men as *dad.* Learning the limits of word reference is part of the emerging semantic knowledge of the child. Interestingly, when children begin to acquire grammatical knowledge about word endings, or inflections, they typically over-extend; producing *breaked* for 'broke' and *taked* for 'took'. Such over-generalisations indicate that children are not simply copying adults since they will not have heard these forms, but generating rules of their own.

Approaching two years old, children begin to produce two-word utterances which frequently make primitive sentence structures, for example *cat jump* (subject + verb), *eat it* (verb + object) but which can also be expansions of holophrases, *more cookie, there potty.* Simple negatives also emerge, combining *no/not* with another word, *no sit, not there*, and also simple questions using intonation *Daddy gone?* After a few months these two-word utterances fill out to a kind of **telegraphic** speech, so called because they sound like the forms one finds in telegrams *Daddy got car* (subject + verb + object), *You go bed now* (subject + verb + object + adjunct). We also find some of the more regular inflections occurring for the past tense and plural, and more sophisticated questions using 'wh' words, *Where daddy gone?*

If we put the child's learning process in the context of universal grammar, then part of what the child is doing is tuning into the structure and content of his/her language. Already by year one s/he has determined which sounds are necessary even though s/he may not be able physically to make them yet. Then in years two and three the child is acquiring a lexicon, a vocabulary of words, and learning about the specific word order expected in the native language. As we saw in Chapter 5, a variety of possibilities exist in the world's languages, although many of the principal choices come down to an either/or distinction. So the child has to decide whether their language is a 'head-first' or a 'head-last' language, a 'pro-drop' or a 'null-drop' one. If we imagine starting out with a set of innate principles about language then part of what children are engaged in is adjusting the parameters of those principles according to the input they receive. After that, other things fall in or out accordingly.

In the case of English it is noticeable that children begin by learning open-class words (see Chapter 5): nouns, verbs, and adjectives. In contrast, closed-class, or function words, such as prepositions, conjunctions, determiners, and pronouns, come later. Thus the telegraphic nature of their utterances, as we have observed. What this suggests is that grammar is acquired gradually. Children are 'bootstrapping' (Aitchison, 1996)) their way into language, making do with a few grammatical distinctions, plurals, and past tenses, before acquiring the rest of the system. They also make do with a limited amount of meanings. Studies from around the world have shown that in the early stages of language acquisition children talk largely about objects, people, and actions and their interrelationships. So they are concerned with pointing things out (demonstrative function), where things are (locative function), what they are like (attributive function) and who owns them (possessive function), as well as who is doing what to whom (agentive function). These are some of the basic functions of language on which sentence relations are built. Their presence at a very early stage suggests that semantic awareness is an integral part of mental grammar. When children learn words they are slotting them into semantic categories which will form the basis of syntactic structures in their native languages.

By about four years of age children are beginning to produce full sentences with clauses strung together using linking devices, *cos*, *and*, *so* and employing many more grammatical words and morphemes. Also more frequent are adult type questions and negatives. And by five many children are in the sorting out stage, separating out irregular plurals and past tenses from regular ones: *He gave the cheese to the mice*, instead of *He gived the cheese to the mouses*. By now they are capable of expressing many more meanings than at age three and although a lot remains to be learnt, the major stages of acquisition have been accomplished. In later years they will learn more sophisticated cohesive devices to link sentences together using a greater range of conjunctions and logical hinges. They will also learn more complex patterns of clause subordination and how to produce passives. And, of course, there will be an explosion of vocabulary. By the early teens the critical period for language acquisition is over. The centres of the brain which are responsible for language are now formed and our native language is as natural to us as our clothing. At the same time, unless we are one of those fortunate children to have been brought up in a bi-lingual environment, the rest of the world's languages will always be slightly foreign, however hard we work. But what still lies ahead of us is the richness of our native language's written record and the wonders of adult literacy.

Conclusion

Human consciousness has been called the 'final frontier'. Understanding the human mind and its relation to brain function remains the holy grail of neuroscience. We have already come a long way in understanding how different parts of the brain are responsible for a variety of physical, emotional, and intellectual phenomena. But in the last analysis we are still only observing. Knowing how the brain does what it does is another matter. It may be that one day we shall have progressed far enough to translate a thought or an emotion into a chemical equation, but I doubt it. For at bottom, what we are investigating is the link between the material and the non-material world. It's an ancient quest, and one in which, despite the strides already made, considerable gaps remain. Language is at the forefront of the new brain science because, more than any other human activity, it has both a material and a non-material dimension. It's both abstract and concrete. Ironically, the evidence it is throwing up comes from examining language failure rather than success. Stroke victims and the like still form the core of much investigation. But equally, as we have seen, the study of children's amazing facility in acquiring language is offering us fresh insights into the creative capacity of the brain. At the moment our best model for this is drawn from computer science. But this discipline itself is undergoing enormous changes. The question of old has been 'what is the difference between animals and humans?' In the future, however, it may well be 'what is the difference between humans and automata?' It's a fair guess that language will be as central in facing that dilemma as it has been in facing the earlier one.

Notes

1   Some models add a further layer and suggest the presence of a lexical processor in addition to a phonological one. In this case, the job of the phonological processor is simply to identify the speech sounds and that of the lexical processor to determine the words.
2   The symbol * is used to indicate an unacceptable sequence.

7 Conclusion
The House of Being

Language is the house of being
MARTIN HEIDEGGER (*Letter on Humanism*, 1947)

Language rules, OK?

Language is the definitive human attribute on which rests our distinction from the rest of the animal kingdom. That, in a nutshell, has been the major theme of this book. In the words of the twentieth-century existentialist philosopher Martin Heidegger, language is 'the house of being', because it is in language that we live and move and have our being. But to say that, is to establish limits as well as possibilities. In Chapter 1 we saw how the evolution of our capacity for language transformed the world by enabling us to conceptualise experience in an entirely new way. 'Language endows nature with meaning' we said. Being able to name things means that objects, events, and activities exist in a coherent and orderly relation to each other, and to us. To name something is to bring it into existence cognitively. The world exists for the language user as knowledge. At the same time, however, it's important to remember that things are not meaningless in the absence of language. It would be an enormous act of hubris to maintain that. One of the themes of this book, alongside the transformative power of words, has also been their limitations. We can never really know things in themselves. We can only know them, as the philosopher Immanuel Kant argued, as we experience them to be. Language helps us to articulate, reflect upon, and communicate experience, but it does so by providing us with a substitute for it. It's inevitably experience at one remove. The world that is named is also the world that is tamed. 'How do you know', asks the poet William Blake, in one of his sudden bursts of illumination 'but that ev'ry bird that cuts the airy way, is an immense world of delight, clos'd by your senses five?' The answer, of course, is that we don't.

Houses, as Heidegger knew full well, are not only places to live in, they are also places of confinement. They are as much containers, privileged spaces with their own barriers, as well as their own freedoms. Every day of our lives we are faced with the twin problems both of expressing what we mean and of conveying that meaning to others. The choices which we have at each stage of this process are staggering: choices of words, syntax, intonation, medium, to name a few. And at the same time we have to negotiate what is being communicated to us and respond appropriately. Even in the simplest conversation we are engaged in very complex discourse strategies. At a minimum these will include monitoring what we have just said, assembling items for our current utterance, and planning ahead for future ones. No wonder there are so many false starts, hesitations, and sentence fillers. Using language, in other words, although a great boon, is also a great worry.

All of which makes it surprising that we use language as much as we do. It's a phenomenon that Susan Blackmore explores in her book *The Meme Machine.* 'Why,' she asks 'do we talk so much?' Like all apparently artless questions – 'why is there something rather than nothing?' 'Why can't I feel someone else's pain?' – the question is not as odd as it seems. We know that all communication takes an enormous amount of energy, particularly talking. And yet a considerable part of each day is spent in an activity which, strictly speaking, is probably expendable. Most of us are inclined to be lazy but, despite this, we are compulsive communicators. It may be, as we discussed in Chapter 1, that our need for language is linked to the evolutionary demands of living in large groups. We need language to service our relationships. But there is an alternative possibility, which is that rather than us using language, language uses us. Most of us at some point in our everyday experience have the uncanny feeling that we are not in our right minds; more particularly, that we are not in control of our minds. In the case of some unfortunate people this experience is so overwhelming that they feel someone else is in control: they are classified as schizophrenic. But in a milder manner it is the common lot of us all. The scientist Richard Dawkins, a person one would expect to exhibit a high degree of mental control, is on record as saying he is sometimes prevented from sleeping by a tune which comes unbidden into his head. The surprising thing about this melody is that it is not one he likes, quite the reverse. In some way it has infected his mind like a virus. This is a simple instance of something which happens all the time. Things swim into our minds, apparently from nowhere, and proceed to take them over. On occasions the consequences can be extraordinarily creative. The entire plot of the Harry Potter books came to the novelist J.K. Rowling on a train journey looking out of a window, thinking of nothing in particular. Such an experience is technically called **autocatalytic**. In other words, ideas give birth to new ideas of their own volition. It is what we mean by creativity. In the past, writers have spoken of feeling inspired and have invoked the muse, and, sometimes, God.

In recent years these experiences have become the source of a new approach to the transmission of knowledge called **memetics**. **Memes** are units of information which have the power of self-replication. The novelist Victor Hugo said 'nothing can resist an idea whose time has come'. From this perspective almost anything has the potential to be a meme. If we think of the things which possibly make up our own mental landscape – belief in equality, the importance of family, the power of love – in many cases they are things we have acquired without realising it; 'a style/Our lives bring with them' the poet Philip Larkin calls them. It isn't until we are forced to inspect them under the stress of experience, or through some process of critical enquiry, that their meme-like status emerges. According to memeticists ideas and beliefs are caught not taught. Certain things take hold because it is in their nature to do so. They spread from mind to mind contagiously. Originally, their power derives from the way they correspond to fundamental human needs and drives: the need for food, shelter, respect, and love. But once generated they become self-sustaining. We build churches, go to war, and write masterpieces in their name. And memes also sometimes die. They go out of fashion, lose their currency, or in some cases manage to reinvent themselves.

What has all of this to do with language? Simply this: in memetic theory language is one of the principal ways by which memes are spread. We have only to think how much of our conversation is constructed out of acquired phrases and ritualised expressions copied unthinkingly. Much of the phatic language we touched on in Chapter 3 is of this sort. Expressions such as *at the end of the day, in the nick of time* and *it's not rocket science,* are used by people who don't know anything about rocket science let alone what a 'nick' is. We think in formulaic utterances which operate as a verbal shorthand for more complex ideas. *Take care, Have a nice day,* and *Alright?* are the convenience food of the linguistic world which have replicated themselves successfully across social, class and gender boundaries to the broad generality of native English speakers. Personally we may not like them, but it doesn't stop us using them.

Memes spread because our minds are geared to learn by imitation. Humans are great copiers. We copy gestures, facial expressions, and sounds. These are passed on from parent to offspring quite unconsciously. Indeed a good percentage of everything we do and say is imitated. Not unnaturally, some theorists have drawn a comparison here between memes and those other great replicators, genes. Just as genes produce biological copies, memes produce cultural ones. Unlike genes however, we do not know what memes are made of, nor where they live in the human brain. No one has yet cracked the memetic code in the way geneticists have the genetic code. All we can do at present is use the idea as a metaphor to explain the way humans have culturally evolved. Even so, it remains an intriguing and fertile possibility. If we think for a moment of the genetic distinction between phenotypes and genotypes it fits quite neatly the different types of culturally copyable information. In biological terms genotypes are the set of coded instructions contained within the gene for producing our bodies. Successful codes are copied across generations and result in the family resemblances we see in photographs and pictures. Phenotypes are the particular outcomes of those instructions, the long noses, fair hair, and brown eyes of individual family members.

Most of the time all we can do with memes is track their phenotypes as they spread horizontally across societies and vertically down the generations. This is what linguists do when they look at stylistic usages, accent patterns, dialectal varieties and so forth. These are features which are 'caught' and transmitted by social contact. But the linguist is ultimately interested in the genotype, the underlying code which generates these phenotypes. It's here that meme theory is interesting because it suggests two ways in which information is passed between minds. Richard Dawkins (in Blackmore, S., 1999) illustrates the difference between these by analogy with the children's game of Chinese whispers. If we imagine a drawing of a Chinese junk shown to a child, who is asked to make her own copy of it, and that copy being shown in turn to a second child who is asked to make a copy, and so on until the twentieth child, the resulting picture is likely to be unrecognisable. Copies of copies inevitably result in considerable degradation. This kind of copying is how some people used to think children learnt their native language. They simply learnt to imitate what they heard around them. But it has a very low success rate. A more successful way of passing information is to pass on the instructions: the genotype. To go back to the Chinese junk analogy. If the first child is shown how to construct a paper junk and then when she has mastered the technique shows the second child how to make one, and so on down the line, then, although individual junks may vary in quality, there is every possibility of the twentieth being as good as the first.

So what we do when we acquire our native languages is to copy the set of instructions for producing it. But the difference between this and the Chinese junk analogy is that we do so, not by being explicitly shown how, but by exposure to the actual phenotypes. The genotype makes a copy of itself almost automatically. Our minds are literally taken over. In other words, language is transmitted memetically. If this is so it is an important qualification to the current genetic hypothesis of how we acquire language. This, as we have seen in earlier chapters, proposes that language is coded into our genes so that we are born primed for language. But it doesn't say anything about *how* it is encoded. What memeticists like Susan Blackmore suggest is that the code is in the form of memes, that is, that genes are the carriers of memes. In which case it may be that evolution is meme driven rather than gene driven. In other words, that genes are the agents of change, rather than the cause of it. All of this is highly speculative. But as we enter a new millennium speculation is fast becoming the order of the day. Theories about the existence of parallel universes and the possibility of time going backwards are aired with increasing frequency by serious academics. We are becoming used to the possibility that our universe is stranger than we previously thought. It now looks, for example, as though our solar system is uniquely geared towards the creation of life: that we live in a designer universe. Just what this means for other planetary systems is unclear but as far as our own is concerned it is likely to have consequences for our received view of our origin, and ultimate destiny. Some years ago the scientist Carl Sagan imagined an alien spacecraft surveying our planet from outside the earth's atmosphere and trying to establish who the inhabitants of this new planet were. He suggested they would come to the conclusion we were made of metal, were capable of moving at speeds of up to 70 miles an hour and lived in convoys. To a large extent we see in nature what we are capable of seeing. We shall probably not get to the point suggested by Douglas Adams in *The Hitchhiker's Guide to the Galaxy* of regarding the earth as a giant computer designed by mice to discover the answer to life, the universe, and everything, but, just possibly, we may discover that what drives evolution forwards is not the selfish gene but the selfish meme, that is, that our world is sustained by the transmission of information, a suspicion some of us have had for a while. Paradoxically, it may be that evolution's greatest triumph has been the production of beings capable of understanding it. Since the evolution memeplex[1] was let out of its box by Darwin it has proceeded to dominate the mental landscape of the western world. The key agent of that domination has been language.

The future of language

But while language itself has taken over the world, individual languages are in a much less healthy state. 'Globalisation' is a phenomenon with potentially massive consequences for linguistic diversity. Estimates of the number of languages in the world vary from between 3000 and 10,000, but if we take a mid-point, then there are probably between 6000 and 7000 languages. The majority of these, according to the Foundation for Endangered Languages, are 'vulnerable not just to decline but to extinction' (Crystal, 2000). 'Language death' as it has come to be called is one of the more recent phenomena of our time. At the beginning of the twenty-first century we have a rapidly growing world population (around six billion) and a steadily diminishing number of languages. According to David Crystal four per cent of the world's languages (about 25) are spoken by 96 per cent of the population. Of the 6–7000 languages around the world, 4000 are spoken by less than 20,000 people and a quarter are spoken by fewer than 1000. Over the course of this century experts estimate that something like two languages will die out every month. There is, as Crystal points out, the distinct possibility of half the world's languages disappearing by the year 2100, and of a world with only one language a few hundred years hence.

Should any of this matter? If it's possible for a single language to fulfil all our language needs, then surely we shouldn't worry about the disappearance of a few thousand minority languages around the world. We might indeed be able to reverse the curse of Babel. But it's important to disentangle the issues here. There's a very good case for an international lingua franca in the modern world. The last time the European world had such a language was several hundred years ago. Then Latin was the language which scholars, gentlemen, and merchants used to communicate across ethnic and national boundaries. The success of Latin was due originally to the success of the Roman empire in dominating and subjugating nations world wide. After the demise of the Romans it remained for centuries as the lingua franca of Europe, largely because it was the language of literature and religion.

The offices and services of the Catholic Church, which up until the end of the medieval period moulded the spiritual and intellectual life of Europe, were all in Latin. Today, English looks most likely to step into the vacuum left by the long, slow death of Latin. Like Latin it has become an international language as a consequence of imperial conquest. The British empire of the nineteenth century was the largest the world had ever seen, spreading English to the four corners of the globe. With the dismantling of that empire we might have expected English to shrink back again, but it had the fortune to be at the forefront of another kind of conquest. The economic muscle of America saw to it that English became, from the 1950s onwards, the most important language internationally, in the fields of commerce, technology, and education.

The lesson of all this is that the success and survival of languages depend on commercial and political power. The centralisation of power which is taking place globally is one of the principal reasons why so many smaller languages are threatened with extinction. But the emergence of a lingua franca doesn't of itself mean that other languages have to die. We need a lingua franca in today's world as an aid to intelligibility, but languages fulfil other needs too. One of these is the need for personal and social identity. Language is a major force in expressing people's sense of rootedness. Indeed, as David Crystal points out, there is plenty of evidence of languages diverging rather than converging. For a long time the people of Yugoslavia spoke a language called Serbo-Croatian, but since the bloody civil wars of the last decade of the twentieth century, the various ethnic groups have begun to diverge linguistically: the Bosnians call their language Bosnian, the Croats call theirs Croatian, and the Serbs call theirs Serbian. And in Scandinavia, although Danish, Norwegian, and Swedish are largely mutually intelligible, speakers see the varieties as separate languages, and they are regarded, internationally, as such. Our sense of who we are, both as individuals, and as members of social and cultural groups, is signalled by our language. As the American academic Christopher Looby comments, nations are 'made' not 'born', 'And they are made, ineluctably, in language.' All languages are different. Obviously so, in terms of their vocabulary and pronunciation, but also in terms of their grammar and usage. It is possible to say things in one language which are very difficult in another. According to the novelist E.M. Forster 'Nothing will translate' the Italian word *sympatico* (*Where Angels Fear to Tread*). The best Forster can offer us is a lengthy paraphrase by one of his characters: 'The person who understands us at first sight, who never irritates us, who never bores, to whom we can pour forth every thought and wish, not only in speech but in silence – that is what I mean by sympatico.'

The need to differentiate our language from that of others is equally as strong, if not stronger than, our desire to speak with one tongue. There is undoubtedly a tribal element to language, as there is with most other facets of our social existence, from supporting football teams to following New Age movements. The important thing is not to allow tribalism to close down the natural avenues by which languages change and develop. France, for example has recently tried to protect its language from the inroads of English by passing a law making it illegal to use an English word, in official contexts, where a perfectly good French word exists. We can find similar anxieties among British people who object to American vocabulary pushing aside native English terms (*truck* instead of *lorry*, *elevator* instead of *lift*). But lan-

---

Evidentials

All languages have their own idiosyncrasies. Tuyuca, a South American language, has a system of evidentials which allows speakers to indicate the evidence for statements being made. In the following example the basic translation is 'He played soccer', but the small particle at the end enables an additional meaning to be conveyed:

Visual:	*diiga ape-wi*
	'I saw him play soccer'
Non-visual:	*diiga ape-ti*
	'I heard the game and him, but I didn't see it or him'
Apparent:	*diiga ape-yi*
	'I have seen evidence that he played soccer – such as his clothes in the changing room – but I did not see him play'
Secondhand:	*diiga ape-yigi*
	'I obtained information that he played soccer from someone else'
Assumed:	*diiga ape-hiyi*
	'It is reasonable to assume that he played soccer'

CRYSTAL, 2000

guage invasions are one of the ways in which healthy languages expand. The history of English is largely the story of periodic invasions in which vocabulary items from all over the globe have been silently assimilated into the word hoard. Native speakers can justly echo the words of the Romanian proverb, 'Our language is one great salad'.

Throughout the world languages are fighting for survival against pressures deriving ultimately from the power bases of a global market economy. But, equally, the world is experiencing an unprecedented growth in demands for greater regional and sub-regional autonomy and for recognition of the rights of minorities. Language is at the forefront of this battle, and is in many respects a mirror of it. What the future holds is uncertain, but experience suggests that, for an ever increasing number of us, it will be bilingual, that a lingua franca, based on some kind of global English, will co-exist alongside a resurgence of interest in mother tongue languages. If so, it will be a situation strangely reminiscent of the end of the Middle Ages when all over Europe, national languages emerged from under the shadow of Latin. The world will probably never get back to its pre-Babel days. We define ourselves as much by our differences as our similarities. That is a key factor in our humanity. And one which should enable us to see what happened at Babel as a blessing, not a curse. Should we be in danger of thinking otherwise there is the salutary lesson of the babel fish in Douglas Adams's *The Hitchhiker's Guide to the Galaxy*. The babel fish is an automatic translation device which, when inserted into the ear, enables what is said to be heard in the listener's native language. Unfortunately, Adams comments, 'by effectively removing all barriers to communication between different races and cultures [the babel fish] has caused more and bloodier wars than anything else in the history of creation'.

Accepting change

The key challenge for all of us in the new millennia will be to live with change. Technology is transforming our lives at an alarming pace and its effect on language is proving to be just as transformatory. 'Living languages are in a continuous state of change,' comments the writer Peter Howard, 'Only dead languages stay still.' But change, as we know from other areas of life, is not always comfortable. It's often tempting to look back to a golden age, when things seemed better. And so it is sometimes with language. Conservative writers frequently talk about declining standards and hark back to periods of British national life when language appeared to be more under control. But if you examine any period of history closely enough you see there has never been a time when controversies about language use have not worried people. As long ago as the fourteenth century, in his translation of a Latin work called *Polychronicon*, John of Trevisa was lamenting that 'the language of the land is impaired and some use strange stammering, chattering, snarling and harsh gnashing'. And, for some people, not a lot has changed. If we were to narrow down attitudes to language we could probably do so in terms of two competing myths. One is that languages, rather like wine, improve with age. They get larger vocabularies, and richer, more varied, means of expression. The difficulty with this view is that languages do not progress in the way the sciences do. We can say that physics post-Einstein is an improvement on Newtonian physics as an explanation of how the universe works. But how can we measure contemporary English against Elizabethan, or neoclassical English? All we can say is that certain possibilities existed then which don't now, and vice versa. The same goes for the second myth, namely, that languages decline with age. Since the time of Samuel Johnson this has arguably been the dominant view among traditional grammarians, and it would probably be echoed widely in the popular mind. But, again, it repeats the mistake of the first in thinking of language as some kind of substance which must either improve or degenerate. Both myths are effectively twin sides of the same coin, and the debate between them is as fruitless as trying to decide whether we are better human beings now than we were in the past. If we need a myth of language to sustain us then we could do worse than adopt the one suggested by T.S. Eliot, 'Our language, or any civilized language,' he says, 'is like the phoenix: it springs anew from its own ashes.' Rather than seeing languages as progressing or decaying we should see them as in a constant state of renewal. That at least would be truer to the creative principle which informs them.

Languages change because of two sorts of reasons. The first are 'language internal' and have to do with the particular mechanics of a language, its sound system grammatical distinctions, and semantic possibilities. The second are 'language external', and are a consequence of the social, political, and cultural changes which affect its users: invasions, discoveries, Acts of Parliament, diseases, inventions, and so forth. The interaction of internal and external pressures on English over the centuries has produced a language of extraordinary range and flexibility. It has, as we know, become a world language on a scale no one could have foreseen. As such the current pressures on it are of an almost incalculable kind. There is an irony in all of this, which is that just as the nation responsible for English is declining in importance its language is becoming more widespread. If, as the linguist R.M. Dixon says 'A language is the emblem of its speakers', we must expect enormous changes from this turn in the fortunes of English. To return to the words of Eliot: 'For last year's words belong to last year's language/And next year's words await another voice.' (*Four Quartets*).

Note

1   The name given by meme theorists to a group of related memes.

Bibliography

Aitchison, J. (1987) *Words in the Mind: An Introduction to the Mental Lexicon* (Oxford: Blackwell).

Aitchison, J. (1996) *The Seeds of Speech* (Cambridge: Cambridge University Press).

Attridge, D. (1982) *The Rhythms of English Poetry* (London and New York: Longman).

Austin, J.L. (1962) *How to do Things with Words*, eds Urmson, J. and Sbisa, M. (Oxford: Clarendon Press).

Baron, N. (1981) *Speech, Writing, and Sign: A Functional View of Linguistic Representation* (Bloomington: Indiana University Press).

Bateson, G. (1972) *Steps to an Ecology of Mind* (San Francisco: Chandler Publishing Company).

Berko, J. and Brown, R. (1960) 'Psycholinguistic research methods'. In Mussen, P.H. (ed.) *Handbook of Research Methods in Child Development* (New York: Wiley).

Berne, E. (1968) *Games People Play* (London: Penguin).

Blackmore, S. (1999) *The Meme Machine* (Oxford: Oxford University Press).

Bloom, H. (1998) *Shakespeare: The Invention of the Human* (New York: Riverhead Books).

Bloom, R., Borod, J., Obler, L. and Gerstman, L. (1992) 'Impact of emotional content on discourse production in patients with unilateral brain damage', *Brain and Language*, 42(2): 153–64.

Bloomfield, L. (1933) *Language* (New York: Holt, Rinehart & Winston).

Brooks, R.R. and Wakanker, V.S. (1976) *Stone Age Painting in India* (New Haven, CT: Yale University Press).

Brown, K. and Miller, J. (1991) *Syntax: A Linguistic Introduction to Sentence Structure* (London: Routledge).

Byrne, R. and Whiten, A. (eds) (1988) *Machiavellian Intelligence* (Oxford: Oxford University Press).

Cheney, D.L. and Seyfarth, R.M. (1990) *How Monkeys See The World* (Chicago: Chicago University Press).

Clanchy, M. (1993) *From Memory to Written Record* (Oxford: Blackwell).

Clark, H. and Clark, E. (1977) *Psychology and Language: An Introduction to Language* (New York: Harcourt Brace Jovanovich).

Coates, J. (1986) *Women, Men and Language* (London: Longman).

Corballis, M. (2002) *From Hand to Mouth: The Origins of Language* (Princeton and Oxford: Princeton University Press).

Coupland, N. and Jaworski, A. (eds) (1997) *Sociolinguistics: A Reader and Coursebook* (London: Macmillan – now Palgrave Macmillan).

221

Crystal, D. (1987) *The Cambridge Encyclopedia of Language* (Cambridge: Cambridge University Press).

Crystal, D. (1995) *The Cambridge Encyclopedia of The English Language* (Cambridge: Cambridge University Press).

Crystal, D. (2000) *Language Death* (Cambridge: Cambridge University Press).

Crystal, D. and Crystal, H. (2000) *Words on Words: Quotations about Language and Languages* (London: Penguin).

Dawkins, R. (1998) *Unweaving The Rainbow* (London: Penguin).

Dunbar, R. (1996) *Grooming, Gossip and the Evolution of Language* (London: Faber and Faber).

Fairclough, N. (1996) 'Border crossings: discourse and social change in contemporary societies'. In *Change and Language*, BAAL 10 (Clevedon: Multilingual Matters).

Fasold, R. (1990) *The Sociolinguistics of Language* (Oxford: Blackwell).

Firth, J.R. (1937) *The Tongues of Men* (London: Watts).

Fish, S. (1989) *Doing What Comes Naturally* (Oxford: Clarendon Press).

Fishman, P. (1980) 'Conversational insecurity'. In Giles, H., Robinson, W.P. and Smith, P. (eds) *Language: Social Psychological Perspectives* (Oxford: Pergamon Press).

Fishman, P. (1983) 'Interaction: the work women do'. In Thorne, B., Kramarae, C. and Henley, N. (eds) *Language, Gender and Society* (Rowley, MA: Newbury House).

Frances, N.W. (1967) *The English Language: An Introduction* (London: English Universities Press).

Freeborn, D. (1986) *A Course Book in English Grammar* (London: Macmillan – now Palgrave Macmillan).

Freeborn, D. (1992) *From Old English to Standard English* (London: Macmillan – now Palgrave Macmillan).

Freeborn, D., French, P. and Langford, D. (1993) *Varieties of English*, 2nd edn (London: Macmillan – now Palgrave Macmillan).

Gardner, H., Brownell, H., Prather, P. and Martino, G. (1994) 'Language, communication, and the right hemisphere'. In Kirshner, H.S. (ed.) *Handbook of Neurological Speech and Language Disorders* (New York: Marcel Dekker).

Goodman, S. and Graddol, D. (eds) (1996) *Redesigning English: New Texts, New Identities* (London: Routledge).

Gregory, M. and Carroll, S. (1978) *Language and Situation* (London: Routledge & Kegan Paul).

Griaule, M. (1998) 'Weaving and the word'. In Rasula, J. and McCaffery, S. (eds) *Imagining Language: An Anthology* (Cambridge, MA: MIT Press).

Grice, P. (1991) *Studies in the Way of Words* (Harvard: Harvard University Press).

Halliday, M.A.K. (1985) *Spoken and Written Language* (Melbourne: Deakin University Press).

Howard, P. (1986) *The State of the Language* (London: Penguin).

Hymes, D. (1962) 'The ethnography of speaking'. In Gladwin, T. and Sturtevant, W. (eds) *Anthropology and Human Behaviour* (Washington, DC: Anthropological Society of Washington. Also in Fishman, J. (ed.) (1968) *Readings in The Sociology of Language* (The Hague: Mouton).

Hymes, D. (1972) 'Models of the interaction of language and social life'. In Gumperz, J. and Hymes, D. (eds) *Directions in Sociolinguistics* (Oxford: Blackwell).

Jackendoff, R. (1993) *Patterns in the Mind: Language and Human Nature* (London: Harvester).

Jesperson, O. (1922) *Language: Its Nature, Development and Origin* (Oxford: Oxford University Press).

Johnson, M. (1987) *The Body in the Mind: The Bodily Basis of Meaning, Imagination and Reason* (Chicago: University of Chicago Press).

Johnson, S. in Bronson, B.H. (ed.)(1958) *Samuel Johnson: Rasselas, Poems and Selected Prose* (New York: Holt, Rinehart & Winston).

Joyce, J. (1966) *A Portrait of the Artist as a Young Man* (London: Penguin).

Keller, H. (1923) *The Story of My Life* (London: Harrap & Co.).

Knight, C. (1990) *Blood Relations; Menstruation and the Origins of Culture* (New Haven, CT: Yale University Press).

Lakoff, G. and Johnson, M. (1980) *Metaphors We Live By* (Chicago: University of Chicago Press).

Lakoff, R. (1975) *Language and Woman's Place* (New York: HarperCollins).

Leech, G.N. (1966) *English in Advertising: A Linguistic Study of Advertising in Great Britain* (London: Longman).

Leech, G.N. (1983) *Principles of Pragmatics* (London: Longman).

Leet-Pellegrini, H. (1980) 'Conversational dominance as a function of gender and expertise'. In Giles, H. Robinson, W.P. and Smith, P. (eds) *Language: Social Psychological Perspectives* (Oxford: Pergamon Press).

Lieberman, P. (1998) *Eve Spoke: Human Language and Human Evolution* (London: Norton & Co.).

Lloyd, G.E.R. (1990) *Demystifying Mentalities* (Cambridge: Cambridge University Press).

Locke, J. ([1690]1964) *An Essay Concerning Human Understanding*, Woozley, A.D. (ed.) (London: Fontana).

Manguel, A. (1996) *A History of Reading* (London: Collins).

Obler, L.K. and Gjerlow, K. (1999) *Language and the Brain* (Cambridge: Cambridge University Press).

Olson, D.R. (1994) *The World on Paper* (Cambridge: Cambridge University Press).

Ong, W. (1982) *Orality and Literacy* (London: Methuen).

Pinker, S. (1994) *The Language Instinct* (London: Penguin).

Pinter, H. (1968) *A Slight Ache and other Plays* (London: Methuen).

Quirk, R. (1962) *The Use of English* (London: Longman).

Radford, A. (1988) *Transformational Grammar a First Course* (Cambridge: Cambridge University Press).

Radford, A. (1999) *Linguistics: An Introduction* (Cambridge: Cambridge University Press).

Schneiderman, E. and Saddy, J.D. (1988) 'A linguistic deficit resulting from right-hemisphere damage', *Brain and Language*, 34: 38–53.

Schultz, M. (1975) 'The semantic derogation of woman'. In Thorne, B. and Henley, N. (eds) *Language and Sex: Difference and Dominance* (Rowley, MA: Newbury House).

Searle, J.R. (1976) The classification of illocutionary acts', *Language and Society*, 5: 1–23. Reprinted in *Expression and Meaning: Studies in the Meaning of Speech Acts* (Cambridge: Cambridge University Press, 1979).

Sperber, D. and Wison, D. (1986) *Relevance: Communication and Cognition* (Oxford: Blackwell).

Talbot, M. (1998) *Language and Gender: An introduction* (Cambridge: Polity Press).

Toolan, M. (1996) *Total Speech: An Integrational Linguistic Approach to Language* (North Carolina: Duke University Press).

Trudgill, P. (1983) *On Dialect: Social and Geographical Perspectives* (Oxford: Basil Blackwell).

Trudgill, P. (1990) *The Dialects of England* (Oxford: Blackwell).

West, C. and Zimmerman, D. (1983) 'Small insults: a study of interruptions in cross-sex conversations between unacquainted persons'. In Thorne, B., Kramarae, C. and Henley, N. (eds) *Language Gender and Society* (Rowley, MA: Newbury House).

Index

A

Adams, D., 214
accent, 119–20
acceptability
in language, 146
accommodation theory, 60, 127
Achard, M., 139
Adams, D., 214, 218
agrammatism, 179
Aitchison, J., 6, 8, 17, 25, 162, 164, 186, 194, 207
alphabet
history of, 100–4
Anglo-Saxon
highly inflected, 159–60
aphasia
Broca's, 177, 179–80
conduction, 183
Wernicke's, 180–1
arbitrariness
concept of, 149
association
power of, 46–9
Attridge, D., 31
Auden, W.H., 88, 173
Augustine, St. *The Confessions*, 92
Austen, J., 64
Austin, J.L., *How to do Things with Words*, 65
autism, 19–20

B

babel fish, 218
Bakhtin, M., 3
Baron, N., 38
Bateson, G., 38
Berko, J., 204
Berne, E., 108
Bernstein, B., 90
Bishop Wilkins, 150
Blackmore, S., 211, 213, 214
Blake, W., 210

Bleasdale, A., 122
Bloom, H., 95,
Bloom, R., 185
Bloomfield, L., 161
Bodine, A., 134
border crossing, 75
brain
assymetry of, 182–3
and language, 176–82
left hemisphere
dominance, 182–6
right hemisphere
processing, 184–6
size important for
language, 4–5
Broca, P., 176–7
Broca's area, 177
Brooks, R., 96
Brown, K., 195
Byrne, D., 18
Burgess, A., 35

C

Carroll, L., *Through the Looking Glass*, 43
case
property of language, 159–60
Cheney, D., 12
children's truce terms, 131
chimpanzees
and language, 28–9
Chomsky, N., 119, 146, 148, 166, 168, 169, 191, 201
Clanchy, M., 88, 93
Clark, H. and E., 206
coarticulation, 144
Coates, J., 137
collocation, 48
communication
language and, 34–71
non-verbal, 38
paralinguistic, 38, 56
competence,

communicative, 54–60, 113, 116, 170, 186
linguistic, 13, 39, 90, 143–4, 159, 186
Condillac, 21
Conrad, J., 1, 17
constituents, 153, 158
convergence, 60
cookie theft picture, 179
cooperative principle, 60–4
Corballis, M., 30
covert prestige, 122–3
Crystal, D., 99, 133, 160, 215, 216, 217

D

Dawkins, R., 25, 211, 213
dialect, 119–20
different from 'language', 131–2
dialect continuum, 130
dialect mapping, 130–2
Dickinson, E., 72
diglossia, 120
displacement, 12, 33
Dixon, R.M., 220
double articulation, 25–6, 33
double negative, 122, 146
duality of patterning, 145
Dunbar, R., 4, 5, 10–12, 15, 22

E

Egyptian hieroglyphics, 100
elaborate code, 91
electronic-mail, 80–5
Eliot, G., 19
Eliot, T.S., 34, 53, 219, 220
estuary English, 124, 125, 129
ethnography of
communication, 111–12

evidentials, 217
evolution
  genetic variation in, 8–9
  significance of climate
    change for, 9–10

F

Fairclough, N., 75
Fasold, R., 110, 111, 113,
  118, 135, 136, 138, 139
Faulkner, W., 64
Feiffer, J., 36, 133
Field, E., 145
figurative language, 50–3
Firth, J., 48, 101
'fis' phenomenon, 204
Fish, S., 56
Fishman, P., 138, 139
foregrounding, 57
Forster, E.M., 216–7
Francis, N., 44
Freeborn, D., 75, 121, 127,
  130
Fry, S., 81–3

G

Gardner, H., 185
gender pattern, 139–41
'Genie', 202
genetic hypothesis, 201
gesture
  inherently symbolic, 205
  inspiration for language,
    30
Giles, H., 127
given/new, 171
Gjerlow, K., 178, 181
glottal stop, 124, 125
Golding, W., *The
  Inheritors*, 5
Goodall, J., 22, 29
Goodman, S., 82, 83, 85
Goody, J., 87
Graddol, D., 82, 83, 85
grammar
  communicative, 169–72
  constituent structure,
    167
  functional, 171–2
  generative, 157
  knowledge of, 145–8
  mental, 200

is organic, 147
  related to glamour,
    172–3
  transformational, 167–9
  universal, 162
Gregory, M., 90
Griaule, M., 3
Grice, P., 60
  maxims of cooperation,
    185–6
grooming
  and language, 14–17

H

Halliday, M., 12–14, 171,
  205
Heidegger, M., 210
high amplitude sucking,
  202
Holmes, O.W., 44, 57
holophrastic utterances, 26,
  206
Householder, F., 59
Howard, P., 149, 218
Hugo, V., 212
Humboldt, W. Von, 149
Hymes, D., 111, 114
hypertext, 78–80

I

idiolect, 3
image schemas, 53
implicature, 60
inference, 58–60
inflection, 160, 163
isoglosses, 130–1

J

Jackendoff, R., 180, 183,
  189, 190, 193, 201
Jakobson, R., 163, 182
Johnson, M., 50–3
Johnson, S., 44, 104, 106,
  219
Jonson, B., 148, 175
Joyce, J., *A Portrait of the
  Artist as a Young Man*,
  40

K

Keller, H., 27–8
Kierkegaard, S., 63
Knight, C., 31

L

Labov, W., 119, 124–7,
  139, 141
Lakoff, G., 50–31, 153
Lakoff, R., 134–5, 137
language,
  an artificial sign system,
    40
  and the brain, 3–5
  like chess, 26, 148
  considered magical, 2
  descent of, 10–14
  design features of, 33
  and discrimination,
    132–3
  the 'dress of thought',
    194
  electronic, 76–80
  future of, 215–18
  and gender, 134–41
  and gesture, 30
  and lying, 17
  is modular, 153–4
  nineteenth–century
    explanations of, 11
  phatic, 16, 107–9, 212,
  rules of, 147
  slipperiness of, 36–7
  and thought, 24–6,
    192–4
language acquisition,
  200–8
  first year of, 203–6
  holophrases, 206
  telegraphic speech, 207
language death, 215
language processing,
  186–97
  parallel-interactive
    model, 196
  serial-autonomous
    model, 196
language universals,
  159–66
  implicational chains, 164
  noun phrase accessibility
    hierarchy, 164
Larkin, P., 154, 212
larynx, 6–7
Leech, G., 63, 69, 74, 170

left brain hemisphere, 182–6
lexicon, 41, 153
linguistic variables, 124
literacy
  inherently dynamic, 88
  origins of, 95–100
  psycho dynamics of, 87
  restructures consciousness, 95
Lloyd, G., 103
Locke, J., *An Essay Concerning Human Understanding*, 36
logic
  formal, 54
  natural, 55
logical connectives, 54
logical form, 167
logograms, 86, 103
Looby, C., 216
'Lucy', 5–10
Luria, A., 89

M
Malagasy
  information concealment in, 111
Malinowski, B., 16, 31, 107–8
Manguel, A., 92
maximum variation of function, 121
Mcluhan, M., 37, 74
McNeill, D., 201
meaning
  conceptual, 47
  connotative, 47
  denotative, 46
  exists separately from language, 191–2
  importance of context, 37–8
  indeterminacy of, 39, 60
  problem of interpretation, 38
Melanesian
  number system, 164
  pronoun system, 161
memetics, 212–15
mentalese, 167, 194
Meredith, G., 109

metaphor, 50–3
Miller, J., 195
Mills, C.W., 127
Milroy, L., 140–1
minimum variation of form, 121
mind
  definition of, 175–6
mood, 66–7
multi-media texts, 80

N
names
  the power of, 26–9
Neolithic revolution, 95
Newman, R., 56
non-prevocalic 'r', 126–7, 128, 129
non-standard English, 121
noun
  abstract, 43
  proper, 43

O
Obler, L., 178, 181
observer's paradox, 127
Olson, D., 88, 90, 94, 96, 97, 98
Ong, W., 74, 86, 87, 88, 94, 95, 102
onomatopoeia, 40
orality
  secondary, 74
Orwell, G., 36, 193
  newspeak, 36
over-extension, 206

P
Page, Le, 128
paradigmatic, 150
paralanguage, 31
paralinguistic function, 38, 56
participant observation, 127
Pelligrini, L., 139
Perelman, S.J., 108
performance, 144
phatic language, 16, 107–9, 212
phoneme, 144, 152, 203
phonograms, 99
phonotactics, 152

phrase
  noun, 156
  prepositional, 156
  verb, 156
pictograms, 98–9
Pinker, S., 106, 167, 194
Pinter, H., 109–10
politeness principal, 63, 69
Polychronicon, 219
Preisler, P., 138
presupposition, 57–9
principles-and-parameters theory, 166
print,
  anonymity of, 77
  development of, 91–5
  psychodynamics of, 95
prosody, 56
proto-language, 13, 22, 205
proto-writing, 99
public colloquial style, 170

Q
Quirk, R., 108, 194–5

R
Radford, A., 153, 198
reading
  private compared to communal, 92–3
Reagan, R., 121
received pronunciation, 125
reference, 41–2
  endophoric, 90
  exophoric, 90
register, 48–9
relative clause
  occurrence in language, 164–5
restricted code, 91
Rich, A., 50
right brain hemisphere, 184–6
Rosetta Stone, 100
Rowling, J.K., 212

S
Saddy, J., 186
Sagan, C., 214
Sankoff, G., 140

Sapir–Whorf hypothesis, 192
Saussure, F. de., 41–2, 150, 152, 154, 182
Schneiderman, E., 186
Schultz, M., 137
Searle, J.R., 65
selection restrictions, 154
semantic features, 47
semantic fields, 49
semantic space, 43
sense, 42–3
  conceptual, 47
  and force, 55
  grammatical, 43
  lexical, 43
  relations, 45–6
sentences
  complex, 157
  constituents of, 155
  garden path, 197
  kernel, 166,
  major/minor, 170
  traditional definitions of, 170
  units of style, 170
Seyfarth, R., see Cheney
Shakespeare, W., 57, 95
Shaw, B., 104
signification, 41–2
signifier/signified, 42
signs
  words are, 39–41
Snow, J., 83
social networks, 141–2
sociolinguistics, 119–23
speech
  errors, 198–200
  public colloquial, 74

scripted, 72–6
and writing, 85–91
speech acts, 55, 64–70, 74
speech communities, 71, 112–14
Sperber, D., 52
Spooner, Rev. W., 199
standard variety
  of language, 121–2, 146
Stoppard, T., 143
structuralism, 45
style-shifting, 124
syllabaries, 103
syntagmatic, 150
syntax, 152

T
tactical deception, 22–3
Talbot, M., 134
Taylor, B.L., 108
texting, 84–5
thematic arrangement, 57
theme/rheme, 171
theory of mind, 18–24, 186
Thomas, D., 48
thought
  and consciousness, 21
  and language, 24–6, 192–4
Toolan, M., 16, 31
transitive/intransitive, 147–8
tree diagram, 155, 158
Trevisa, J., 219
Trudgill, P., 110, 119, 121, 122–3, 124, 128–9

U
under-extension, 206
universal grammar, 162–6, 203

pro drop, null drop parameter, 166
uptalk, 138

V
Vegetative sounds, 203
verbicide, 44
voluntarism, 21

W
Wada test, 183
Wakankar, V., 96
Watt, I., 87
well-formed/ill-formed, 146
Wernicke, C., 177–8
Wernicke's area, 177
West, C., 139
Wheelock, J.H., 206
Whiten, A., see Byrne
Wilson, D., 62
Wittgenstein, L., 2, 34, 45
Wodehouse, P.G., 109
words
  associations of, 46–9
  are artificial signs, 40
  reference of, 41
  signification of, 41
writing,
  alphabetic, 100–4
  becoming technologised, 76
  compared to talking, 89
  proto, 99
  Sumerian tablet, 98

Y
yod dropping, 123

Z
Zimmerman, D., 139